THE STARTING POINT
OF CALVIN'S THEOLOGY

The Starting Point
of Calvin's Theology

George H. Tavard

WILLIAM B. EERDMANS PUBLISHING COMPANY
GRAND RAPIDS, MICHIGAN / CAMBRIDGE, U.K.

Wm. B. Eerdmans Publishing Co.

255 Jefferson Ave. S.E., Grand Rapids, Michigan 49503 /
P.O. Box 163, Cambridge CB3 9PU U.K.

Printed in the United States of America

05 04 03 02 01 00   5 4 3 2 1

Library of Congress Cataloging-in-Publication Data

Tavard, George H. (George Henry), 1922–
The starting point of Calvin's theology / George H. Tavard.
p.   cm.
ISBN 0-8028-4718-8 (pbk.)
1. Calvin, Jean, 1509–1564. Psychopannychia. 2. Calvin, Jean, 1509–1564.
Institutio Christianae religionis. 3. Reformed Church — Doctrines.
4. Theology, Doctrinal. 5. Soul.
I. Title.

BX9418.T38 2000
230′.42′092 — dc21
00-035430

www.eerdmans.com

Contents

Abbreviations

ARCIC	Anglican-Roman Catholic International Conversations
BA	*Bibliothèque augustinienne*
COD	*Conciliorum Oecumenicorum Decreta,* Basel: Herder, 1962
CR	*Corpus Reformatorum*
DS	Denzinger-Schönmetzer, *Enchiridion Symbolorum,* 32nd edition, Freiburg: Herder, 1963
Imit.	*De imitatione Christi*
Inst.	*Institutio christianae religionis*
RSV	*Revised Standard Version* of the Bible
SC	*Sources chrétiennes*
S.T.	*Summa theologiae*

Introduction

S ince the initiation of bilateral dialogues, in the wake of Vatican Council II, between the Catholic Church and other churches or families of churches, Catholic theologians have met with the heirs of Calvin's theology gathered in the World Alliance of Reformed Churches. Beginning in 1970, these dialogues have brought together Catholics chosen by the Pontifical Council for the Promotion of Christian Unity and Protestants selected by the World Alliance of Reformed Churches. Similar conversations have taken place on a smaller scale in several countries, notably in the United States, where conversations started in 1965, and in France. More recently the Pontifical Council for the Promotion of Christian Unity has sponsored meetings between Catholic theologians and unofficial representatives of evangelical traditions that maintain a more conservative interpretation of Calvinist principles.

While I have not been part of these dialogues, I have followed the work being done in this important section of the ecumenical landscape. And I cannot avoid being puzzled by the absence of memorable results that would be on a par with the achievements of ARCIC-I and -II and of the dialogue of the Catholic Church with the Lutheran World Federation or with the World Methodist Council. The modern conversations between Catholicism and Calvinism have had the least impact on the ecumenical situation as a whole. A first series of meetings (1970-1977) issued a report of a rather general nature entitled "The Presence of Christ in Church and World." This text mentions Calvin once, in relation to christology and the *extra calvinisticum,* that is, the doctrine that, being the eternal Word of God, Christ is present not only in his body but also outside his body. A second series (1984-1990) produced a joint confession of faith, with a number of reflections on "Christ, Justification, and the Church." A third series started only in 1998. These long interruptions have not nurtured a focused attention on essential problems.

The picture looks different if one takes account of the unofficial *Groupe des Dombes,* named after its usual meeting place, a Trappist abbey north of Lyons, in France. This dialogue, which includes Reformed, Lutheran, and Catholic theologians from French-speaking countries, began as early as 1937. The remarkable documents that have issued from it come the nearest to substantive agreements between Catholics and disciples of the Continental Reformers who endorsed the Second Helvetic Confession (1566). These documents are generally cast in the form of invitations to conversion, a mode of thought that is close to the heart of Calvin's own theology. Compared with the fruitfulness of the *Groupe des Dombes,* the relative sterility of the official meetings seems to reflect the absence of the voice of Jean Calvin himself in their debates, a voice that is easily detectable, however, in what the *Groupe des Dombes* has been saying to the churches.

For many years I have been an occasional reader of Calvin's *Institutio religionis christianae* in both Latin and French, along with a number of his biblical commentaries. I have also given courses on the theology of the *Institutio.* And I have seldom left Calvin's writings without gaining further insights, not only into the coherence of his Christian vision, but also into the very substance of faith and the essential structures of Christian thought.

The present volume is a modest endeavor, not indeed to restate the major features of Calvin's theology, a task that has been done many times, but to open a way of entrance into his thought that may be more congenial to the Catholic mind than delving right away into the finished product of the final edition of the *Institutio.* The attempt to grasp the totality of Calvin's theology as it is found in this last edition is of course tempting for readers of the *Summa theologica* of Thomas Aquinas, who may find it intriguing to compare two systems of Christian thought. The way I intend to follow is more historical. It is also somewhat new. I have wished to detect how Calvin himself entered into the Reformed or, should we say, the Reforming way of thought that he transmitted to posterity. The key, I suggest, will be found — paradoxically perhaps — in Calvin's first theological writing, an inquiry into the question of the immortality of the soul.

Chapters 1 to 6 analyze the structure of and the ideas expressed in this short volume. Chapters 7 to 10 relate some major features of Calvin's theological system to his early investigation of the immortality of the soul.

* * *

Many thanks are due to the personnel of the libraries of the following institutions of the Boston area, in which most of my research has been carried out: Harvard Divinity School, Andover-Newton Seminary, St. John's Seminary, the University of Boston College. I have also consulted the library of the Pontifical College Josephinum in Columbus, Ohio, and, through interlibrary loans, the libraries of the University of Illinois at Chicago and the Historical Library in North Newton, Kansas.

* * *

I wish to dedicate this book with gratitude to a Calvinist line among my maternal ancestors. My great-grandfather, Auguste Wasser (1825-1903), was baptized in the Reformed Church of Alsace in the small village of Saulxures (Bas-Rhin). In his adult life he worshiped in the "temples" of St. Dié, Strasbourg, and Nancy.

SOLI DEO GLORIA

Assumption Center   GEORGE H. TAVARD
Brighton, Massachusetts

I

Psychopannychia

The short Latin work entitled *Psychopannychia* is the first theological work of Calvin to have been written, and the second to have been published. It was composed, as Calvin reports in the "letter to a friend" that serves as a preface to the printed edition, at the request of "several pious persons"; and it does not seem to have been originally destined to publication. A first version, never printed, and now lost or, rather, incorporated in the second, was composed during Calvin's sojourns around Angoulême and in Orléans in 1534. The second version, finalized in Basel in 1535-36, may have been printed in 1536 in Basel, although this seems doubtful and no copy of an early printing has survived. It was printed in 1542 in Strasbourg, and again in Geneva in 1545.

The prefatory letter, dated "Orléans, 1534," goes back to the first version. Calvin was invited by friends to refute the strange opinion that the soul falls asleep at the death of its body and wakes up at the final resurrection. He waited some time before taking up the matter, for he expected such a peculiar idea to have no success. It soon became obvious, however, that the false doctrine was spreading far and wide. Calvin then considered it his duty to take up the pen in defense of the true doctrine, namely that the soul neither sleeps nor dies at bodily death, but remains fully alive as it is taken up in the Lord. Although Calvin did not at the time specify all the ins and outs of what he considered to be orthodox doctrine, he already felt strongly that it was his duty to defend the true Christian revelation. This conviction would remain with him all his life. More than a pastor (he never asked for ordination), he became a lecturer, commentator, preacher, and author. The circumstances in which he thus served the church forced him to become a prophet.

*　　*　　*

Psychopannychia has not been one of the favorite books of students of the Reformation. Indeed, the French *Psychopannychie*, printed in Geneva in 1558, was not directly Calvin's work but was apparently done under his supervision, and remained the only translation in any language until an English version came out in 1851.[1] A German version was published only in 1996.[2] Like the translations, studies of the little volume and its teaching have been slow in coming. The most thorough investigations of it were published in Germany in 1932, 1991, and 1996. The first was the long introduction to a new edition of the text by Walther Zimmerli.[3] The second, a doctoral thesis, was presented by a Korean scholar, Jung-Uck Hwang, at the Kirchlische Hochschule in Wuppertal.[4] Hwang's introductory chapter provides an overview of previous studies. The third, done by Wilhelm Schwendemann,[5] includes a critical survey of Zimmerli's work. These volumes support specific theses about the nature and structure of *Psychopannychia*, which will be examined further on.

The composition of *Psychopannychia* received a good deal of at-

1. Henry Beveridge, trans., *John Calvin. Tracts,* vol. 3 (Edinburgh, 1851), pp. 413-90.

2. Wilhelm Schwendemann, *Leib und Seele bei Calvin. Die erkenntnistheoretische und anthropologetische Funktion des platonischen Leib-Seele-Dualismus in Calvins Theologie* (Stuttgart: Calwer Verlag, 1996). The German text of *Psychopannychia* has its own pagination — 1-79 — following p. 415.

3. Walther Zimmerli, *Psychopannychia von Joh. Calvin (Quellenchriften zur Geschichte des Protestantismus* 13) (Leipzig: A. Deichert, 1932).

4. Jung-Uck Hwang, *Der junge Calvin und seiner Psychopannychia,* Europäische Hochschulschriften. Reihe XXIII. Theologie. Series XXIII, vol. 407 (Frankfurt-am-Main: Peter Lang, 1991).

5. Schwendemann, *Leib und Seele bei Calvin.*

tention in Doumergue's classic life of Calvin.[6] The study of Calvin's theology by François Wendel,[7] however, did not speak of it. In his masterful study of "the young Calvin," Alexandre Ganoczy drew on *Psychopannychia* to illustrate Calvin's readings in Angoulême and to point to his early antagonism to the anabaptists.[8] In 1975 Ford Lewis Battles's introduction to his English translation of the *Institutio* of 1536 presented *Psychopannychia* as a polemical piece that would have been implicitly directed against the Roman doctrine of purgatory,[9] though without giving it prominence in the panorama of Calvin's early writings. William Bouwsma's portrait of Calvin did not speak of it, even when examining the nature of the soul.[10] Since 1991, however, French-speaking scholarship has opened intriguing perspectives on Calvin's investigation of the state of the soul after death. Brief though suggestive notes were offered in an essay by Bernard Roussel;[11] and, in a chiefly literary study of Calvin's corpus, Olivier Millet paid careful attention to *Psychopannychia*.[12]

6. Emile Doumergue, *Jean Calvin, les hommes et les choses de son temps,* 7 vols. (Geneva: Slatkine Reprints, 1969), vol. 1, pp. 466-68, 584-85.

7. François Wendel, *Calvin. Sources et évolution de sa pensée religieuse* (Paris: Presses Universitaires de France, 1950).

8. Alexandre Ganoczy, *Le jeune Calvin. Genèse et évolution de sa vocation réformatrice* (Wiesbaden: Franz Steiner Verlag, 1966), pp. 74, 77-78.

9. Ford Lewis Battles, *Institution of the Christian Religion* (Atlanta: John Knox Press, 1975), pp. xxxii-xxxvi. The assumption that Calvin is attacking the notion of purgatory has no foundation; the problem is not touched in *Psychopannychia*.

10. William J. Bouwsma, *John Calvin: A Sixteenth Century Portrait* (New York: Oxford University Press, 1988), pp. 78-79. The description of the soul is taken chiefly from the *Institutio* of 1559, I, ch. 15, and from *Brève instruction contre les erreurs des Anabaptistes* (Geneva, 1544; Latin translation by Nicolas des Gallars *Adversus anabaptistas,* issued in Strasbourg in 1546).

11. "François Lambert, Pierre Caroli, Guillaume Farel — et Jean Calvin" (1530-1536), in Wilhelm H. Neuser, ed., *Calvinus Servus Christi* (Budapest: Presseabteilung des Ráday-Collegiums, 1988), pp. 35-52. Hans Scholl's investigation of twentieth-century Catholic studies of Calvin confirms that little or no attention has been paid by them to his early teaching on the soul: *Calvinus Catholicus. Die katholische Calvinforschung im 20. Jahrhundert* (Freiburg: Herder, 1974).

12. Olivier Millet, *Calvin et la dynamique de la parole. Etude de rhétorique réformée* (Paris: Editions Champion, 1992), pp. 439-47. Millet noted: "Zimmerli's introduction is the only monograph consecrated to this first theological essay by the Re-

The basic importance of *Psychopannychia* derives from the fact that it was the very first writing in which Calvin intended to speak as a theologian. Although he may have been reluctant, at the time of writing, to present himself to the public as a polemicist in matters theological, he felt pushed by conscience to express his thoughts in defense of the true faith. Calvin himself at the beginning of *Psychopannychia* provides an elaborate description of the pressures he felt from unidentified friends, who urged him to refute the denial of the immortality of the soul by a group of anabaptists. Hence what Millet calls the "eminent ambiguity" of the preface, which can be read as humanistic rhetoric in the framework of the old Church, and also as a formulation of the deepest convictions of a reformer[13] on the question of the soul's immortality. Although it was not long before Calvin no longer felt the need to justify his taking up the pen in defense of and for the elucidation of true Christian doctrine, a twofold attitude of personal shyness and assertive certitude remained typical of most of his later works.

In his biography of the great reformer, Bernard Cottret offers a rich insight into the latent importance of the work.[14] Cottret asks the obvious yet generally neglected question: Why was Calvin so excited about the obscure doctrine of a few anabaptists who affirmed the sleep or the death of the soul? On the one hand, Calvin's later diatribes against the anabaptists, whom he systematically identified as the worst enemies of true Christianity, suggest that his distrust of the "radical reformation" was deeply rooted in his thinking; and *Psychopannychia* shows the early emergence of these roots in Calvin's acquaintance with the reforming movement. On the other hand, Calvin may also have been personally troubled by the question of the sleep of the soul. In refuting the anabaptists on this point he may have laid to rest a personal anguish. If this was so, however, the exact nature of this anguish cannot be identified with certainty, though the experience of a near contemporary of Calvin may sug-

---

former" (p. 442, note 10). In fact, Hwang's careful study had been published in 1991.

13. Millet, *Calvin*, p. 444.

14. Bernard Cottret, *Calvin. Biographie* (Paris: Editions Jean-Claude Lattès, 1995), pp. 89-94.

gest a possible interpretation. St. François de Sales (1567-1622) struggled with despair in his youth when he was somehow haunted by the thought that he was not numbered among God's elect. To judge by the concerns of *Psychopannychia,* Calvin's anguish, if there was one, may have been related to a more metaphysical fear of annihilation. One cannot rule out that the overcoming of a similar anguish was among Calvin's personal motives when he faced the doctrine of these anabaptists, whoever they were.

*   *   *

Why, then, did Calvin begin his distinguished theological career with the relatively peripheral topic of *Psychopannychia?* The German editor of the 1932 edition suggests elements of an answer, which, however, he does not develop at length. He starts his introduction with the first lines of the *Institutio christianae religionis* of 1559:

> *Tota fere sapientiae nostrae summa, quae vera demum ac solida sapientia censeri debet, duabus partibus constat, Dei cognitione et nostri. Caeterum, quum multis inter se vinculis connextae sint, utra tamen alteram praecedat, et ex se pariat, non facile est discernere.*

> (Nearly the whole sum of our wisdom, which must be held to be particularly true and solid, consists of two parts, the knowledge of God and of ourselves. Besides, since they are connected by a multitude of links, it is not easy to discern which precedes the other and gives it birth.)

That there is a close connection between knowledge of God and knowledge of self had been clearly seen by St. Augustine, as explained in his early spiritual writing, the *Soliloquia.* Augustine's wording — *noverim me, noverim te*[15] — suggested that a certain self-knowledge comes first, and that it leads to, or implies, a certain awareness of God. This was in keeping with the experience of neo-

---

15. *Soliloquia,* II, i, 1, BA, vol. V, *Dialogues philosophiques* (Paris: Desclée, 1948), p. 86.

Platonist contemplation that Augustine was to describe in book VII of the *Confessions,* which was itself inspired by Plato's descriptions of the spiritual ascent.[16] The Platonic way of ascent starts from the contemplation of bodily beauty, whence it passes on to the contemplation of spiritual beauty, and further to a perception of the ineffable beauty of the first and highest Principle. In the writings of Plotinus, this first Principle is called "the One" (τὸ ἀεν), an expression that Augustine renders through the neutral term *Idipsum,* "It itself." *Idipsum,* the supreme though impersonal Being, is above all, inexpressible. Augustine had traveled the neo-Platonic way of ascent when, after being initiated to the search for wisdom by Cicero's *Hortensius,* he had read some of the "books of the Platonists." At the time he was enthralled by reflection on the divine *Logos,* but, as he noted in the *Confessions,*[17] he had not yet perceived the importance of the incarnation of the Word.

It is not easy, Calvin remarks, to discern which comes first, the knowledge of self or the knowledge of God. This hesitancy, if it was one, did not last long. It nevertheless shows that Calvin's point of departure was not that of an adept of mystical Platonism. His humanistic researches, which had climaxed in his study of Seneca, had turned his thought toward Stoicism and problems of law and politics rather than Platonism and questions of personal spirituality. In any case, the interest that Calvin felt in Augustine's approach to self and to God, and thereby to Christian theology, could hardly derive from his own university formation in the Faculty of Law. It resulted rather from the judgment that Seneca's Stoic approach, which had its proper field in the realm of politics, was in need of a complement when the nature of the soul came into question. This complement Calvin found precisely in Augustine's account of his own more interior itinerary. In spite of this, however, the order in which Calvin ranks God-knowledge and self-knowledge is in a sense the reverse of what Augustine had written in the *Soliloquies.* It is the reverse in that Augustine's *Noverim me, noverim te* becomes Calvin's *cognitione Dei ac*

---

16. As in *Phaedo, Phaedrus, The Banquet.* I analyzed this experience in *Les Jardins de saint Augustin. Lecture des Confessions* (Paris: Editions du Cerf, 1988), pp. 25-39.

17. *Confessions,* IX, iv, 11.

nostri. It is in myself, Augustine had noted, that I know God, and the better I know myself the better I will know God. Such a *noverim me* may bring up the question of immortality if I go on to ask, Do I know if my soul is truly immortal? If the question is properly answered it will lead to *noverim te:* I shall know something of you, the eternal Creator of my soul. It is striking, however, that Calvin's theological reflection in the *Institutio* does not start from self-knowledge as such, but rather from the knowledge of God that is revealed in Jesus Christ. Nonetheless, Calvin's approach is exactly that of Augustine insofar as both are eager to know nothing other than God and the soul, as Augustine had written: "I want to know God and the soul. — Nothing more? — Nothing at all."[18] The chief difference in the starting point of the two theologians is that, unlike Calvin, Augustine does not seek to establish the nature of the soul on the basis of its immortality but rather on that of its potential for knowledge.

Calvin's investigation of the soul as implied in its survival of bodily death could not be without relevance to the theological system he began to construct in Basel and Geneva at the very time when he was revising his text on the soul for publication. The opening sentence of the first edition of *Institutio christianae religionis* was not substantially different, though it was shorter, than that of 1559: *Summa fere sacrae doctrinae duabus his partibus constat: cognitione Dei ac nostri,*[19] that is, "The near-totality of sacred doctrine resides in these two parts: the knowledge of God and of ourselves." This tying together of God-knowledge and self-knowledge remained intact through the successive, and successively enlarged, editions of Calvin's *opus magnum*. Now the temporal nearness of *Psychopannychia* and the first *Institutio* as they were composed and published hints at a hidden connection between the theme of the first — the soul and its immortality — and the starting point of Calvin's systematic theology: God-knowledge and self-knowledge.

If this is correct, then it seems astonishing that Calvin's *Psycho-*

18. *Deum et animam scire cupio. — Nihilne plus? — Nihil omnino. Sol.,* I, i, 7, BA, Dialogues philosophiques V, p. 36.

19. *Calvini Opera Selecta,* vol. 1, ed. Peter Barth (Munich: Chr. Kaiser Verlag, 1926), p. 37.

pannychia has been so little considered in the Calvinist theological tradition. If one surmises that the theologians' research has been more or less guided by ecclesial concerns, then one is tempted to put a degree of blame on the Reformed and Presbyterian Churches for neglecting a writing that could throw light on Calvin's major theological work. Responsibility for such neglect is likely to be shared by theologians and by church administrators.

*   *   *

As a newcomer to the theological field when he tackled the problem of immortality, Calvin acted with prudence and submitted his essay to a number of friends and acquaintances, some of whom were known to him only by reputation. Among those who received a copy were the Alsatian reformers Wolfgang Capito (Köpfel, 1478-1541) and Martin Bucer (1491-1551), Calvin's cousin Robert Olivétan (1506-1538), translator of the Bible, and the great humanist Lefèvre d'Étaples (c. 1455-1536). In a response addressed to Martianus Lucanus (Calvin's humanistic pseudonym)[20] Capito gave it as his opinion that an attack on a small heretical group would give this sect an undeserved publicity. He also recommended that Calvin's first publication reflect a more mature exegesis of biblical texts than was contained in the essay on the immortality of the soul.[21] Bucer likewise advised the author not to publish this writing, at least for the time being. This was hardly an auspicious beginning for a young aspiring theological author.

20. The humanists liked to adopt names that had a meaning in one of the ancient languages. Felix Capella Martianus was a Latin poet of North Africa in the fifth century, author of an encyclopedic poem, *Satiricon,* and Marcus Anneus Lucanus (39-65), a young Latin poet of Spain, author of an epic historical poem, *Pharsalia,* or *Belli civilis libri decem,* who lived in Rome and was put to death by Nero. The two words may have been evocative of war (related to *Mars,* the god of war) and of light (related to *lux*), thus suggesting "victorious light." Another possibility is that *Lucanus* is related to *luca* (elephant), which would then suggest "fighting elephant." In either case the appellation is not inappropriate in light of Calvin's determination to fight for the truth.

21. These and the following details are borrowed from Zimmerli's introduction, pp. 7-9.

8

One gathers from a letter written on 3 September 1535 to his friend Libertet — Christopher Fabri (1508-1588), one of Guillaume Farel's collaborators in the reformation of the city of Basel — that Calvin revised and possibly rewrote his essay some time after receiving these critiques. As Calvin also mentions in a later letter (1 October 1538), Bucer changed his mind later and urged the author to publish his dissertation on the soul. Nonetheless, for a number of reasons the work was not printed before 1542. Among those reasons one may list Calvin's travels to Ferrara and his temporary return to France; his work on Olivétan's translation of the Bible, for which he wrote a prefatory letter in Latin and an introduction, and which he began revising for further printings; his more original work on the first version of *Institutio christianae religionis;* the new orientation his life took in 1537 when he began to lecture on the Bible in Geneva; and the bankruptcy of the Genevan printer Michel du Bois. The book was printed by Wendelin Rihel in Strasbourg in 1542, under the title *Vivere apud Christum non dormire animos sanctos, qui in fide Christi decedunt. Assertio.*[22] In the same year Calvin published his first catechism for the Church of Geneva. This was six years after the first Latin edition of *Institutio* (March 1536), one year after the first French edition of the same (1541), and one year before the second Latin edition (1543), at a time when Calvin must have already been at work on this second edition. The original letter to a friend, dated 1534, served as prefatory epistle, and was followed by an "address to readers" dated "Basel, 1536."

A second edition, with slight alterations and additions, was issued in 1545 in Strasbourg by the same printer, who devised the more exotic and impressive title, *Psychopannychia, qua refellitur quorundam imperitorum error, qui animas post mortem usque ad ultimum judicium dormire putant.*[23] *Psychopannychia* is a composite Greek word formed by combining the noun ψυχή (soul) and the feminine adjective παννύχια (active all night long), meaning therefore something like "soul awake at night." In the same year of 1545 Calvin pub-

---

22. Rodolphe Peter and Jean-François Gilmont, *Bibliotheca Calviniana. Les oeuvres de Jean Calvin publiées au XVIe siècle*, vol. 1 (Geneva: Librairie Droz, 1991), pp. 113-16.
23. Peter and Gilmont, *Bibliotheca Calviniana*, vol. 1, pp. 201-3.

lished the French version of his second *Institutio*. Only in 1558, after a number of requests by Guillaume Farel, was a French translation printed in Geneva by Conrad Badius, under a title that must have puzzled unscholarly readers, if any ventured into the pages of the book: *Psychopannychie*.[24] That there was a great interest in this text among French-speaking readers is manifest, as the first printing was soon followed, in the one year 1558, by another one.

*   *   *

The original draft of *Psychopannychia* was composed in what was for Calvin a transition period. Calvin had left Paris after the challenging address that was made on 1 November 1533 by the new Rector of the Sorbonne, Nicolas Cop, for the opening of the academic year. Since Nicolas Cop was not a theologian but a physician, the more conservative doctors of the Sorbonne had searched among Cop's friends and acquaintances for a likely author of his theological speech, the Lutheran leanings of which were clear enough. Calvin, who was among the suspect, had felt it wise to put a sizable distance between himself and the authorities in Paris. He had traveled south at a leisurely pace, arriving in January 1534 at the home of his humanist friend, *chanoine* Louis du Tillet (born c. 1509). Louis, a priest, was pastor in the little town of Claix, and his family owned a large mansion in the neighboring city of Angoulême. Calvin spent a few months in this house, where an extensive library was at his disposal. A good part of his first draft on the soul must have been composed there.

It was during his sojourn in the du Tillet mansion that Calvin paid a visit to the residence of Marguerite de Navarre at Nérac, in April of the same year, although he cannot have met Marguerite herself, who was away in Normandy in the spring of 1534.[25] Marguerite

---

24. *Psychopannychie. Traité par lequel est prouvé que les âmes veillent et vivent après qu'elles sont sorties des corps, contre l'erreur de quelques ignorants qui pensent qu'elles dorment jusques au dernier jugement.* See Peter and Gilmont, *Bibliotheca*, vol. 2 (1994), pp. 684-87. The text was reprinted by Paul-Louis Jacob in *Oeuvres françaises de Calvin* (Paris: Gosselin, 1842), pp. 25-105.

25. Doumergue, *Calvin*, vol. 1, p. 404.

10

d'Angoulême (1492-1549), Queen of Navarre through her second marriage, was the devout and reform-minded elder sister of King François I (king, 1515-1547). She was herself a humanist and a religious poet, close to the enlightened Bishop of Meaux, Guillaume Briçonnet (1470-1534), who promoted the Renaissance and sympathized with the reform movement, and with whom she corresponded on matters of her conscience. Gérard Roussel (1480-1550), her chaplain and court preacher since 1526, was a student and friend of Lefèvre d'Étaples, whose library he would soon inherit. He was not reluctant to preach about justification by faith, as he did in the Lenten sermons he delivered in 1533 at the royal chapel of the Louvre palace in Paris, in the presence of the king and the queen. Marguerite defended her chaplain from the charge of heterodoxy when this was questioned, and all the more so as her own poem, *Le miroir de l'âme pécheresse,* printed in 1531 in Alençon, was included in an index of forbidden books that was issued in November 1533 under the authority of the Sorbonne. When the king enquired about the reason for this outrage to his sister, an embarrassed faculty of theology denied all responsibility.[26] Calvin regarded Roussel as a friend until, in 1536, the king honored his sister by promoting her chaplain Roussel to the bishopric of Oléron, and he, to Calvin's horror, accepted the promotion.

It is most likely that on the occasion of his visit to Nérac Calvin read Marguerite's recently published theological poem, *Dialogue spirituel en forme de vision nocturne.*[27] Her first lengthy venture into poetry, the piece had been inspired at the end of 1524 by the death from rubella of her beloved niece, the king's eight-year-old daughter Charlotte (1516-1524). This had been a time of sadness at the court and of personal trial for the king's sister. The young queen, Claude de France (1499-1524), already the mother of seven children, had

26. The index commission was composed of two members of the Parliament of Paris and two professors at the Sorbonne; the decision had to be approved by all faculties of the university sitting separately. On this episode, see Hwang, *Der junge Calvin,* pp. 40-59.

27. Renja Salminen, ed., *Marguerite de Navarre. Dialogue spirituel en forme de vision nocturne,* Annales Academiae Scientiarum Fennicae, Series B, tome 27 (Helsinki: Suomalainen Tiedeakatemia, 1985).

died on July 26. At the time the king was away on his Italian campaign. The queen-mother Louise de Savoie, the mother of Marguerite and of François I, was herself sick and largely unable to exercise the regency of the kingdom in the absence of the king. It was Marguerite, who was then married to the Duke of Alençon,[28] who had to protect the king's interests in matters political as well as familial. She took care of the princess Charlotte, who died in her arms on September 8. In her distress Marguerite bared her soul in several letters to Briçonnet, and also in the poem, *Dialogue spiritual en forme de vision nocturne,* which she kept from printing until she had it printed in 1533, along with the second edition of her better known *Miroir de l'âme pécheresse.*

The vision described in the poem is of the princess Charlotte now in heaven. The dialogue is between the soul of the princess and her aunt, still mourning on earth. This long poem of 1260 lines, in the form of the *terza rima* used by Dante in the *Divine Comedy*[29] and recently imported from Italy, is entirely based on the Christian belief that the soul is immortal, and that, at least for those who share the true faith, it lives in God after bodily death. The poem was composed between September 1524 and the battle of Pavia in February 1525, after which Marguerite was too occupied and preoccupied to find the leisure necessary to such a writing. François I, captured at the battle of Pavia, was a prisoner of his arch-enemy, Emperor Charles V. His sister Marguerite assumed the additional task of getting him freed, and she traveled to Spain to negotiate with the emperor, who released him in January 1526.

In 1533, Calvin, who had mourned the passing away of his father in May of 1531, could easily be sensitive to the tone, the feelings, and the doctrine of Marguerite's *Dialogue spirituel,* so that his acquaintance with the poem may well have triggered the outrage he felt when confronted by denials of the immortality of the soul. It is

---

28. She would be widowed in April 1525, and would marry the King of Navarre, Henri d'Albret, in January 1527.

29. Marguerite, whose mother was Louise de Savoie, knew Italian, though she did not speak it well. The poem shows traces of the influence of both Petrarch and Dante. See Carlo Pellegrini, *La prima opera di Margherita di Navarra e la terza rima in Francia* (Catania: Francesco Battiato Editore, 1920).

undoubtedly true that Calvin never became close to the king's sister. Although they later exchanged a few letters, he never enjoyed with her the sort of spiritual friendship that marked his relations with her cousin Renée de France, Duchess of Ferrara. Moreover, in 1537, he would identify Marguerite's chaplain, Gérard Roussel, as a notorious Nicodemite, who did not dare to follow his reforming convictions to their logical end when he was offered promotion in the Church. By the same token Calvin may have regarded Marguerite also as a Nicodemite, for she tolerated Roman practices in spite of her basic agreement with the doctrines of the reformers. He never said so in public, however, whatever his private thoughts about the king's sister.

* * *

Meanwhile, on the occasion of his visit to Nérac Calvin was able to converse with the aging Lefèvre d'Étaples, Roussel's mentor. He must also have discussed the religious situation with the wide circle of the queen's guests and visitors, and it may have been from them that he heard for the first time about strange doctrines being spread abroad by anabaptists and by the people he later called *libertins spirituels*.

In May of 1534 Calvin traveled back to his hometown of Noyon. On the eve of his twenty-fifth birthday when he would become officially major (he had been born on 9 July 1509), he had to choose a way of life. Did he wish to join the clergy or to remain a layman? Only on condition of seeking ordination and a clerical career could he keep the ecclesiastical benefices that had hitherto enabled him to be fairly free of financial concerns. The alternative was to give up his entitlements and to shift for himself as a lay person. On May 4 he informed the canons of the cathedral of Noyon of his renunciation of all his benefices. The rights to the income of the chapel *de la Gésine*, which he had enjoyed since the age of twelve, were sold for a small sum. The benefice of the parish of Pont-l'Evêque he gave away to a friend. On the one hand this was hardly a lucrative operation; on the other, there was in it no hint of an attraction to the cause of the reformers, though it showed his lack of interest in a church career.

It was after the disastrous *placards* affair of October 1534 that Calvin decided it would be safer for him to leave the country, at least for some time. *Placards,* or posters advocating a given theological position, were popular among the reformers, who could claim Luther's Ninety-five Theses as a precedent. But while the Ninety-five Theses were in Latin and intended for a scholarly disputation, the posters that were occasionally put up in Switzerland and France had the more popular purpose of propaganda. Posters denouncing the Mass as an abomination, composed by a Frenchman, Antoine Marcourt[30] (d. 1561), who at the time was preaching in Geneva, appeared simultaneously in the cities of Paris, Rouen, Orléans, Blois, and Tours. In addition, the same text was also posted up in some of the royal residences, including the château d'Amboise, where the king was himself staying at the time. This bold but rather foolish venture was apparently an endeavor to bring François I's religious policy at home in harmony with his foreign policy. In January the king had met with the most prestigious of the Lutheran princes, the young landgrave Philip of Hesse (1504-1567), in the Lorraine city of Bar-le-Duc. He had promised to support the Schmalkald league of Lutheran princes against their militant Catholic emperor, Charles V. In this the king's motivation was purely political. At home, however, he found no reason to alter his predecessors' policy of allegiance to the papacy, an allegiance that was still moderated by restrictions on papal power in the king's territories, on the model of the Pragmatic Sanction of Bourges.

While the posting as such may have made sense from the point of view of the reformers, targeting the king's own residences was entirely foolish, since it could only be viewed as a personal attack on the royal person. As an indication of the strength of the reforming movement in France, however, this was highly effective; the impres-

---

30. Gabrielle Berthoud, *Antoine Marcourt, Réformateur et pamphlétaire, du 'Livre des Marchans' aux Placards de 1534* (Geneva: Droz, 1973). Marcourt was one of the four preachers who were brought to Geneva after Calvin was expelled from the city on 23 April 1537. The four of them, however, were never able to function in peace, and they abandoned Geneva in 1539, Marcourt leaving on 21 September. The Magistrates begged Calvin to return. Henceforth Calvin considered Marcourt a personal enemy!

sion spread rapidly at the court that a huge conspiracy was at work. There were, however, two miscalculations in this bold enterprise. First, the mere suspicion of a conspiracy was bound to provoke the king's anger. Second, the title of the poster, in the sarcastic style of Marcourt's more substantive works, sounded more provocative than persuasive: *Articles véritables sur les horribles, grands et insupportables abus de la Messe papalle.*

The *placards* were posted in the night of 17 October 1534, around two or three in the morning. Within one month some two hundred sympathizers of the reforming movement had been arrested, and twenty-four of them were eventually tortured and then burnt as unrepentant heretics. Calvin fled in time. Traveling from Poitiers with Louis du Tillet, he found his way to Strasbourg and eventually to Basel, a university town in which he hoped to find a quiet niche as a dedicated scholar.[31]

The date of the *placards* scandal suggests a *terminus ad quem* for the first version of the book on the soul, for after this date the ceremonies of the Mass became such a hot topic that Calvin could hardly avoid expressing an opinion about them. In fact, the printed edition neither contains nor implies any criticism of the papacy or of papal doctrines, and it does not differ in substance, and only slightly in form, from the standard medieval approach to theological reflection. Admittedly, although the final shape of the book was published when Calvin was quite engaged on his reforming career, it did not allude to the "abominations" of the Mass. This could simply be due to the author's more scholarly than polemical or pastoral concerns when he stayed in Basel, before he was directly involved in the care of souls. Moreover, as a careful craftsman of language in both French and Latin, Calvin did not usually mix the genres of his writings, though his indignation at the doctrines of Michael Servetus would lead him to include violently polemical passages in the later editions of *Institutio christianae religionis.* In any case Calvin

31. The route Calvin followed to Strasbourg may have gone through Metz or, more likely, further south through Pont-à-Mousson; in a place that his biographer Théodore de Bèze calls Desme (presumably the modern Delme), one of Calvin's servants ran away with his purse and a horse (Doumergue, *Calvin,* vol. 1, p. 468).

would soon address questions relating to ceremonies and to the Mass in two letters respectively addressed to Nicolas Duchemin, whom Calvin had known as a student in Orléans, and to Gérard Roussel. There is, however, no reason to think that the first form of *Psychopannychia* made any allusion to such matters.

After staying in Basel for about one year, Calvin paid a visit to the Duchess of Ferrara in March 1536. The duchess, Renée de France (1510-1575), was the daughter of the late King Louis XII (king, 1498-1515), to whom François I had succeeded when, by virtue of the Salic law, Renée was barred from her father's succession. François's father, Charles d'Angoulême, was her first cousin. Like François's sister Marguerite, Renée de France was one of the great ladies of the Renaissance. She had married Hercule II d'Este, Duke of Ferrara, on 28 June 1528. Her sympathy with the Reformation attracted Protestant exiles to the ducal court, despite the duke's hostility to the new movements. She was a friend and protectress of the Italian evangelicals. The poetess Vittoria Colonna (d. 1547), who was herself devoted to the reforming movement and active in the evangelically oriented Oratories of Divine Love, had visited the duchess some time before.[32] Calvin stayed only a short time at the court in Ferrara. He left suddenly after Good Friday (14 April), when the very orthodox Duke of Ferrara was infuriated by the young Frenchman's refusal to venerate the cross during the traditional ceremony.[33] Calvin's hasty departure has been attributed to fear of being identified if the duke got too curious about his wife's guests, Calvin having traveled to Italy incognito. It is more likely, however, to have been prompted by the desire to make a quick visit to France while a safe journey was still possible. The Edict of Coucy, signed by François I on 16 July 1535, gave six months to the exiles to come back in peace into the kingdom. April 1536 was clearly beyond the six months' grace, but the return to a harsh policy was not immediate.

At any rate, Calvin's brief visit to Ferrara was sufficient to incite

32. On Vittoria Colonna, see Eva-Maria Jung-Inglessis, *Il Pianto della Marchesa di Pescara sopra la Passione di Christo*, in the *Archivio Italiano per la Storia della pietà*, vol. 10 (Rome, 1997), pp. 115-204.

33. Ganoczy, *Le jeune Calvin*, p. 101.

the duchess to correspond with him all her life long. In these letters Renée consulted the reformer as a theological adviser and spiritual guide. He encouraged her to remain steadfast in the true faith when she was examined by the Roman Inquisition and, on 6 September 1554, found guilty of heretical leanings. Confined by her husband to a small part of the palace with two servants, she outwardly relented, receiving communion from a Jesuit priest on 23 September. After the duke's sudden death in 1559, however, Renée retired to her castle at Montargis, in France, which she made a haven for Calvin's followers.

Meanwhile, still in the company of Louis du Tillet, Calvin traveled back to Noyon. He did not stay long in his native town, however, for the Edict of Coucy had a condition he was not willing to meet: The returning exiles had to abjure their errors if they wished to settle down.[34] Along with his sister Marie and his brother Antoine, Calvin arrived in Geneva in the summer of 1536. The party had intended to travel to Strasbourg, but a new outbreak of hostilities between the King of France and the emperor rendered the crossing of Lorraine hazardous. Though not yet incorporated in the kingdom, the three bishoprics of Metz, Toul, and Verdun generally tended to favor the King of France. The bishopric of Metz was rather tolerant of Protestants. But the dukes of Lorraine were both loyal to their sovereign the emperor, and quite hostile to the reforming movements. Calvin and his party made a long detour south through Burgundy and the Swiss territory, stopping in Geneva for a few days. It was then that Guillaume Farel persuaded the magistrates of the city to hire Calvin as a lecturer in the Bible.

*   *   *

To the unsuspicious reader *Psychopannychia* looks like a theological investigation of the scholastic type on a point that had been occasionally debated, though never given prominence, in medieval tractates, until Latin Averroism at the end of the thirteenth century denied the individuality of the intellect agent through which, in

---

34. Doumergue, *Calvin,* vol. 1, p. 586.

Aristotelian philosophy, the mind is able to perceive what is universal in the singularity of beings. When this happened it became important for orthodoxy to determine the state of the soul between individual death and the resurrection of the flesh. As we shall see, it became common among the humanists to examine the problem of the soul. When he turned his attention to this question, Calvin took sides against some unnamed authors or preachers that he designated under the generic title *anabaptists* or *catabaptists* — a term previously used by Zwingli — to which he added the unflattering remark, "whom to name is enough to suggest all sorts of scandals."[35] *Psychopannychia* thus constitutes a first salvo in Calvin's unrelenting polemics against *les fantastiques* — Luther's *Schwärmer* — who, under the pretense of reforming the Church, destroy some of the essential Christian doctrines.

In the letter that opens *Psychopannychia*, Calvin cites a few precedents for the doctrines he is going to oppose.[36] In the early Church there were some Christians in Arabia, mentioned in Eusebius's *Ecclesiastical History* and Augustine's *Liber de haeresibus*. In the fourteenth century there had been John XXII, pope in Avignon from 1329 to 1334. And now there were anabaptist conventicles. The most interesting of these cases is undoubtedly that of John XXII. In three sermons that he preached in November and December 1331 and January 1332, the pope interpreted the apocalyptic image of the "souls of the saints waiting under the altar" (Apoc. 6:9) as meaning that, before the final resurrection, the souls of the dead can see the human nature of Christ in its risen state, but do not see God and do not enjoy the beatific vision. However, the King of France, Philippe VI (Philippe le Bel, king, 1328-1350), had ordered an inquisitorial investigation of this doctrine, and the Sorbonne had declared it erroneous. The pope had then submitted the question to a commission of cardinals. A few days before his death he had, in the bull *Ne super his* (3 December 1334), retracted his previous opinion. His successor,

---

35. *Istud rursum lectores omnes (si qui tamen erunt) memoria tenere volo catabaptistas (quos ad omne genus flagitiorum designandum nominasse satis est) esse praeclari hujus dogmatis auctores* (Zimmerli edition, p. 108).

36. Zimmerli, pp. 16-17.

Benedict XII (pope, 1334-1342), had "defined" the opposite doctrine: After the resurrection of Christ and before the resurrection of their body, the souls of the just are truly in heaven, where they do see "the divine essence in an intuitive and even face to face vision" (constitution *Benedictus Deus*, 29 January 1336).

Calvin, however, does not examine the nuances of John XXII's views. He is concerned about current doctrines, not about past opinions that did not last. His indignation is not directed at the pope or at the Roman Church, but at extremists among the radical reformers, anabaptists or catabaptists who are endangering the reform of the Church by promoting unorthodox teachings that contradict the Scriptures and the theological tradition. He therefore does not discuss, as John XXII did, how much of God the just souls do contemplate. He does not even, as he might have done later, take occasion of the pope's fall from the true tradition to attack the Roman primacy. He is entirely concerned about refuting two assertions more radical than John XXII's: First, the souls of the dead, since they cannot function without a body, are asleep in death; second, the soul dies along with its body, until both are brought back to life on the last day.

*   *   *

Calvin hardly referred, in *Psychopannychia,* to debates about the soul other than those directly related to the opinions he wished to refute. He designated his adversaries with derogatory terms — slumberers, hypnologues, hypnosophists, soul-killers — that are more descriptive of his hostility than indicative of their identity. Yet he so carefully discussed their arguments and so thoroughly examined the New Testament texts that could have a bearing on the question that we have to wonder if something else was not at stake in composing this book — something besides the wish to refute false conceptions of eschatology and to destroy an opinion that had never been popular and had little chance of appealing to many of the Christian faithful. In fact, it was fashionable among humanists of Calvin's day to dream of writing the definitive study on the immortality of the soul; and as we shall see, Calvin in this respect was no exception.

II

The Renaissance Debate on the Soul

Willingness or eagerness to refute erroneous doctrines may not have been Calvin's only motivation in composing, if not in publishing, his essay on the immortality of the soul. There must have been another powerful motive, one that had its origin in the humanistic circles in which the young Calvin cut the figure of a promising Law scholar. Indeed, the soul — *animus* or, indifferently, *anima* — had for more than a century occupied a unique place in Renaissance literature. It would have been the normal thing, for an aspiring humanist who wished to establish his credentials, to express his thoughts on the question of immortality in a scholarly and persuasive *De anima*. More specifically, two fundamental questions relating to the soul loomed large on the philosophical horizon of the time.

First, there was a historical point: Did Aristotle in his *De anima* (Περὶ ψυχεί) teach the immortality of the soul? Among the great scholastics of the thirteenth century, Bonaventure had denounced "the philosophers" in general and Aristotle in particular as denying the immortality of the soul and taking for granted the eternity of the world. Thomas Aquinas on the contrary had affirmed the opposite in regard to Aristotle's understanding of the soul. In between, John Duns Scotus had presented Aristotle as undecided on the question of immortality. In spite of Thomas's immortalist interpretation, however, it was by no means evident, two centuries later, that the Thomist version of Aristotelianism was historically correct. Secondly, a more substantive speculative problem lurked in the historical discussion: Whatever Aristotle's position, is the human soul in fact mortal or immortal?

The opinions of philosophers at the end of the Middle Ages, that is, of the professors who taught in the faculties of Arts of the main universities, were all the more divided, as neither Avicenna nor Averroes, both of them Muslim commentators on Aristotle, had considered the soul immortal in its singularity. For if it is true, as they thought, that there exists only one intellect agent for the whole of humanity, the singularity of each human person does not extend to the highest intellectual operations of the mind. In this case, whatever the nature of the human *animus,* it cannot possibly share the spirituality of the intellect agent and, not being spiritual, it cannot be immortal. Precisely, in spite of episcopal and papal pressure against their popularity, these non-Christian philosophers provided favorite readings in the faculties of Arts and in the *studia* that featured chairs of *philosophia naturalis.*

In fact, St. Thomas's philosophical assertion of the immortality of the soul ran into difficulties precisely on the point of singularity. Since the hylomorphic anthropology defended by Aquinas did not attribute the individuality of the human person to its form but to its matter, individuality was not attached directly to the soul, but to the soul's union with the body. In this case one may well wonder what happens to it at death, when the soul leaves the body. Duns Scotus and the later Franciscan school generally escaped the dilemma by positing *haecceitas,* a "thisness," in each human, which resulted from a substantial *forma corporeitatis,* a "form of corporeity," itself distinct from, though inseparably united with, the intellectual or spiritual form. As he denied the plurality of substantial forms in one human being, Thomas had effectively closed this door. The ensuing problem, however, though looming large in philosophy, had little impact in theology, since the teachings of the New Testament on rewards and punishments in the next life, on the resurrection, and on the eternal kingdom of God, necessarily implied a created soul that was immortal. Dismissed in theology, the question remained on the philosophical agenda: Is the immortality of the individual soul rooted in nature as such, and rationally demonstrable? Or is it an additional divine gift that is known theologically, not philosophically, by faith, not by reason?

An extreme philosophical tradition existed, which deliberately operated with no reference to the Christian faith. This had originated in the teaching of Siger de Brabant (c. 1235-1284) at the University of Paris. Siger had himself applied his version of Averroism to the soul in his *Questiones de anima,* when he had run into Thomas Aquinas's quite opposite interpretation of Aristotle. Thomas, who tackled Siger's central idea in his opusculum, *De unitate intellectus contra Averroistas,* considered Siger a distorter of true Aristotelianism.[1] Meanwhile, Bonaventure's last major work, *Collationes in Hexaëmeron,* took the form of a multi-sided presentation of Christian eschatology, in opposition both to the historico-trinitarian speculations of Joachim of Fiore (c. 1135-1202), and to the world outlook that was becoming fashionable in the faculty of Arts of the University of Paris.

In the later Middle Ages the theological tradition could draw on the official condemnation of Siger de Brabant in 1277 by the Bishop of Paris, Etienne Tempier. In spite of this Siger's interpretation of Aristotle and Averroes remained alive for a long time. The prolonged survival of Latin Averroism, and the continuing assertion of the mortality of the soul by philosophers, led two general councils of the West, the Council of Vienne (third session, 6 May 1312) and the Fifth Council of the Lateran (eighth session, 19 December 1513), to intervene in the name of the Church in favor of the immortality of the soul.

The Council of Vienne labeled "erroneous and inimical to the truth of the Catholic faith" the notion that "the substance of the rational or intellectual soul is not truly and by itself the form of

---

1. Thomas wrote abundantly about the soul and against the Averroists, e.g., *Questio disputata de anima* (*Quaestiones Disputatae,* vol. 3 [1925], pp. 91-206); *De unitate intellectus contra Averroistas* (*Opusculum* V, in Pierre Mandonnet, ed., *S. Thomae Aquinatis Opuscula Omnia,* vol. 1 [Paris: Lethielleux, 1927], pp. 33-69). Thomas declares: *Averroes non tam fuit Peripateticus quam Peripateticae philosophiae depravator* (*De unitate,* p. 50).

the human body,"[2] and it branded as heretical the thesis that "the rational or intellectual soul is not by itself and essentially the form of the human body." But if indeed the substance of the rational soul is the form of the human body *per se et essentialiter,* as the council said, how can it survive in the other world without the body that is essential to it? If theologians could be expected to suspend their judgment on this matter, it ran against the grain to do so in a philosophical context. In spite of the conciliar statement, therefore, diverse forms of Averroism remained alive in humanist circles and in many faculties of Arts. In the first half of the sixteenth century the debate was particularly active in the universities and *studia* of northern Italy. The discussion reached a high point in the *studium* of Padua, when the Fifth Lateran Council examined the problem again.

*   *   *

While we cannot examine all the details of the controversy, the importance of the question for a young humanist in the first decades of the sixteenth century may be underlined by a brief survey. In the theology of the schools, the *via moderna* had, since William of Ockham, considered the immortality of the soul as rationally unprovable, though certain by virtue of the Christian faith. In this case, however, what were the proper relations between, on one side, theology and faith and, on the other side, rational philosophy, *philosophia naturalis?* If it was not difficult for theologians to admit the coexistence of two tracks for the human mind, one philosophical or natural, the other theological or supernatural, it was harder to admit that the conclusions reached on both sides were equally true, though at different levels, if they stood in mutual contradiction. According to the fourth canto of *Inferno,* Dante Alighieri (1265-1321), passing through limbo, saw Aristotle at the center of an admiring

2. The text of the thirty-eight conciliar decrees was never formally promulgated. It was revised by popes Clement V and John XXII, and sent by the latter to the universities. The reference to the soul is in the first decree, *Fidei catholicae,* which is directed against the errors of Petrus Johannes Olivi (Joseph Alberigo et al., *Conciliorum Oecumenicorum Decreta* [henceforth, COD] [Basel: Herder, 1962], p. 337).

circle of ancient philosophers. On the outskirts of the circle were several medical doctors:

> Ipocràte, Avicenna, e Galïeno,
> Averoìs, che 'l gran comento feo.[3]

It was in hell, however, that Dante saw the "heretics,"[4] namely, those philosophers who, following Epicure, denied the immortality of the soul.

The nature and the immortality of the soul thus remained major philosophical questions commonly discussed among the humanists through the fourteenth and fifteenth centuries,[5] though, busy as they often were with linguistic and philological problems of Latin, Greek, or Hebrew relating to the ancient texts, the humanists did not generally look into metaphysical perspectives. As was still the case with Erasmus, their philosophical reflections usually remained within the limited horizon of morals, thus following a safe way between two strands that could be considered extreme: the mystical and the metaphysical. There were indeed mystical musings in the spirituality of *devotio moderna*. There were also metaphysical speculations in the circles that cultivated the writings of Avicenna or Averroes. Both strands could cause bishops and scholastic theologians of the old school — *antiqui* — to raise their eyebrows when researchers veered off, or seemed to veer off, the middle path of the theological tradition. This did happen, on the mystical side, among the *illuminati* or *alhumbrados*, and on the metaphysical side, in universities and *studia* in which the study of the Arts prescinded from faith and theology. When this happened it was tempting, though ultimately unconvincing, to avoid the hazardous perspectives opened

3. Alberto Chiari, ed., *La Divina Commedia* (Milan: Casa editrice Bietti, 1977), Canto IV, vv. 143-44, p. 28. The *Divine Comedy* was completed in 1317.

4. *Eresïarche* (Canto IX, v. 127, p. 55), translated as "Arch-Heretics" by Laurence Binyon in *The Portable Dante* (New York: Viking Press, 1975), p. 50.

5. In the next few pages I am indebted to Giovanni di Napoli, *L'immortalità dell'anima nel Rinascimento* (Turin: Società editrice internazionale, 1963), and its abundant Latin quotations.

in philosophy by making a distinction between two types of truths, philosophical and theological.

A sort of standoff between two types of truths seemed necessary to the autonomy of *philosophia naturalis,* and by the same token to the independence of the *studia* in which commentaries on Aristotle and his commentators occupied the center of the curriculum. Given the spread of Ockhamism and Nominalism in theology, the separation between reason and faith allowed philosophers to go their own way regardless of the theological certainties of revelation. Thus it was that, with the career of Paolo Nicoletti da Udine (1372-1429), Padua became a hotbed of Averroism, which spread therefrom to other intellectual centers in northern Italy. Many of the ensuing tractates on the soul were either chiefly Platonist or chiefly Aristotelian, or they attempted a synthesis of the two great systems. Some followed Greek or Muslim commentators, notably Alexander of Aphrodisia, Avicenna, and Averroes. All of them drew on St. Augustine, many on St. Thomas, St. Bonaventure, and more recent scholastics. Whether they were more theological or more philosophical, they constituted a library that could hardly escape the attention of an eager student of humanistic ideas in the spirit of the Renaissance, as Calvin had shown himself to be in his edition and commentary of Seneca's *De Clementia.*

*   *   *

Tractates such as *De anima, De immortalitate animae,* and related titles multiplied through the fourteenth and fifteenth centuries. This was all the more central a topic for Renaissance humanists as it evoked the germane question — also carefully examined — of "the dignity of man," *De dignitate hominis.* Human nature as such was at stake in the debate on the nature of the soul. The exaltation of human nature followed the assertion of the soul's immortality as a necessary corollary. And the corollary showed a tendency to replace the originally more limited question of immortality. In this sense the *De dignitate et excellentia hominis* (1452) of Gianozzo Manetti (1396-1459) inspired a multitude of similar essays *De dignitate hominis.* Bartolomeo Fazio (1400-1457), whose *De excellentia et praestantia hominis,* written between 1448 and 1450, grounded human dignity in the traditional Christian eschatology,[6] acquired a wide audience. Nonetheless, the theological demonstration of the soul's immortality did not do away with the desire to find a philosophical proof of it.

Philosophically, the affirmation of immortality can be based on the capacity to think. One did not only ask, however, "Is *animus* mortal or immortal?" One went on to wonder, "Is *anima* divine?," for immortality, within as well as without the Christian faith, is one of the traditional attributes of God. It is then logical to consider that one who shares immortality with God is also, in a sense that philosophers and theologians may wish to qualify, divine. Or, starting from the spirituality of the soul that is implied in the capacity to think, and affirming spirituality also as an essential attribute of God, one could end up with the striking formulation of the Florentine Cristoforo Landino (1424-1498): "Such is the divinity of our souls that nature itself compels us to believe them immortal."[7] If, however, there is a *divinitas animi,* and a human being is what the soul is, then man is himself in some sense divine. As Agostino Dati (1420-1479) argued, "All the meaning and permanence of human life lies in knowing and acknowledging the immortality of the soul."[8] This line of thought found a willing echo among some of the Greek humanists who settled in Italy after the fall of Constantinople to the Turks, notably Cardinal Basil Bessarion (1403-1472) and Giovanni Argiropulo (1415-1487).

A Platonist theological and philosophical approach was revived in Florence through the writings of Marsilio Ficino (1433-1499), who brings us nearer to Calvin's theological problematic. On the one hand, Ficino's most voluminous book, *Theologica platonica de immortalitate animorum* (1482), gave the soul's immortality the central place in philosophy. On the other hand, Ficino drew attention to the

---

6. As is stated in the prologue of his book, Fazio's intent was to complete the work of Innocent III (pope, 1198-1216), who, after writing *De miseria humanae conditionis,* intended to compose a *De dignitate naturae humanae,* in which he would show that if the human condition is indeed miserable, human nature as such enjoys a high dignity. This was never written.

7. Napoli, *L'Immortalità,* pp. 114-20.

8. Napoli, *L'immortalità,* p. 111.

relationship — the dialogue, as he called it — between God and the soul as to a question that ought to be central to the concerns of every human being. On this matter he composed a *Di Dio e anima* in Italian and a *Dialogus inter Deum et animam theologicus* in Latin. His *Oratio ad Deum theologica,* which he promised to himself that he would pray every day, expressed his personal commitment to an ongoing interior dialogue with God. In this, Ficino reiterated and reinterpreted what St. Augustine had presented in the *Soliloquies* as "the shortest and most perfect prayer": *Deus semper idem, noverim me, noverim te*[9] ("God ever the same, may I know myself, may I know you"). Self-knowledge and God-knowledge are inseparable. Since God is ever the same, my knowing God has itself to be a permanent feature of my being. It follows that the dialogue between God and the soul that begins in this life cannot be suspended by death but requires immortality. Augustine had himself demonstrated the point in the *Soliloquies:* Since the truth is eternal, so is the soul that knows it.

When Giovanni Pico della Mirandola (1463-1494) composed a *De hominis dignitate* to introduce the nine hundred theses that he proposed to defend in Rome on the feast of the Epiphany, 1487,[10] the debate on human dignity acquired a strikingly modern accent. God, according to Pico, invited Adam to define himself in total liberty, for he created Adam in mid-world, "neither celestial nor terrestrial, neither mortal nor immortal," in such a way that Adam himself had the liberty to decide what he would become. The choice lay between degeneration to the level of beasts and regeneration to the divine level. Thus the human soul, incarnate in a body, unites the high and the low, and it cannot properly grasp anything unless it first understands its core nature, its inner reality, as *imago Dei.* In this perspective Pico picked up the theme of man as the *copula* that hyphenates the high and the low. This notion itself derived from the older medieval view of the human being as a microcosm in which

---

9. *Soliloquia,* II, i, 1, BA, Dialogues philosophiques V (Paris: Desclée, 1948), p. 86.

10. The disputation was not authorized by Pope Innocent VIII, as a theological commission he had appointed objected to thirteen of the theses. Pico later explained that these theses did not all express his own opinion. In a quasi-scholastic exercise it was proper to debate ideas *secundum Averroem* as well as *secundum Plotinum.*

the macrocosm of the universe is summarized and reflected. Pico also extended the union of the high and the low beyond the universe. There is, as he perceived it, a *copulatio, colligatio,* between God and the human soul in the present life, which prepares their eternal unity, so that the ultimate dignity of the soul lies in its deification. Immortality is inscribed in the soul's very structure as a destiny that ought to be freely chosen.[11]

In the first decades of the sixteenth century a less spiritual twist was given to the discussion of the soul's immortality by the humanist Pietro Pomponazzi (1462-1525), a professor of *philosophia naturalis* in Padua, who lectured a number of times on the soul, notably in 1494-95, 1499-1500, 1503-6, 1513-14, and 1517-18. His *Tractatus de immortalitate animae* is from 1516. Originally Pomponazzi was a rather hesitant Averroist, who eventually veered toward the interpretation of Aristotle held by Alexander of Aphrodisias, a teacher in Athens around the year 200 B.C. Following Alexander, Pomponazzi denied the individual immortality of the soul as a philosophical datum. His immensely erudite writings drew on the scholastic tradition as well as on classical philosophy, and he did not reject the Church's teaching that the soul is immortal. Methodologically, however, he was determined to examine the question of the soul strictly as a philosopher, *remoto lumine fidei,* prescinding from the light of faith. Philosophically, he concluded, one cannot know the soul well enough to decide whether it is immortal or mortal by nature.

Such ideas could not go unchallenged. Pomponazzi was taken to task by other distinguished humanists. His *De immortalitate animae* caused turmoil in Venice, where it was condemned by the patriarch, Antonio Contarini (d. 1524, patriarch in 1508), and by the senate. Among the many critiques of Pomponazzi that followed, the *De immortalitate animae* (1517) of the future cardinal Gasparo Contarini[12] (1483-1542) deserves a special mention, if only because

11. Henri de Lubac, *Pic de la Mirandole. Etudes et discussions* (Paris: Aubier-Montaigne, 1974), esp. pp. 161-93.

12. A distinguished layman who was a humanist and a theologian, Gasparo Contarini became a diplomat at the service of Venice and then of the pope, and Pope Paul III made him a cardinal of the Holy Roman Church in 1535. He was a member of the *Consilium de reformatione ecclesiae* that gave its report in 1537. Calvin

Pomponazzi listed it as *prima contradictio* — the first contradiction — of his teaching. Contarini had studied in Padua under Pomponazzi himself. His book, known at first in manuscript form, did not carry an indication of authorship. He admitted finding himself at first convinced by Pomponazzi, but turning against him through further study of Aristotle and Thomas Aquinas. It became evident to Contarini "that the human intellect cannot be one and the same in all humans," and that "the human soul is simply immortal, although this is less than the immortality of pure spirits."[13] That is, the nature of understanding requires the spirituality and immortality of the intellect, which is identical with the soul. There followed an exchange of writings, Pomponazzi responding with an *Apologia prima,* to which Contarini retorted with a *De immortalitate animae liber secundus,* based on philosophy alone. Pomponazzi answered again with *Apologia secunda* (1518), which in turned provoked the entry of many a theologian into the fray.

The official Church also was led to intervene once more, in part because Pomponazzi's theses ran contrary to the dogmatic tradition, in part also because, as they gained notoriety, they caused scandal in non-philosophical circles. In the constitution *Apostolici regiminis,* which was promulgated in December 1513 by Leo X (pope, 1513-1521), the eighth session of Lateran Council V recalled the teaching of the Council of Vienne on the soul as the form of the body, and rejected two philosophical notions: first, that "the soul is mortal"; second, that "there is a single soul for all humans."[14] The first reason that was given for this condemnation was strictly philosophical: "Since it is not only, by itself and essentially *(per se et essentialiter),* the form of the human body, ... but it is also immortal, and, given the multitude of the bodies in which it is infused, it is in-

---

met him in 1541 at the Colloquy of Regensburg, where Contarini headed the papal delegation and Melanchthon the Lutheran delegation.

13. *Duo vero, quemadmodum puto ego, de intellectu homano naturalis ratio efficaciter ostendit. Horum alterum est quod intellectus humanus unicus in omnibus hominibus esse non potest, ut putavit Averroes. Alterum vero, quod anima hominis simpliciter sit immortalis, licet deficiat ab intelligentiarum immortalitate. Neque arbitror in duobus his Aristotelem dubitasse ullo pacto* (cited in Napoli, *L'Immortalità,* p. 281, note 9).

14. COD, pp. 581-82; DS 140-41.

dividually multiplicable, multiple, and destined to multiplication."[15] In addition, the council denied the possibility that these notions could be true philosophically while they were erroneous in the light of revelation. More precisely, they contradicted Scripture and the Church's belief in the incarnation, in the mysteries of Christ, and in the resurrection of the flesh.

The conciliar language suggests an underlying question that could possibly be ignored by philosophers, but to which theologians were bound to react. In the warmth of their defense of the immortality of the soul, did not the Christian humanists tip the balance in favor of human self-exaltation? Did they not nurture a new version of Pelagianism that was profoundly un-Christian? Relying as it did on the achievements of human reason, the methodology of the humanists was hardly equipped to bring this matter up. It is not unreasonable to think, however, that sensitive Christian consciences could feel caught on the horns of a new dilemma: either the soul's immortality or true creatureliness! either the arrogance of self-satisfaction or Christian humility before God! This may well have been part of the reason why the small group of anabaptists Calvin had in mind when he wrote *Psychopannychia* solved the problem by simply denying the natural immortality of the soul and seeing resurrection as pure grace.

Though Calvin did not in his treatment of the soul directly allude to the philosophy of Pomponazzi or to the decrees of the Fifth Lateran Council, he could not have been unaware of the academic discussions that had agitated the philosophical world for over two centuries. Granted, then, that the young Calvin was eager to consolidate his scholarly standing by writing, in humanist fashion, on the immortality of the soul, his sense of the Christian tradition and his growing interest in true doctrine led him to accept his friends' challenge. He would refute the anabaptists, and he would do so without falling into the Pelagian trap. For such a task, however, the predominantly philosophical methodology of the humanists would not do. Calvin's beginning evangelical interests militated against using a

15. . . . *verum et immortalis, et pro corporum quibus infunditur multitudine singulariter multiplicabilis, et multiplicata, et multiplicanda sit.*

merely rational method. From the standpoint of Renaissance humanism, therefore, what he did was profoundly revolutionary: He chose to confront the thesis of the death of the soul on the sole grounds of Scripture and of the testimonies of the early Church. In this perspective he had to rely on revelation and theology, for it is the revealed knowledge of God that is the key to real self-knowledge.

Little help could be found for such a task in the early writings of the main reformers. Given the general imprecision of the Old Testament about the state of the dead, and vague allusions in the New Testament to "the bosom of Abraham" and the opposite destinies of Dives and Lazarus, a certain agnosticism would seem to be permissible as to the exact nature of the kingdom of Jesus, the paradise promised to the good thief. Indeed, this agnosticism corresponded fairly well to Martin Luther's reluctance to speculate about the life of the soul after death, a reluctance that led a few authors, and already in the seventeenth century, to include Luther among Calvin's adversaries in *Psychopannychia*.[16] Admittedly, Calvin could find hints in Melanchthon's long dissertation on the invocation of saints that constitutes article XXI of the *Apology for the Confession of Augsburg* (1532). Melanchthon's denial of the legitimacy of praying to the dead implied the conviction of their continuing life in God after bodily death. It also implied the pious belief that the saints do pray for the Church, coupled, however, with a total uncertainty, given the silence of Scripture, as to their capacity to hear our prayers.

Ulrich Zwingli (1484-1541), who had himself been a devoted humanist, had never, unlike Calvin, envisioned a career in the new knowledge. Ordained a priest in 1506, he had been the pastor in the town of Glarus for ten years. In that capacity he had served as chaplain to those of his parishioners who had enlisted as mercenaries at the service of the fighting pope Julius II (1503-1513) in the wars of northern Italy. At the battle of Marignano (1515), however, the Swiss had been soundly beaten, after which they had changed loyalties and passed over to the service of the winner, the King of France, François I. Disgusted with this reversal of allegiance, however,

16. Thus François Garasse, *La Doctrine curieuse des beaux esprits de ce temps, ou prétendus tels* (Paris, 1623).

Zwingli had left Glarus to become chaplain to the popular pilgrimage of Our Lady of Einsiedeln, and in 1518 he had been made rector of the main church in Zürich, the Grossmünster. While he was actively involved in pastoral care he had found time to cultivate the scriptural dimension of Renaissance studies, and he had acquired a distinguished library of humanist writings. He was not attracted to philosophy, however, but to biblical studies in Greek. He had several of his sermons printed. And when the possibility of reforming the Church in depth emerged on the horizon he sided with the reforming party.

It was in 1523 that Zwingli publicly endorsed the Reformation, when, against the vicar general of Constance, Johannes Faber (1478-1541), he presented and defended sixty-seven theses in which he explained his doctrinal position and denied all religious authority to the bishops and the pope. In 1525, at Guillaume Farel's suggestion, he composed his central work, one of the great books of the Reformation, *Commentarius de vera et falsa religione*. Dedicated to a humanist of a different stripe, King François I of France, this book was composed chiefly *ad usum Galliarum,* "for use in the Gauls," where Renaissance humanism still was, in spite of Calvin's little known study of Seneca, more literary and spiritual than philosophical or theological. Centered on Christ and his work, the *Commentarius* naturally assumed the immortality of the soul without having to muster philosophical arguments for it. Among many other shorter works[17] Zwingli had, in July 1527, published a denunciation of the "catabaptists": *In catabaptistarum strophas elenchus.* Calvin was presumably acquainted with this piece.

On the whole, the well-known reformers of Germany and Switzerland were by no means a major source for Calvin in the matter of the soul's immortality. By contrast, Calvin may well have taken cognizance of the interest that some of the Catholic opponents of the Reformation showed in the question. In fact, the year 1534 had seen

---

17. The most important are, *Auslegung und Gründe der Schlussreden* (1523); *Von göttlicher und menschlicher Gerechtigkeit* (1523); *Ein kurz und christliche Anleitung* (1523); *Der Hirt* (1524); *Ad Carolem imperatorem fidei ratio* (1530). Zwingli had a number of his sermons printed.

the appearance of several new works in defense of the traditional position on the immortality of the soul. The Dominican Thomas de Vio (Cajetan, 1458-1534), Luther's constant adversary, treated the question in his *Commentarius de Ecclesiastes,* as also the Spanish Franciscan Alonso de Castro (1495-1558) in his ambitious *Adversus omnes haereses.* Calvin may also have been acquainted with the *Nugae* of the French humanist Nicolas Bourdon, and with a relevant letter of Etienne Dolet (1509-1546), all of these works published in 1534. Adding to these Marguerite d'Angoulême's poem, *Dialogue spirituel en forme de vision nocturne,* one obtains an impressive harvest of immortalist writings that were flourishing in France when Calvin was still there. Indeed the question of the soul had become a hot topic, a point that could not have escaped Calvin when he started thinking about the future *Psychopannychia.*

An older contribution to the debate on the soul had come to light very close, geographically speaking, to Angoulême and Nérac. The Spaniard Raymond de Sebonde (d. 1437), a former chancellor and professor of *sacra pagina* at the University of Toulouse, had entered the debate on the soul with a *Liber creaturarum sive de homine,* published in 1436. This humanist from Barcelona, a doctor in medicine as well as a philosopher, was to become one of the intellectual mentors of Montaigne (1533-1592). There is in fact an uncanny similarity between a major thesis of Raymond de Sebonde and the opening chapter of the first *Institutio.* Sebonde exploited the Bonaventurian theme of the "books" written by God.[18] Where Bonaventure had three books, however — *natura, anima, Scriptura* — Sebonde had only two. Along with the book of Scripture God gave the "book of nature," which Sebonde called the "book of creatures," each creature being "a letter written by the finger of God,"[19] and *homo,* man, the principal letter. The book of the soul was thus included by Sebonde in the book of nature. Or, one could say, the book of nature and the book of the soul had collapsed into one.

The central theme of this *liber creaturarum* was the knowledge of

18. The line from Bonaventure to Sebonde may have passed through the Spanish Franciscan Raimundo Lullo (d. 1315).

19. Napoli, *L'Immortalità,* p. 76, note 88.

God, a knowledge that Sebonde also considered to be inseparable from self-knowledge. The science *(scientia)* of the book of creatures, Sebonde had written,

> has no need of any other science or art; it does not even presuppose grammatical logic or any of the seven liberal arts, or physics, or metaphysics, because it is primary and is necessary to every man, and it orders all the others toward a good end and toward true human usefulness. For this knowledge teaches man to know himself.[20]

Human self-knowledge includes awareness of immortality and of the perpetuity of the human will, which are required as a matter of justice in regard to merit and demerit. Sebonde pays no attention to the quarrels between Averroists and their critics. His concern is for true knowledge of God and of the self, and his method is to search for what is evidently implied in the structure of the self.[21]

Whether Calvin was directly acquainted with the work of Raymond de Sebonde is not certain, though it is a reasonable hypothesis. The *Liber creaturarum* may well have been on the shelves of the du Tillet library. It may have provided one of the sources of Calvin's theological point of departure.[22]

*   *   *

In his edition and commentary of Seneca's *De clementia,* Calvin the humanist had done painstaking work in all the sciences that contribute to the study of ancient texts, such as Latin philology, gram-

---

20. Napoli, *L'immortalità,* p. 76, note 87.

21. *Quidquid probatur de aliqua re per ipsammet et per naturam ejus maxime certum est* (Napoli, *L'Immortalità,* p. 76, note 89).

22. The soul remained a concern of the Renaissance in Spain as well as in Italy and France. Juan Luis Vives (1492-1540), a Spanish disciple of Erasmus and a friend of Thomas More who lived in Flanders and England after studying in Paris, composed a *De Anima* in 1538. This work "is often described as laying the foundations of modern empirical psychology" (E. Allison Peers, *St. John of the Cross and Other Lectures and Addresses, 1920-1945* [London: Faber and Faber, 1946], p. 80).

matical analysis, logic, rhetoric, and history. He had compared the text and ideas of Seneca with the writings of other authors: ancient ones like Virgil, Quintilian, Cicero, Suetonius, and Plutarch; recent ones like Erasmus, Lefèvre d'Étaples, Guillaume Budé, and many others. He had also examined the principles of politics as seen in the light of Stoic philosophy. The intellectual world of the Renaissance in which he was so much at ease, however, could not hold Calvin's attention once he began to read the Christian Scriptures eagerly, with the help of an increasing knowledge of Greek and Hebrew. In the Bible Calvin included the Christian apocrypha, which, in keeping with medieval practice, he recognized as truly edifying and spiritually useful. Yet he could not help finding the inspired text obscure and difficult, at least when compared with a philosophical composition like that of Seneca. As Cottret puts it, "the Bible is too old a text in too new a world."[23] The word of God is hard to read. No wonder that the anabaptists, lovers of novelties, men of small intelligence and of no common sense, perverts who twist everything out of shape, seemed to be wallowing in confusion! Since "the word of God is not new . . ."[24] it does not appeal to novelty seekers. Furthermore, if the word of God saves those who receive it, it also condemns those who do not accept it. As he composed *Psychopannychia,* however, Calvin's beginning devotion to the biblical writings found comfort in the philosophy of the soul that had been emphasized in Platonism and had remained in the background of Stoicism.

The commentary on *De clementia* duly noted the superiority of the soul over the body. Seneca had briefly remarked that the "whole body is at the service of the soul."[25] He had seen an analogy between the prince and the multitude of his people on the one hand, the soul and the body's many organs on the other. The human composite, body and soul, is somehow similar to human society. In his commentary, however, Calvin paid more attention to the soul than to the political analogy that St. Paul had used in 1 Corinthians 12 to il-

23. Bernard Cottret, *Calvin. Biographie* (Paris: Editions Jean-Claude Lattès, 1995), p. 91.

24. *La parole de Dieu n'est pas nouvelle.* . . .

25. Ford Lewis Battles and André Malan Hugo, eds., *Calvin's Commentary on Seneca's De Clementia* (Leiden: E. J. Brill, 1969), p. 78.

lustrate the unity of the body of Christ in its many members. He confirmed the soul's dominion over the body. "The human soul," Calvin wrote, "is something tiny and minuscule, seen by no eyes,"[26] while the body is massively visible and beautiful. The soul is simple, the body varied. The body has strength and natural vigor, yet *penes animum est temperatura,* that is, "control of the body is with the soul." Ancient philosophers disagreed as to the soul's whereabouts in the body, a problem that Calvin did not attempt to solve. Rather than in the location of the soul he was interested in its activity, namely, in the various sorts of human desires that had been recognized by philosophers: natural, sensitive or animal — which are themselves inferior or superior — and rational. These desires, Calvin remarked, "so contradict one another that we would be pulled apart unless Dame Reason were in charge."[27]

*   *   *

Once he had discovered that he could follow the Bible and throw his lot with the Christian faith without giving up the requirements of reason, Calvin the theologian and biblical commentator did not pursue, though he never retracted, his humanist concerns. That he remained a humanist at heart is manifest in his careful use of Renaissance Latin. It is also clear in the craftsmanship that he brought to his compositions in French and in the translations he made of his Latin writings, which is all the more admirable as he really was the first to give a theological dimension to the French language.[28] He could receive the word of God with trust and explain it with precision while remaining within the bounds of rational sobriety before the divine revelation.

Calvin's central concern when he proceeded to refute anabaptist mortalism may be identified further. Is the soul, after death, asleep

26. Battles and Hugo, *Commentary on De Clementia,* p. 90.

27. . . . *nisi domina ratio praefecta fuerit* (p. 94).

28. Calvin's posthumous rival for the souls of the peasants of the Valais, a Swiss canton in the Rhône Valley, St. François de Sales (1567-1622) — Bishop of Geneva who could never reside in his episcopal city — also wrote in distinguished French, but in spiritual rather than systematic theology.

until the resurrection and the last judgment? There is really no need to be anxious about this, unless one wonders in the first place what this soul is that is said by some anabaptists to fall asleep at death. Since I live now in my body, how can I be sure that my soul is other than body, that it does not die when the body dies? This amounts to posing the fundamental question of self-identity. Having already been a distinguished Latinist for quite a while, Calvin knew that *animus* and its feminine equivalent, *anima,* connote the principle of life,[29] even though he would not formulate this principle in the hylomorphic terms of Aristotelian philosophy. One may ask, however: When life goes out, what happens to *anima?* While to modern ears the question may sound like a Zen koan, it presupposes a fundamental concern about the nature of the self, a concern that can be put very personally: What is my soul? What, ultimately, am I?

Neither Calvin's public career nor his writings suggest that once he had embarked on his reforming career he ever entertained any hesitancy about his providential calling or about his identity as a prophet at the service of the reform of the Church. In spite of a native shyness he conveyed a high sense of certainty about himself, his interpretation of the Bible, his systematic elaboration of theology, his denunciation of the fanatics and of Michael Servetus. But such a certainty may well have covered up what could have been a crisis of identity at the very time when Calvin came to agree with the judgment of the reformers that a true Christian believer cannot follow the Roman pontiff with a good conscience, that the Roman Mass is filled with blasphemies, and that the Roman priesthood is an abomination in the eyes of God. Already in 1534, on the way from Angoulême to Noyon with a small party, Calvin had celebrated the Lord's Supper on a Sunday, not by attending Mass, but by presiding at a *manducation* in a cave near the city of Poitiers.[30] In spite of this, the extent to which Calvin rejected the Roman system at that moment is still debatable, since no anti-Roman feeling is expressed either in the introductory letters or in the main text of *Psychopannychia.*

29. Whence our term "animation."
30. Emile Doumergue, *Jean Calvin, les hommes et les choses de son temps,* 7 vols. (Geneva: Slatkine Reprints, 1969), vol. 1, pp. 459-61.

An anti-Roman suspicion, soon to turn into a conviction, was growing in Calvin's mind in the years 1535 to 1536. This is manifest in the letters to his two humanist friends Nicolas Duchemin and Gérard Roussel, promising reformers who, to Calvin's horror, accepted promotion in the Church of Rome. Both had been attracted to the reform of the Church that was afoot in humanist circles, and they had even spoken or written in its favor — notably on Luther's doctrine of justification by faith alone, which functioned at the time as a test of the will to reform the Christian life and doctrine. Yet Duchemin had recently begun to climb the Roman ecclesiastical ladder, as he had agreed to be made *officialis* in the diocese of Le Mans. Meanwhile, Roussel, chaplain to Marguerite d'Angoulême, had accepted ordination as Bishop of Oléron. This was a normal promotion for a priest who was deeply appreciated by the king's beloved sister, and it put him well on the way to high ecclesiastical honors. But this was precisely what distressed their friend Calvin: How free would political and ecclesiastical entanglements leave the new bishop to follow the gospel? Calvin's letters to these men are so full of invectives against the Roman system that they appear to be both spontaneous expressions of anxiety for his two friends and the fruit of a growing anger at the Roman system.

*   *   *

If his readings and reflections had possibly led Calvin to abandon some Catholic practices of devotion and some Catholic doctrines even before the address of Chancellor Cop in November 1533, his careful investigation of the nature of the soul in *Psychopannychia* may well show that in the eyes of some French adherents of the Reformation he was already a trusted guide in regard to doctrine. But it also points to a lingering personal problem. The fidelity to Rome of some of his close friends, not only Duchemin and Roussel, but also, in 1537, Louis du Tillet, could not leave him indifferent. It led him to expose the Nicodemites, men and women who, like Nicodemus in the Gospel of John, do not dare to declare themselves openly for what they know in their heart to be the true doctrine.

Nicodemites or not, their decision to stay with the old Church while hoping for internal reform, rather than search for new ecclesial structures and a reformulation of doctrine, came to Calvin as a personal challenge: it suggested that his own choice was mistaken. It may also have hinted that he had himself lingered, though for a short time, as a Nicodemite. Writing about the immortality of the soul provided him with the balance he needed to keep his theological sanity, to say nothing of his psychological peace, in a period of external turmoil and presumably of personal stress.

III

Does the Soul Sleep?

The prefatory letters of *Psychopannychia* — to a friend, and to the readers — carefully delineate the scope of Calvin's purpose[1] in this short work. The letter to a friend is dated from Orléans in the year 1534. Since most of that year was spent with Louis du Tillet in Claix and Angoulême, where Calvin had access to his host's extensive library, the friend in question is likely to be du Tillet himself. As to the place, Orléans was on the way to Noyon when Calvin traveled from Angoulême to his hometown to dispose of his benefices.

We need not decide if Calvin was already bent on seeking exile when he wrote this letter, and still less if in his heart he had already joined the cause of the Reformation. When his rooms at the Collège Montaigu were been raided by the royal police after Nicolas Cop's notorious address of November 1533, he had safely retired to the south. After the *placards* affair, however, it was not hard to know that the king was truly angry, and Calvin may well have felt a natural desire for safety, if he thought of himself as somehow belonging in the camp of those who would be identified as subversive of the accepted order, and this whether or not he had a hand in the composition of Cop's speech. The exact moment when Calvin made the leap

---

1. These letters are analyzed at length in Jung-Uck Hwang, *Der junge Calvin und seiner Psychopannychia*, Europäische Hochschulschriften. Reihe XXIII. Theologie. Series XXIII, vol. 407 (Frankfurt-am-Main: Peter Lang, 1991), pp. 91-128, 128-60.

from the enlightened humanism of the Seneca commentator to a determined opposition to the leadership of the Bishop of Rome is far from certain. Yet his sojourn in Angoulême and his work in the du Tillet family library had considerably deepened his knowledge of the theological questions raised by the reformers. His visit to Nérac is a sufficient token of his interest in the religious side of the humanist movement to suggest that he was considering the likelihood of a personal call to devote his life to the gospel and the reform of the Church.

*   *   *

As he introduces his writing on the soul, Calvin recalls that he has been alerted for quite some time already to the spread of a false doctrine about the soul, which, much to his surprise, has now gained considerable ground among some advocates of the reform movement. At first he could not identify these people, for he had not read their pamphlets but only bits and pieces *(notulas quasdam)* that he had gathered from a friend. Yet he knew enough to call them *animicidae*[2] and, keeping the Greek word, ψυχοκτόνοι, "assassins of the soul." The question they raised struck him as so important that he was afraid of making himself "a traitor to the truth" *(veritatis proditor)* if he did not refute their doctrine. Their teaching is so pernicious that it does not allow him to write with his usual sobriety. He will nevertheless attempt to stay within the bounds of moderation as he refutes them. And he heartily wishes that someone would discover a way *(ratio)* that could force this "polluting evil to recede before it crawls farther each day like a cancer!"[3]

After providing the brief overview of the emergence of the doctrine in question, which was sketched in the previous chapter, Calvin identifies its contemporary advocates as anabaptists and, in the last lines of the book, as catabaptists. He briefly states a few principles that he intends to apply in the theological argumentation that

---

2. *Psychopannychia*, Zimmerli edition, p. 24. (My references being to Zimmerli's edition, I will not repeat his name each time.)
3. *Psychopannychia*, p. 16.

41

follows. He will not venture into expressions of hatred, contempt of persons, or impudence, for he does not wish to give offense to anyone. He bemoans the sorry spectacle of people who give free rein to an insane desire to bite and hurt others, and meanwhile "who tearfully cry that you are breaking the unity of the Church and violating charity if you touch them with the tip of your finger."[4] Calvin, however, does not "recognize unity except in Christ, or charity unless Christ is its link. For the reason to preserve charity is that faith remain for us holy and integral."[5] Since charity is ordered to faith it should not be used as a pretext to delay the refutation of untruth.

This letter amounts to a statement on the urgency of responding to the challenge about the soul that Calvin attributes to some of the anabaptists.

*　　*　　*

The address to the readers is dated "Basel, 1536." This was the year when Calvin sent the text to a printer, although the printing was delayed by a series of mishaps for another six years. The author has now found shelter in Switzerland. He has revised and, to an extent that is impossible to gauge, rewritten his essay. From his letter to Libertet[6] of September 1535, we learn that this revision has consisted essentially in moving much of the material around, suppressing some points, adding a few others.[7] Calvin has also moderated the original tone and language of his essay, for he is now eager not to shock "the delicate ears" of "many good people" who have been led astray "by excessive credulity or by ignorance of Scripture," and who "do not sin obstinately or maliciously"[8] in professing their error. If a few vehement expressions still remain, they will serve to show the importance of the is-

---

4. *Psychopannychia*, p. 17.

5. *His responsum sit, primum, nullam nos agnoscere unitatem nisi in Christ, nullam caritatem nisi cujus ipse sit vinculum* . . . (pp. 17-18).

6. Christopher Fabri, as above, ch. 1, p. 9.

7. *Non multis quidem aut additis aut expunctis sed prorsus inverso ordine, quamquam pauca quaedam sustuli, alia addivi, mutavi etiam nonnulla* (quoted in Hwang, *Der junge Calvin*, p. 182).

8. *Psychopannychia*, pp. 18-19.

sue, for Calvin is now dealing with "that most pernicious flock of anabaptists," who deserve much more violent language! A subdued style, however, better fits his purpose, since he intends to "draw those who do not wish to be pushed,"[9] attracting them to the right way rather than shaming them into it.

Having briefly indicated the qualities that are to be desired in the writer of such a piece, Calvin turns to several qualities that ought to be present among the readers. In doing so he makes use of the standard medieval device inspired by Aristotelian logic, with which the scholastics were wont to attribute four causes to their theological work. The topic that is treated acts as material cause; the qualities of the work constitute its formal cause; the intended purpose is the final cause; and the author is the efficient cause. Calvin, however, who is not addicted to the philosophy of Aristotle, simplifies this scheme by reducing it to a contrast between author and reader — roughly, the efficient and the final cause — in which he also manages to include the style or qualities of the author's work. As he turns to the qualities to be desired in the readers of his work Calvin remembers that his commentary on Seneca's *De clementia* was not a publishing success, and it is with a nice touch of humor that he addresses his readers, "if there are any."[10] They should bring to the reading of these pages "a healthy judgment and a soul like a seat prepared for the truth."[11] While novelties have great attraction for some people, "we must reflect that there is only one voice of life, that comes from the mouth of the Lord."[12] Our ears should be closed to all other voices, for we know that "his word is not new; and that which was from the beginning is and always shall be."

There nevertheless are subversive characters who, "as they put the word of God to a perverse use, and call its teaching a novelty when it comes to light, bend also like reeds to whatever wind." Calvin asks rhetorical questions that are destined to bring the readers to acknowledge the supremacy of the word of God. Does learning

9. *Trahere posset eos qui duci nolint* (p. 19).
10. . . . *si qui futuri sunt* (p. 19).
11. . . . *integrum judicium . . . et animum quasi paratam veritati sedem* (p. 19).
12. *Sed debemus cogitare unam esse vocem vitae, quae est ex ore domini* (p. 19).

Christ consist in "listening to any sorts of doctrines, even true ones, without the word of God?" What does a person *(homo)* really own besides vanity? One should always follow the examples of the early Christians, who, "when they received the word, scrutinized the Scriptures" (Acts 17:11). Today, however, "we receive the word of God with I know not what laziness or rather what contempt." Through the centuries one is able to see the spectacle of so many uneducated persons who tragically show off their ignorance. They want to be known as Christians because they have touched a few chapters of the commonplaces *(loci communes)*. In the first half of the sixteenth century this expression was used to designate the topics of theology; in fact, the first systematic theology written in a Lutheran context was Melanchthon's *Loci communes,* published in 1521. But acquaintance with a few theological notions is not sufficient to master theology. To know one or two of these commonplaces is itself a form of ignorance. And it is exhibited precisely by the anabaptists, who, to avoid the shame of seeming to be ignorant, vaticinate[13] about everything with absolute confidence! Indeed, this impudence has been at the origin of so many schisms, so many errors, so many scandals to our faith, so many occasions for "blasphemies against the name and the word of God among the impious," that as soon as "we have learned three syllables we are inflated by a pretense of wisdom into being rich and kings to ourselves, yet we do not burst!"[14] But, Calvin asks rhetorically, "is that the way to learn? to turn and twist the Scriptures so as to serve our libido, to submit to our own sense, than which nothing is more stupid?" If this is the way the Scriptures are read, it should cause no surprise that so many sects are mushrooming among those who at first gave their name to the gospel and to a renewal of the word.

What should be done? To a confession of coming somewhat belatedly to the truth Calvin adds a determination to follow the Word of God where it will lead, and he invites his willing readers to enter with the same disposition: "As to us, brothers, warned by so many examples we are coming so late to wisdom. Let us always hang onto

---

13. . . . *quasi ex tripode* (p. 20): as from the hot seat of the Pithia in Delphos.
14. *Psychopannychia,* pp. 19-20.

the Lord's mouth and add nothing to its wisdom or mix some of our wisdom with it, lest like a yeast it corrupt the entire dough." Let us rather "offer ourselves to the Lord as the disciples he wants to have, poor, void of personal wisdom, knowing nothing, willing to know nothing except what He will teach."[15] Only those who are empty of vanities can be filled with heavenly wisdom. In choosing this as the fundamental principle of his search for the truth Calvin echoes the words of St. Paul in 2 Corinthians 12:10: "Whenever I am weak, then I am strong."[16] He also stands squarely in the medieval tradition of the *via negativa* or, as it was called by Nicolas of Cusa, of *docta ignorantia*. Some three to four decades later St. John of the Cross will give it a striking formulation: In order to have all, *todo*, I must have and be nothing, *nada!*[17]

*   *   *

New though he is to theological writing, Calvin has already found his critics. At the time when he revises his text on the immortality of the soul he is also working on the first form of his *Institutio christianae religionis*. Although his still unpublished writing on the soul has been seen by few readers, the rumor is already abroad that Calvin is about to publish an attack on the catabaptists, for there are those, as Calvin says, "who criticize my project *(consilium)*," who blame him for making a mountain out of a mole-hill, "starting huge fights about nothing." It is not nothing, however, he responds, "to see the light of God extinguished by the devil's darkness." And in any case, "this question" — the matter of the soul's sleep, death, or awakened survival — "is more important than is believed by many." At this point, Calvin does not explain the importance of it, since this should be made obvious by the argumentation of the book. As to himself, he has attempted to defend the truth. He nonetheless remains quite modest as to the outcome of his endeavors: "Whether I

15. *Psychopannychia*, pp. 20-21.
16. Translation as in RSV.
17. *Ascent of Mount Carmel*, Bk. 1, ch. 13 in *The Collected Works of St. John of the Cross* (Washington: ICS Publications, 1991), pp. 149-51.

have succeeded I do not know; I certainly intended to do so and I gave it my best. May others, if they have something better, contribute to the common good."

Since this address to the readers of the book functions as an introduction it really serves two purposes, which emerge from two points that are made in it. On the one hand Calvin indicates where he sees his place, so far, in the evangelical movement of reform. He wants to be a voice crying against distortions of the gospel that are spread by the anabaptists. Writing the *Psychopannychia* in Latin, he does not expect to be read by the ordinary people whose access to scholarly debate is limited by their exclusive use of a vernacular language. In this Calvin follows the example of Martin Luther and the first reformers, whose early writings were read, where available, by the well-educated, those who at least had a reading knowledge of Latin, and hardly by the people at large. His intention is to alert potential leaders, scholars, and educated persons to the dangers represented by the anabaptist movement. While he already projects himself as a teacher of the truth that has been revealed through Christ, he does not pretend to act as a minister in the formal sense of the term, and still less as an organizer or an administrator.

On the other hand Calvin outlines the theological method that he intends to use. The word of God in the Bible will be his guide and his judge. The style and tone will be sober, even though Calvin will write in his highly polished Renaissance Latin. He will not indulge in excessive speculation. Even then, however, he will in fact take scholastic treatises as models for his argumentation about the state of the soul, for he is about to proceed through four steps that are germane to the scholastic method: explanation of a thesis, analysis of the state of the question, presentation of arguments, refutation of counterarguments. Additional precisions on method are given at the beginning of the treatise. In any disputation, we are told, the topic must have been honestly examined by the speaker, and clearly explained to the reader. And since no one is likely to admit defeat in a controversy as long as it remains possible to play games with distinctions and evasions, the adversary must be pushed to the point where he is forced to give up, and he should be tackled, so to say, in hand to hand combat so that he cannot possibly escape.

Nothing has been said in this that would distinguish Calvin's theological method from the general approach of medieval theology. The relevance of tradition to the determination of doctrinal questions is far from rejected. Calvin appeals to tradition in his argumentation. A long presentation of patristic doctrine is introduced with the sentence, "Thus also did those who treated of God's mysteries with moderation and reverence transmit them to us by hand."[18] Indeed Calvin declares: "Let us always hang on the word of the Lord and let us not add to his wisdom or mix with it something of our own."[19] I do not find any evidence in *Psychopannychia* that by the time it was published Calvin had endorsed a reformed conception of reliance on scripture alone.[20] One may even say that Calvin's appeal to the Lord's wisdom as expressed in the word remains vague if it is compared with the clarity of Thomas Aquinas's earlier formulation of the scriptural principle. The Angelic Doctor had explicitly taught that only "authorities" taken from Scripture can provide apodictic arguments in theology,[21] and furthermore that only from the literal sense of Scripture, expressing the author's intention, and not from allegorical senses, can valid arguments be drawn.[22] Among the authorities of the tradition from whom Calvin argues at length, in the present work, are Tertullian, Irenaeus, John Chrysostom, Augustine, Cyril of Alexandria, Eusebius of Caesarea. He also quotes, or refers to, Cyprian, Origen, Ambrose, Jerome, Hilary of Poitiers, Basil, Gregory the Great, Bernard of Clairvaux. It is somewhat sche-

18. *Haec etiam nobis per manus tradiderunt, qui parce et reverenter tractarunt dei mysteria* (p. 83). This formula is even more forceful than that of the Council of Trent: *. . . traditionibus . . . quae . . . quasi per manus traditae ad nos usque pervenerunt . . .* (session IV, 8 April 1546: DS 1501). The word *quasi*, "as though," implies that the transmission by hand is an analogy. Calvin's formulation is more direct: The Church Fathers did transmit the doctrine to us by hand.

19. *Pendeamus semper ex ore domini et nequid ad ejus sapientiam addamus aut admisceamus de nostro* (p. 20).

20. Jung-Uck Hwang insists that Calvin goes strictly by Scripture alone in his argumentation, I do not think this is correct.

21. *Auctoritatibus autem canonicae Scripturae utitur proprie, ex necessitate argumentando* (S.T., I, q.1, a.8, ad 2).

22. *. . . omnes sensus funduntur super unum, scilicet litteralem, ex quo solo potest trahi argumentum, non autem ex his quae secundum allegoriam dicuntur* (S.T., I, q.1, a.10, ad 1).

matic, yet not incorrect, to say, with Jung-Uck Hwang, that Calvin follows a theological line that goes from St. Paul to Irenaeus and to Augustine.[23]

One cannot endorse Hwang's judgment, however, that in 1534 Calvin still admitted the Catholic rule that the Vulgate is "the only lawful edition of the Bible," while by 1536 "it is evident that the Vulgate had lost its absolute authority."[24] First, there never was a rule in the Middle Ages that the Latin Vulgate was the only lawful edition of the Bible. At no time was the authority of this text treated as absolute. The scholastics knew well enough that it was not the original inspired text but only a translation, even if they believed it had been made by St. Jerome and was sanctified by long ecclesiastical usage. Secondly, that Calvin quoted from the Vulgate in 1534 and from other Latin texts in 1536 does not identify him as a partisan of the Reformation. It simply shows that, as a good humanist, he kept his eyes on several editions and translations, among which he could choose which one seemed to provide the best text.[25]

*   *   *

Theological authors of the sixteenth century seem to have overestimated their readers' logical capacities. Except for those who still maintained the largely obsolete scholastic pattern of divisions and distinctions, they mostly left the structure of their writing to be discovered and reconstructed by eventual readers. Though Calvin will depart from this practice in the successive editions of his *Institutio*, his *Psychopannychia* was no exception to it, despite his expressed determination to bring "the simplest clarity" *(quam simplicissima perscuitate)* to the problem of the soul. Millet suggests that this work

---

23. Hwang, *Der junge Calvin,* pp. 311, 342.

24. Hwang, *Die junge Calvin,* p. 158.

25. The decree of the Council of Trent on the Vulgate *(vulgata editione bibliorum),* of 8 April 1546, did not even claim absolute authority for it; it simply stated that this *vetus et vulgata editio* (where *vulgate* means "widespread"), "that has been approved for use in the Church for so many centuries," should not be rejected by anyone under any pretext (DS 1506).

"is forgotten today because it is terribly technical."[26] While it is technical in its careful argumentation and in the details it accumulates, the overall structure of *Psychopannychia* can be reconstructed fairly easily. Zimmerli highlights the hinges of this structure in the footnotes of his edition. After a methodological introduction (pp. 22-26) the book is divided into two parts. Part I (pp. 26-61) establishes that the soul is a substance by itself. Part II (pp. 61-108), in a more polemical style, refutes the adversaries' argumentation point by point.

As Jung-Uck Hwang endorses this twofold division he also gives a more detailed analysis of the arguments, which leads him to say that Calvin gave *Psychopannychia* an extremely elaborate structure. As he sees them, the two parts of the book are strictly parallel, following an identical order of the material, in which each positive point in the first part corresponds to a negative counterpoint in the second. The first affirms the true doctrine: the soul lives after bodily death. The second refutes two opinions to the contrary: the soul sleeps and, more lethal, the soul dies after death. Such a strict rhetorical balance would show that Calvin went to great lengths to ensure the literary unity of his work. Each part is subdivided in two parallel sections that would correspond point by point: I.1.1 to I.1.2 parallels II.1.1 to II.1.2; and I.2.1 to I.2.5 parallels II.2.1 to II.4.2. The symmetry, however, is broken twice: at I.3 by the conclusion of the first part, and at II.3 by an "interlude," in which an allegorical interpretation takes the drowned Pharaoh as an image of the mortiferous dark side of the soul.[27]

There are in fact serious problems with this symmetric plan. First, there is another break of the balance of the two parts in I.2.4, which is parallel to two subsections, II.2.3 and II.2.4.[28] Second, another discrepancy is manifest after I.2.2.2, which in Hwang's outline is followed not by 2.2.3 but by 2.1.4. In other words, in the midst of

---

26. "Dans ce texte aujourd'hui oublié, parce qu'il est terriblement technique . . ." (Olivier Millet, *Calvin et la dynamique de la parole. Etude de rhétorique réformée* [Paris: Editions Champion, 1992], p. 442).

27. Hwang's detailed commentary on the text, however, does not expound on this structural parallelism.

28. Hwang, *Der junge Calvin,* pp. 178-81.

his demonstration against the soul's sleep Calvin would have inserted an argument against the death of the soul, though the logical locus of this point should have been after 2.1.3. Third, and this I regard as the main reason not to admit a strict parallelism between the two parts of *Psychopannychia,* Calvin has himself indicated some of the articulations of his work, and these do not fit the proposed outline.

Three conceptions of the hereafter, Calvin explains — the soul's sleep, the soul's death, the soul's life — reflect three understandings of the nature of the soul: It is not a substance; it is a substance so tied to the body that it dies with it; it is a substance in itself (pp. 22-23).[29] After a clarification on philosophy and the meaning of "spirit," which Calvin identifies with "soul," the substantiality of the soul is explained (pp. 25-30), and then supported by biblical arguments (pp. 30-32); its immortality is established from Scripture (pp. 33-41); there follows a description of the promise of peace made to the soul — that it will be at rest in Abraham's bosom (pp. 41-50). It is in this description of the divine promise of peace that Calvin makes his articulations clear:

CALVIN		HWANG'S PLAN
Part I		
Primum . . . (p. 41),	in	I.2.2.2
Cum autem . . . (p. 44),	in	2.2.2
Christus resurrexit . . . (p. 45),		2.2.3
Aliud argumentum . . . (p. 48),	in	2.2.3
Praeterea . . . (p. 49).		2.2.4

In a more polemical and longer second part, Calvin faces the adversaries' arguments:

Part II	
Objiciunt primum . . . (p. 61),	II.1.1.1
Objiciunt secundo . . . (p. 65),	2.1.1
Tertio loco afferunt . . . (p. 71),	2.2

29. The reference is to Zimmerli's edition.

Although Calvin has already refuted a number of objections, he next proceeds to an additional systematic rebuttal:

Painstaking as Hwang's analysis has undoubtedly been, it seems to have missed several features of the book. As an experienced rhetorician Calvin may indeed have been concerned about achieving a careful balance between exposé (Part I) and refutation (Part II). This contrasted parallelism, however, does not account for the whole structure of his essay, for the first part is not homogeneous in terms of tone and content. From the beginning on page 22 to the first full paragraph on page 50, Calvin explains and defends what he holds to be the true Christian teaching about the state of the soul after death; and he initiates the debate with the sectarian opponents of the true doctrine with an investigation of the biblical and traditional understanding of the soul's survival after the body's death.

In the second part of his demonstration — from page 61 to the end — Calvin refutes his adversaries' arguments in scholastic fashion. Before this, however, he inserts a series of reflections (pp. 50 to 61) that no longer explain the doctrine and do not yet amount to a systematic refutation of errors. One should therefore distinguish two sections in the first part of *Psychopannychia*. The first is biblical and traditional; it explains the true doctrine in a scholarly and objective mode. The second is couched in a more personal and suggestive mode. It hints at other reasons than the urgency of defending the truth that have determined Calvin to take the task on himself and to make a thorough investigation of the problem.

Hwang's outline locates this personal section in an exposé on the beginning and the nature of eternal life (I.2.4.1-I.3) that is supported by patristic and biblical considerations. He does not see it as offering more than a continued demonstration that the soul is alive and active after bodily death.[30] According to his outline this section is parallel to the statements of Part II about the "holiness and fullness" of eternal life (II.2.3.2-4) and to the following interpretation of some biblical passages (II.4.2). However, the parity between these items of Part II and the topics of the allegedly corresponding section of Part I is far from evident. Indeed, a clever rhetorician may well cloak a personal concern in a philosophical or theological argument. A parallel structure of the texts, however, is hardly detectable here. Nor does Hwang exploit the parallelism in his commentary.

*   *   *

At this point one may take a look at Schwendemann's thesis on the meaning of *Psychopannychia*, as this includes another hypothesis regarding the structure and articulations of Calvin's book.

Schwendemann divides *Psychopannychia* in five sections:

1. Introduction (5 subsections)   pp. 22-26[31]
2. The Creation of Man (6 subsections)   pp. 26-32
3. The Survival of the Soul after Death
   (6 subsections)   pp. 33-38
4. The Story of Dives and Lazarus
   (15 subsections)   pp. 38-61
5. More on the Survival of the Soul
   after Death (11 subsections)   pp. 61-108

The first four sections easily correspond to the first part of the Zimmerli/Hwang outline, the fifth section to the entire second part.

---

30. This demonstration is analyzed in Hwang, pp. 220-29.
31. Schwendemann does not provide the page references.

This makes *Psychopannychia* singularly uneven, the fifth section having approximately the same length as the first four put together. Calvin, however, was a distinguished student of rhetoric and an acknowledged master of his pen, whose aesthetic sense would have recoiled from such carelessness in the organization of his text. Schwendemann attributes the imperfect balance of the work to an underlying intention to refute too many different opponents. In addition, the proposed outline is subordinated to the central thesis that Calvin the humanist entertained a thoroughly Platonic conception of the soul,[32] in keeping with a fairly general trend in the Renaissance. *Psychopannychia* would draw the consequences of this fundamental philosophy in regard to a number of contemporary questions, problems that attracted Calvin's early interest in theology when he was sojourning in the region of Angoulême, and issues that arose in the months of his first solid commitment to the Reformation in Basel and Geneva.

Calvin, however, Schwendemann specifies, was not a neo-Platonist. He owed nothing to Plotinus and the mystical tradition that derived from the *Enneads* and had influenced the major streams of the medieval mystical tradition. His thought had its source directly in Plato as known in the Renaissance, and his acquaintance with the Platonist doctrine of the soul derived chiefly from the *Phaedo.* As Schwendemann sees him, Calvin did not give up his Platonist philosophy when he became a biblical scholar. Rather, he read Paul's σῶμα/πνεῦμα (flesh/spirit) duality in light of Plato's body/soul dualism. The paradox of *Psychopannychia* would then be that while Calvin was arguing from a philosophical basis, he intended his argumentation to be thoroughly scriptural, refuting his opponents on the basis of Scripture alone, with the additional assistance of the Fathers of the Church as witnesses. Calvin's adversaries would have been, on the one hand, some Roman defenders of holy pictures and, on the other, the anabaptist advocates of the sleep of the soul after death.

---

32. Wilhelm Schwendemann, *Leib und Seele bei Calvin. Die erkenntnistheoretische und anthropologetische Funktion des platonischen Leib-Seele-Dualismus in Calvins Theologie* (Stuttgart: Calwer Verlag, 1996), pp. 125-77, with extensive footnotes.

As perceived by Schwendemann, however, Calvin's perspective was not merely philosophical and scriptural. It reached into many other areas of Calvin's concerns. The dualism, body/soul, flesh/spirit, presented an analogy with the structures of Genevan society, a similarity that eventually helped the reformer to face the problems of the city as he tried to shape its life according to the gospel. It also provided a key to Calvin's epistemology, to his antagonism to holy pictures, to his projects for Christian society, and to his conservative convictions on the relative status and tasks of the sexes and their complementarity.

Hwang and Schwendemann are in agreement that the Calvin of *Psychopannychia* argues from Scripture alone. For Hwang this makes him a humanist, for Schwendemann a true Protestant. In this the two scholars strongly differ in their assessment of Calvin's ties to the Reformation at the time of writing this work. Was Calvin still, when he composed his text, a Catholic, though an anxious one, and possibly an unconscious Nicodemite who did not dare to declare himself, as Hwang sees him? Or had he already been a convinced *réformé* for a long time, as Schwendemann perceives? Did he include Lutherans, and maybe Luther himself, in the people whose eschatology he criticized? Hwang esteems this to be quite possible. While Luther was loath to speculate on such questions, concerning which the Scriptures were notably silent, he occasionally used the analogy of sleep as a metaphor that could illustrate the state of the soul between death and the final resurrection. Schwendemann, however, does not see this as a major difference between Luther and Calvin, whose Platonist dualism between body and soul he finds somewhat adumbrated in the writings of Luther.[33]

*   *   *

If we now confine our attention strictly to the exact topic of *Psychopannychia*, the state of the question is relatively simple. Calvin found three opinions on the state of the soul after bodily death among his contemporaries. The first asserts that after death the

---

33. Schwendemann, *Leib und Seele, Exkurs,* pp. 245-47.

soul is asleep, therefore unconscious and inactive, until it wakes up at the resurrection at the end of the world. The second speculates that with the death of the body the soul also dies, until both are brought back to life at the resurrection. For the third, the soul continues to live after death, and to perform those spiritual acts for which the body is not an indispensable instrument, until, at the resurrection, it recovers what St. Paul calls a spiritual body. Clearly, the immediate point at stake hides a deeper question regarding the nature of the human soul. The first view would imply that the soul is an undefined "something." In the second view it would be "nothing less than a substance," but with no life of its own apart from "arteries and lungs" and the other organs of the body, without which it would not be able to subsist. In the third view the soul is a substance in itself apart from its body, without which it is able to subsist.[34]

It would be pointless, Calvin pursues, to look for a solution of the problem of immortality among philosophers, who have entered into endless and fruitless discussions about everything. If Plato has written well *(praeclare)* about the faculties of the soul, and Aristotle has discussed everything with the greatest acumen *(acutissime)*, neither one has explained "what the soul is and where it comes from." Actually, such a view of the contribution of classical philosophers to the sum total of human wisdom is not different from the one that prevailed in most of medieval scholasticism: Plato and Aristotle have spoken well of many rational questions, but they have fallen short of the basic affirmations of Christian wisdom, especially in their denial of the creation of the universe by an almighty God and of the immortality of the soul. This was St. Bonaventure's basic critique of the philosophers,[35] a critique that was only slightly corrected by Thomas Aquinas, who more deeply appreciated the contribution of Aristotle to an objective analysis of nature. One can even say, Calvin adds, in keeping with the opinion of the major Schoolmen, that the whole company of those who profess wisdom has not done any better than Plato and Aristotle, even though the philoso-

---

34. *Psychopannychia,* pp. 22-23.

35. Tavard, *Transiency and Permanence: The Nature of Theology according to St. Bonaventure* (St. Bonaventure, N.Y.: The Franciscan Institute, 1954), pp. 141-65.

phers — and at this point Calvin may be thinking of the many humanists who have pored over the question of the soul — have generally been wiser than the anabaptists, in spite of the fact that these claim to be disciples of Christ.[36]

Soul and spirit, Calvin remarks, are often used in the same sense in ordinary Christian parlance, though they can also be distinguished. Precisely, the first mistake of the catabaptists lies in their literal understanding of biblical passages that should be read metaphorically. For instance, *anima* in Scripture is sometimes used to mean life. In other places it designates the will or desire, which have their origin in the soul. *Anima* can also mean a living person *(homine animato)*. Likewise, taken materially, *spiritus* is the wind or breath. In the prophet Isaiah the word is even used to designate a thing of no importance.[37] In another direction of thought *spiritus* can also mean "that which has been regenerated in us by the Spirit of God."[38] In this sense, when Paul says that "the spirit conspires against the flesh" (Gal. 5:17), he does not mean that "the soul fights with the flesh, and reason with desire," but that it struggles with itself insofar as it is not yet filled with the Spirit of God.[39] It may also happen that soul designates the will and spirit the intellect, as in Paul's perception of a "division between the soul and the spirit" (Heb. 4:12), although some interpreters equate spirit with the essence of the human person, in which the faculties of reason and of will reside, and soul with the "living motion and the senses that philosophers call higher and lower."[40] These diverse exegeses, however, are not cause for fundamental dissent. The main point is to perceive the reality of the soul, whatever name is given to it.

*   *   *

Calvin's first major discussion relates precisely to this point. What is the entity that is called soul or spirit? Calvin finds the basic princi-

36. *Psychopannychia,* pp. 23-24.
37. The text provides no reference.
38. *Psychopannychia,* p. 25.
39. *Psychopannychia,* pp. 25-26.
40. *Psychopannychia,* p. 26.

ple of the right answer in the creation of Adam and Eve as it is reported in the Book of Genesis, at least as the text was understood by St. Ambrose and St. Augustine. The human person was created "in the image and likeness of God" (Gen. 1:26). According to Ambrose and Augustine this image is not in the body but in the soul, notwithstanding the marvelous superiority of the human body over that of animals. It is precisely because "God is spirit" that the divine image cannot be represented by a body.[41] Just as a picture or sculpture of somebody's face should show all the lineaments that are visible in the original, so "should the image of God, by its likeness, form a certain knowledge of God in our souls."[42] Here the soul is not described or defined in itself but in relation to a function. This function relates to the knowledge of God that we obtain from the fact that our soul is an image of God.

Calvin is aware of other identifications of the image of God in us. There are those who locate it in the authority *(imperium)* of Adam over the animals, in which they see a participation in the divine authority over the universe. This was St. John Chrysostom's understanding of the image of God when he argued against the anthropomorphites, who believed that God has a human shape. It is not acceptable, however, because Moses, in Genesis, did not refer the image of God to the human body formed out of the mud of the earth, but rather to the "breath of life" that God breathed into the mud, "so that the image of God would shine in man when he would be complete in all his parts."[43]

Others have seen the divine image in the very breath of life that comes from the Creator. But this is not acceptable either, for there is no radical difference between the breath of life that caused Adam to be and that which the Creator also breathed into animals when the order was given: "Let the earth produce a living soul" (Gen. 1:24). What has come from the earth will necessarily return to it. This, however, is not the destiny of the soul: "The human soul is not from

41. . . . *Deus qui spiritus est . . . nulla corporis effigie repraesentari potest* (p. 27).

42. . . . *ita haec imago Dei debet sua similitudine aliquam Dei cognitionem in animis nostris informare* (p. 27).

43. *Psychopannychia,* p. 28.

the earth, but out of the mouth of God, that is, out of a hidden source."[44] Calvin, a careful Latinist, does not use the same preposition for both cases. Animal life is *de,* "from" the earth, created from the preexisting stuff of earth. The human soul, however, is *ex,* "out of" the mouth of God; it is created externally to the Godhead, out of no preexisting material, by a hidden and secret divine power. From this origin it follows that the soul as image of God must reside *extra carnem.* As Calvin writes, "I want only to obtain one point: The image itself is outside the flesh; otherwise it is not such a great praise to say that humans have been made in the image of God." Scripture, however, insists on this high praise of human creatures, a praise that rebounds to the glory of the Creator since God's external works reflect the divine greatness and attributes.

This line of argumentation follows a principle of medieval theology that had been especially highlighted by St. Bonaventure. It is tantamount to a form of the argument *ex pietate.*[45] This rests on the principle that a theological option is more likely to be true if it reveals and enhances the divine glory than if it does not. Reversely, a theory that ignores or diminishes the divine glory in human eyes is likely to be incorrect. In the present case, the argument *ex pietate* is confirmed by the details of the biblical story. God is shown, on the one hand, as simply ordering the creation of animals and, on the other hand, when the creation of the human race is imminent, as deliberating — calling on the divine wisdom and power, thinking — before bringing out the unique human specimen of Adam. Calvin of course recognizes that these are anthropomorphic images of the divine action. He nonetheless regards them as entirely proper, in that they provide "a magnificent commendation of the image of God" that shines in human beings.[46] "Whatever stupidities are invented by philosophers or by those slumberers, the fact is that nothing carries the image of God except a spirit, for God is spirit."[47]

44. *Anima vero hominis non de terra est, sed ex ore domini, hoc est ex virtute secreta* (p. 28).

45. Tavard, *Transiency,* pp. 203-11.

46. *Psychopannychia,* p. 29.

47. . . . *habemus nihil esse quod imaginem Dei ferat nisi spiritum, ut Deus spiritus est* (John 4:25).

There is no good reason, Calvin believes, to speculate about the exact nature of the image's similarity with its archetype.[48] The lesson of Scripture is clear. Paul relates the image to the new creation (Col. 3:10) and to "putting on the new man" (Eph. 4:24). The created image of God participates in the divine nature, as is stated in 2 Peter 1:4. Calvin, at this point, assumes that the image shares in some of the fundamental attributes of God: "If we wish to express all this in one word, we say that man as spirit has been made participant in the wisdom, justice, and goodness of God."[49]

Like Genesis, yet more briefly, Ecclesiasticus relates the image of God to the soul and not to the body (Ecclus. 17:1). Wisdom calls man immortal because created in the image of God (Wis. 2:2).[50] In any case, "let us retain this image of God in man, which can be seated nowhere but in the spirit." In his next few pages Calvin adduces other biblical texts: 1 Peter 1 and 2; Job 4:19; 2 Peter 1:13-14; Heb. 12:9, 22; 2 Cor. 7:1; 1 Cor. 2:11; Rom. 8:16. That such was the Apostles' doctrine is evident, since Paul declared himself to be a Pharisee (Acts 23), and the Pharisees affirmed the existence of spirit that was denied by the Sadducees. Among the early Fathers Calvin quotes St. Polycarp (c. 69–c. 155), "a disciple of the Apostles," and Melito of Sardis (d. c. 190), who composed a book *De corpore et anima*.

*   *   *

The second major point of Calvin's investigation relates to the soul's state after the death of the body. The soul survives in the next world, where it remains endowed with *sensu ac intelligentia*,[51] "aware-

---

48. . . . . *imaginis similitudo ad suum archetypum.*

49. *Quae omnia cum uno verbo comprehendere volumus, dicimus hominem secundum spiritum factum esse participem sapientiae, justitiae et bonitatis Dei.* The allusion to 2 Peter is not specified by Calvin.

50. "Immortal," translated *inexterminabilis*, "that cannot be killed." This is hardly an accurate version of what Wisdom says, but Calvin refers to these two texts only because his adversaries wrongly argue from them. These books are recognized by Calvin "if not as canonical, certainly as ancient, pious, and accepted by many" (p. 30).

51. *Psychopannychia*, p. 33.

ness and intelligence." Calvin, however, distinguishes this from a mere affirmation of immortality. Immortality as such could be compatible with the belief that the soul lingers in a slumbering state, devoid of its normal activity of moving, feeling, and understanding, to which Calvin adds, with Tertullian, self-awareness. It is precisely this active immortality that is affirmed in Scripture. Calvin comments on Matthew 10:28. Human tyrants can torture and kill the body, but "God alone has such a power over the soul as to send it to the gehenna of fire."[52] When Christ commended his spirit to God (Luke 23:46) and Stephen commended his spirit to Christ (Acts 7:58), they did not merely ask to be kept alive until the final resurrection. When Christ surrendered his spirit (John 19:30), he was not referring to the breath of his lungs!

The descent of Christ into inferno (1 Peter 3:19) is the object of a long comment. As Calvin remarks, Christ, if he preached among the dead, did not address sleeping souls, but living spirits who were able to grasp what he said. His power extended to the living and the dead, to disciples and unbelievers. The fact that the "holy fathers who expected redemption by Christ" are included among those to whom Christ went after his death implies that they were alive, though not in the present visible and temporal world. The state they were in is delicately suggested by the experience of twilight and early dawn: ". . . they looked from afar at the light under a cloud and a shadow (like those who perceive the remains of the day under a prolonged twilight, or sense the coming day before dawn). . . ."[53] But how, Calvin asks, could Christ preach to these souls if he was not himself in his body? That he preached indeed in spirit to the spirits in prison means that the power of his redemptive work was made manifest to the spirits of the dead. The Epistle of Peter, however, does not refer at this point to "the pious, who acknowledged and received the fruit" of redemption, but only to unbelievers, "who received the news to their confusion,"[54] for they were excluded from redemption. Life and death stand in an antithetic relation. Those

52. *Psychopannychia*, p. 34.
53. *Psychopannychia*, p. 36.
54. *Psychopannychia*, p. 37.

who look only at the body judge that people are dead. In God's eyes, however, the dead live in the spirit.

Calvin makes a few additional comments, on Ecclesiastes 12:7, on the fourth book of Esdras 7:12,[55] and on the parable of Dives and Lazarus in Luke 16:22. The details of these comments may be omitted here. Concerning the parable of Dives and Lazarus, Calvin argues from the testimonies of quite a few Fathers of the Church: Ambrose, Gregory, Tertullian, Irenaeus, Origen, Cyprian, Jerome, Hilary, Cyril of Alexandria, Augustine. The partisans of the sleep of the soul regard this parable as pure fiction. Its purpose, however, is to point to the truth, to show that the souls of Dives and of Lazarus are not asleep in death.[56] The exegetical principle involved is then neatly formulated:

> This is the perpetual law of parables: First we must conceive the thing itself as it is proposed. Then we are led from this concept to the purpose of the parable, that is, to the reality itself to which it resembles.[57]

Certainly, Calvin admits, the souls that are separated from their bodies have been promised peace. What Scripture means by this is the "tranquility and security of conscience"[58] that always accompany faith and that are made perfect after death in the kingdom of God. It is the new and intimate conviction of true believers: God, formerly feared as a judge, is now seen to be a father. From children of wrath the faithful have become children of grace. Those who have been touched by the bitterness of sin find consolation in the one

55. The first two books of Esdras belong to the deutero-canonical books of the Old Testament (apocrypha). The third and fourth books, though not generally recognized as canonical in any sense, were also included in many medieval manuscripts and some printed editions of the Latin Vulgate. They were not listed by the Council of Trent among the inspired books (Decree on the Sacred Books and the Traditions, session IV of the Council of Trent, 8 April 1546: DS 1502). Calvin does not comment at this point on the canonical status of 4 Esdras.

56. *Psychopannychia*, pp. 39-41.

57. *Denique haec est perpetua lex parabolae, ut primum concipiamus rem nudam, ut proponitur. Deinde ex ea conceptione deducamur ad finem parabolae, hoc est ad rem ipsam cui accommodatur similitudo* (p. 40).

58. . . . . *conscientiae tranquillitatem et securitatem* (p. 41).

they offended, in whom they will rest and dwell as soon as they have shed the flesh and its concupiscence. Such a peace *(quies)* could well be called sleep, had not this word been corrupted by the lies of false teachers. It is identified in Scripture with Abraham's bosom because the faithful who have died have been "received at the seat of peace along with Abraham, father of the faithful."[59] They are truly in God, together with Abraham. It is in God that the elect are at rest.

Since, at the time of writing, Calvin has recently passed through a painful period of turmoil and troubles, it is no wonder that he waxes eloquent as he describes the soul's repose in God, "this peace that opens the treasures of heavenly grace, which inebriates with the sweetness of the Lord's cup," the "tranquility of conscience in the house of peace," the "rest of the heavenly Jerusalem," the "vision of peace in which the God of peace gives himself to be seen to his peaceful ones."[60] This is also "the sleep and peace of the souls of the living, who assent to the word of God and do not wish their will to come before God, but keep prepared in his hand to follow where he will call." Indeed, "their peace is not complete as long as they expect what they do not see and desire what they have not." What they have in this life is already a quiet desire, "when with assurance *(certo)* they expect what they expect and by faith they desire what they desire."[61] Yet they still miss "the highest and perfect glory of God" that they hope to see. The faithful in this life stand between "the impatience of desire" and "the full and perfect quiet" to which they cannot have access before the day of judgment.

The source of the certainty of the faithful that they will rise at the last day is no other than Christ's own resurrection. "As he died and rose again, so we die and resurrect in him." Christ's death was of the same nature as ours. And this is precisely where the false doctrine of the sleep of the soul challenges the very heart of the Christian faith. The issue becomes christological as soon as one asks, How did Christ die? Could Christ be asleep when he watches over our salvation? Could the one who has the power of life lose it? What

59. *Psychopannychia,* p. 43.
60. *Psychopannychia,* p. 44.
61. *Psychopannychia,* p. 45.

does it mean to say, with the Gospel of John, that "as the Father has life in himself, so he gave it to the Son to have life in himself" (John 5:26)? Being christological, the issue is also necessarily trinitarian: "Since Jesus Christ is Son of God and son of man, what he is by nature as God, that he is by grace as man, so that from his fullness we may all receive, even grace upon grace" (John 1:16).[62]

Calvin notes that St. Cyril agrees with this understanding of the Johannine passage.[63] For greater clarity he also borrows the old trinitarian analogy of the source and the brook: "The font from which all draw, from which rivulets flow and derive, is said to have water in itself, not from itself, but from a source that serves it assiduously, which should suffice for flowing streams and drinking men." The analogy, however, is not applied here to the eternal relations between the First and the Second Person, but to the incarnation and, more precisely, to the relation of the humanity of Christ to the divinity of God the Father:

> When we say that Christ as man has life in himself, we do not say that he himself is the cause of life, but only that all the fullness of life was poured by God the Father into Christ the man. . . . Christ has life in himself, that is, the fullness of life by which he lives and vivifies his own; he does not have life from himself. . . . And as he has life in himself as God, when he assumes man he receives this gift from the Father, to have life in himself also on the human side.[64]

The soul of Christ, Calvin concludes, was "suffused with divine power lest it run into perdition, and his body was kept in the tomb

---

62. *Psychopannychia*, p. 46.

63. *Psychopannychia*, p. 47.

64. *Cum autem dicimus Christum, quatenus homo est, habere vitam in semetipso, non ipsum sibi causam esse vitae dicimus sed hoc tantum omnem vitae plenitudinem a Deo Patre effusam esse in Christum hominem. . . . Ergo Christus habet vitam in semetipso, hoc est vitae plenitudinem qua et ipse vivat et suos vivificet; non tamen habet ex semetipso, quemadmodum ipse alibi testatur, quod vivit propter Patrem* (John 6:57). *Et cum in se ut Deum vitam haberet, ubi hominem assumpsit, donum accepit hoc a Patre, ut vitam ea etiam parte haberet in semetipso* (p. 47).

in view of his rising."[65] He finds support for the true doctrine in the story of Jonas, which he understands metaphorically, the belly of the whale meaning death itself. Likewise, in Genesis 22, Isaac may be taken to represent the soul, the ram signifying the body; the body died, and the soul lived. Only if one does not believe that Christ as man received the gift of total life from God the Father can one maintain that his soul was not alive after he died, unless, with Appolinaris, one denies that he had a human soul.

Along with the doctrines of the incarnation and the Trinity the entire Christian life is at stake in the question of the soul's immortality, for "our life is hidden in Christ" (Col. 3:3). If the soul of Christ did not fall asleep at his death, neither do ours when we die. Christians are in Christ and Christ in them. Therefore, "if it is Christ who lived in them, it is the same who dies in them."[66] Even if the body is a "mass of sin" that has resided in man since the birth of his flesh, there is a "part of man that has been spiritually regenerated."[67] This is what St. Paul called spirit ($\pi\nu\varepsilon\tilde{\upsilon}\mu\alpha$). At the disputation of Lausanne in October 1536, the Bernese minister Pierre Caroli accused the Genevan reformers of not believing that God is one nature and three Persons.[68] The doctrine of the Trinity is in fact manifestly present in *Psychopannychia*. The Christ who is said to be full of grace for our salvation is, Calvin affirms, the Eternal Son of the Eternal Father. His humanity has received the gift of what his divinity possesses eternally. Calvin remarks: "If a gift is made to someone who does not have it, it is to man, not to God, that it is given to have life in him. Since Jesus Christ is Son of God and son of man, what he is by nature as God, that he is by grace as man. . . ."[69]

* * *

Calvin is now about half-way through *Psychopannychia*. He has forcefully established the true and traditional doctrine — founded in

---

65. *Psychopannychia*, p. 48.
66. *Psychopannychia*, p. 49.
67. *Psychopannychia*, p. 50.
68. See below, ch. 10, p. 176, and note 23.
69. *Psychopannychia*, p. 46.

Scripture and supported by the Fathers — of the soul's life after the body's death. He has said little, however, about the essence and the inner structure of the soul, what it is in itself. Regarding the structure, Calvin is of course aware of the many analyses that were made of it in the spiritual and theological writings of the Middle Ages and of the Renaissance. As to the essence of the soul, which had been discussed since Plato and Aristotle put forward their conflicting views of its relation to the body, it would appear to be more difficult to determine than its sheer existence as spirit.

IV

The Nature of the Soul

What we have called the second section in Part I of Calvin's writing against the theory of the soul's sleep or death is still a refutation, but the tone has changed considerably. Rather than a demonstration of a thesis by an appeal to Scripture and the Church Fathers, Calvin opens unexpected vistas into what could be a profound series of insights. Adversarial positions are still denounced, biblical citations are brought in to support what Calvin wishes to say. The Fathers of the Church are cited. Yet the tone has become all of a sudden less assertive and more searching. There is, as it were, one and the same movement of hesitancy and hope. Having demonstrated to his satisfaction the fundamental thesis of his work, that the soul lives after death, or lives in death, Calvin has led his reader to the gate of the soul as to the threshold of an inner sanctum that is still hidden behind a veil. Aware of the remaining unknown, he is not sure how to enter, how to draw the veil, and uncover the soul itself as it is at its core.

*   *   *

The passage begins with the expression of a wish, a longing: *Utinam . . .*, "If only . . ." What Calvin would like to have and to see at the moment is immensely desirable. And yet faith provides no immediate knowledge of it: "If only we could, with the right faith, perceive what the kingdom of God is that is within the faithful already when they live the present life!"[1] Calvin is a distinguished Latinist. He is aware of the double meaning of this wish. Does he affirm that the divine kingdom is present in the heart of the faithful already in this life? Or does he wish to perceive the reality of the kingdom while he himself is still in this life? Knowing that Latin does not use our kind of punctuation, should one erase the first or the second comma? If the first, then Calvin states the doctrine that the kingdom is within; and he wishes to perceive it by experience now, in the present life. If the second, Calvin emphasizes that the kingdom is indeed within us in the present life, before we ourselves pass beyond the veil. One may presume that both meanings are intended. In any case, there is a mystical dimension to this wish, which is not unlike what the *devotio moderna* had placed at the heart of the imitation of Christ: *Audiam quid loquatur in me Dominus Deus.*[2]

What is at stake here is the knowledge of our present participation, by faith, in the kingdom of God. In spite of the current trend to translate this New Testament expression as "the reign of God," the term "kingdom" is entirely appropriate. In its medieval connotations, which were not repudiated by the Renaissance, the word designates the realm of the king's authority: the *rex* reigns in a *regnum* which determines the extent and the limits of royal authority, geographically, politically, and morally. When God is seen as King, this kingdom or king's domain is, in the present life, for Christian believers, within themselves: *intra fideles.* And yet *recta fides,* the true faith, does not reveal its own nature and quality. *Qualis sit,* Calvin would like to know. Precisely, *qualis* posits the question of its quality. What are the qualities, the characteristics, the structures, of the kingdom of God, the sum total of which would constitute and reveal its nature? *Etiam dum hanc vitam vivunt:* What Calvin envisions "even while they live this life" is the eternal life already present in the soul by faith, though in darkness.

---

1. *Utinam recta fide percipere possemus, quale sit regnum Dei, quod est intra fideles, etiam dum hanc vitam vivunt* (*Psychopannychia,* p. 50).

2. *De Imitatione Christi,* III,i,1, Tiburzio Lupo, ed., *De Imitatione Christi. Edizione critica* (Vatican City: Libreria Editrice Vaticana, 1982), p. 133.

Indeed, if true faith showed this, perception would lead to understanding. It would then be "easy to understand eternal life in its beginning."[3] We already have the promise, in John 5:24 — from "the one who cannot be wrong" — that eternal life starts here and now for those who hear the words of Christ. One may then ask, "If the passage into eternal life has been made, why is this life interrupted by death?"[4] Calvin actually wrote: "why do they interrupt this life by death?" But who are "they?" as we, his readers, may well ask. "They" can only be the faithful themselves, who have already passed by faith into an inchoate form of eternal life, but as death strikes they have to interrupt the process and undergo the mysterious event of dying. Eternal life is given, as Calvin shows with suitable quotations from the Gospel of John, not only when one hears the words of the Savior, but also to anyone who "believes in the Son" (John 6:40), to the one who eats his flesh and drinks his blood (6:54), to the one who eats, not manna in the desert, but "this bread" (6:58). Two perspectives are opened by these texts, on eternal life and on the resurrection. The slumberers "hear two, but embrace only one." They look forward to a sort of resurrection. But the word that they do not embrace establishes their error, for Jesus says, "I am the resurrection and the life. Whoever believes in me, even if dead, lives. And all those who live and believe in me will not die for eternity" (John 11:25-26).[5] Those who have faith, who listen to the word and receive the sacraments cannot possibly die. "This we believe, this we expect. But what is left to the heretics, besides their deep sleep until the sound of the trumpet wakes them up, like a burglar who catches them asleep in the dark?"

Confronting the soul-slumberers, who believe the resurrection but deny that eternal life is already given to believers before they die, Calvin asks a fundamental question about the nature of our present participation in eternal life. He is convinced that there is such a participation. He has the unquenchable hope that the present inchoation of eternal life in the faithful will flourish when they die

---

3. *Nam simul facile esset intelligere inchoatam vitam aeternam.*

4. *Si transitus factus est in vitam aeternam, cur eam morte interrumpunt?*

5. *Psychopannychia*, p. 51.

to this world in their body. Yet he would like to know more than faith declares. What is the eternal life of the believing soul, now, this side of death?

*   *   *

Suddenly the response is given, with certainty, yet in a hypothetical form: "And if God is the life of the faithful soul, just as the soul is the life of the body. . . ."[6] In this context the grammatical conditional, "if" *(si),* does not really posit a condition. Like the analogy of the soul — life of the body — it implies the affirmation: God is the life of the faithful soul. Calvin could have said, "since God is the life of the soul," for he has no doubt of it. Yet this certainty opens a profound dilemma of Christian life: We do not know, and we have no way of knowing, how this life of the soul, which is no less than God, is compatible with the harsh fact of bodily death. As long as it is in the body, of which it is the life, the soul never tires of leading it. At death, when the body dies because the soul ceases to be its life, is God so tired that he also gives up being the soul's life? Surely, the soul has great strength as it sustains, moves, and compels the "mass of earth" which is the body. All the greater is God's strength in moving the soul and acting on it, which is so agile by nature!

Here, it would seem, is a hidden truth behind the erroneous hypothesis of the sleep of the soul: God and Christ have revealed so much, and no more. Faith knows that God is the life of the soul, but it does not know what form this life takes when we die. The blessed ones, in Psalm 84, will pass from strength to strength or, as the Hebrew text has it, from abundance to abundance.[7] This shows how absurd is the proposition that the soul vanishes, or that it is no longer active, once it has lost its companion the body. It also leaves the questing soul frustrated in its desire to know how God is its life. This is the soul's basic desire, to know God as its own life, to know

---

6. *Et si fidelis animae Deus est, perinde atque ipsa vita est corporis, quid est quod anima, quamdiu in corpore est, ipsum agitat nec unquam ita otiosa est intentionemque suam remittit, ut non aliqua officii parte fingatur, Deus autem velut agendo fatigatus cessat?* (p. 51).

7. *Psychopannychia,* p. 52.

69

its life which is God, or to know itself as divine life. Calvin wonders about his adversaries' logic: "If they [the blessed souls] always grow until they see God, and from this crescendo they pass on to the vision of God, how do they [the heretics] bury them in drunkenness and profound weakness?" There also remains a not dissimilar question that Calvin does not formulate: If God is himself the life of the soul, and leads it on a continuous ascent to the beatific vision, what does death tell us about the nature of this ascent, of the soul's life, and of the soul itself?

In the Pauline epistles Calvin finds a reflection that is germane to the present one. Naturally he quotes Paul against the catabaptists. At the same time, however, he neatly formulates the question that he is himself unable to answer because the faith as such gives no response to it. We know that if our earthly tent is destroyed "we also have an edifice from God, a domicile not made by hands, that is eternal in the heavens."[8] At this moment, in the present life,

> in this our domicile, we cry, desiring to put on the one that is in heaven, if we are to be found dressed and not nude. And indeed we who are in the present tent cry, feeling oppressed because we do not want to exit but to vest, so that mortality be absorbed by life.[9]

We must all appear before Christ's tribunal, but in what garment? The vestment that will cover our nakedness is evidently Christ himself. The soul-slumberers, however, understand it to be the body "rather than the blessings of God in which we richly abound from the moment of death."[10] The sense of Paul is simple: "We wish to escape from the jail of the body, not to wander in vagrancy shelterless. There is a better house that the Lord has prepared for us, if at least we are found dressed and not naked." Our vestment is the Lord himself (Eph. 6:11). Biblical texts confirm this. The king desires the

8. *Psychopannychia,* p. 52.

9. *Psychopannychia,* p. 53.

10. . . . *Dei benedictiones quibus a morte luculenter abundamus* (p. 53). I take it that at this point *a* does not denote action but time. The French translation says . . . *aux bénédictions de Dieu qui nous sont haillíes en abondance après la mort* (Paul Louis Jacob, *Oeuvres françaises de Calvin* [Paris, 1842], p. 56).

70

beauty of his spouse (Ps. 45:12). The Lord has marked his own, whom he will recognize in death and resurrection (Apoc. 7:8). Our external humanity will see corruption, but our inner humanity will be renewed from day to day (2 Cor. 4:16). Calvin concludes:

> These words tell us, without an interpreter, to struggle in the body and outside the body in order to please the Lord; and that we shall then experience his presence when separated from this body; and that we shall walk, not by faith but by sight, because the weight of the earth that presses on us separates us from God by a great distance, like a wall.[11]

The false doctrine of the soul asleep, however, makes the distance between God and us much greater after death than it is in the present life. It gives us more happiness now than we can receive after we die, for now we are, but then we are not. But such a perspective is not only opposed to the Scriptures; it is also against the Christian experience now. By this alleged lethargy and forgetting of all things in death the souls would lose "whatever suavity of spiritual tasting they have."[12] This is a clear allusion to the traditional doctrine of Christian mystics, originally formulated by Origen in his Commentary on the Song of Songs,[13] that the soul has spiritual senses. It can experience a spiritual tasting, smelling, touching, hearing, and seeing of God, just as it can partake of a sacramental eating of the spiritual body and blood of Christ. Calvin mentions only tasting at this time and, as usual, he remains very discreet, "sober," as he alludes to the intimacy between God and the soul that derives precisely from God being the very life of the creature that has put on Christ as a garment. Yet it is without ambiguity that he envisions the end of the present strife between the soul and the flesh: "Mortification of the flesh is vivification of the spirit."[14]

11. *Psychopannychia*, p. 53.

12. *Ubi autem veternus ille et rerum omnium oblivio animas a morte exceperit, perdunt quamcumque habent suavitatem spiritualis gustus* (p. 54).

13. Origène, *Homélies sur le Cantique des Cantiques* (SC 37, Paris: Le Cerf, 1953), pp. 89-94.

14. *Psychopannychia*, p. 54.

Calvin is still a humanist when his thoughts enter the domain of mystical experience, and as a humanist he is more inclined to follow Plato than Aristotle. It is generally recognized that there are ties between the Book of Wisdom and the "middle Platonism" that acted as a historical link between the works of Plato and their mystical interpretation by the later neo-Platonists. In the Book of Wisdom, which, as we have seen, Calvin placed among the edifying books closely related to Scripture (the deutero-canonicals of the late medieval tradition),[15] he read: "The body is a weight on the soul, and our earthly dwelling is heavy on the mind that thinks many thoughts."[16] Being himself of a weak constitution that needed constant attention,[17] Calvin was at home in the perspective that sees the body as a temporary prison of the soul. But if the body acts as a jail that confines the soul and its actions within strictly drawn parameters, then death must be a liberation. When death happens, Calvin asks rhetorically, "If the body is the soul's prison, if [the soul's] shackles are its earthly habitation, what is the soul that has been freed from prison, that has escaped its chains? Does it not return to itself and, as it were, gather itself?"[18] Then, having been freed, "it is truly spiritual...."[19] And it cannot possibly sleep since it is no longer weighed down by the flesh.

One may ask, what is this spirituality of the soul that is reached only through dying to the material world? As Calvin sees it, there is a basic aspect of freedom at which the soul's capacities are not impeded by its body, when it can "raise itself without the pull of

15. See ch. 2, p. 35.

16. *Corpus enim quo corrumpitur aggravat animam, et terrena inhabitatio deprimit sensum multa cogitantem* (Wisdom 9:15). The New English Bible puts it thus: ". . . a perishable body weighs down the soul, and its frame of clay burdens the mind so full of thoughts."

17. Doumergue, *Jean Calvin*, pp. 11-12, 239, 250-51. Calvin frequently suffered from migraine headaches, throat and lung inflammation, gout, painful colic, etc. . . . In 1561 in a letter to Beza he called himself a "gouty old man" (*vieillard podagre*, p. 250). His anxieties concerning the frailty of human life (Bouwsma, *John Calvin*, pp. 32-65) may have been due largely to his poor health. One of the qualities he required of his future wife was that she would be concerned about his health (Bouwsma, p. 23).

18. *Nonne sibi redditur et quasi se colligit?*

19. *Tum . . . vere est spiritualis.*

72

weight," and "perceive many things in sense and thought unencumbered by impediment." The soul, one could say, though this is not Calvin's language, functions like the angels once it has entered the realm of spirits. And there is another aspect, which can be experienced before death, when the soul's capacities are so wholly attuned to the spiritual realities that it "assents to the will of God and does not feel the tyranny of the flesh opposing it, so that it dwells in tranquility, thinking nothing other than God."[20] In other words, while it still is in the present life the soul has access not only to its natural intellectual powers but also to the higher levels of divine grace and glory that have been described by Christian mystics.

*　　*　　*

The intimacy with God that the Christian soul has experienced in the prison of its body is not abolished by death. Rather, it passes into the heavenly life, in which it continues and increases. When therefore Calvin remarks, "We acknowledge God as being born in his elect and growing from day to day,"[21] he joins together the life of the soul here below, in which God is born by faith, and its life in the hereafter, when the growth of God born in us is unimpeded by the flesh, by ignorance, and by sin. He also acknowledges that there are already those in this world who go "from faith to faith, from virtue to virtue, and who enjoy the fruition of the taste of beatitude when they practice meditation."[22] The expressions that Calvin uses here, *cogitatione Dei, fruere, beatitudinis gustu,* were standard terms in the tradition of the medieval Catholic mystics. They designate the meditation *(cogitatio)* of the beginners and the more advanced, and the tasting and fruition that are felt at higher levels of contemplation. These are the works of God *(opera Dei)* that divine grace performs in the faithful soul that it leads to holiness of life. *Exercerent* is, in ver-

20. . . . *ut consentiat voluntati Dei nec sentiat carnis tyrannidem sibi repugnantem, ut in hac tranquillitate resideat, nihil aliud quam Deum cogitans* (p. 54).

21. *Nos agnoscimus Deum velut nascentem in electis suis et de die in diem crescentem . . .* (p. 54.)

22. *Qui prius ibant de fide in fidem, de virtute in virtutem et beatitudinis gustu fruebantur, cum se in Dei cogitatione exercebant . . .* (p. 55).

bal form, the very term that St. Ignatius Loyola used to designate the "Spiritual Exercises" that he composed in 1522, and which would obtain their first papal endorsement from Paul III in 1548. There is, for Calvin, the same distance between such a soul and its body as there is between heaven and earth.

The slumberers, however, are unable to see all this. In their theory death is more deleterious than it is in reality, for it destroys the divine works that, as was prophesied in Scripture, God operates in his saints.[23] It does more than interrupt the work of God for a moment; it also extinguishes what God has done so far in the soul.[24] Such a doctrine would see the sleeping state as a state of perfection, and it would make St. Paul aspire to a good sleep when he wished to "dissolve and to be with Christ" (Phil. 1:23). Paul, however, "knew that he had another dwelling from God, a house not made by hands, if the house of his earthly dwelling was dissolved."[25] And this was indeed what he hankered after. Calvin concludes from Paul's example: "He who would stop living his own life would be beautifully with God."[26]

As Calvin leads this section of his book toward its conclusion he recalls Jesus' statement that "God is the God of Abraham, Isaac and Jacob, . . . of the living, not of the dead" (Matt. 22:32), and that Jesus rejected the opinion of the Sadducees, who denied both the resurrection of the dead and the immortality of the soul. He then considers the vision of the Apocalypse which shows the souls of Christian martyrs waiting under the altar and clamoring for justice (Apoc. 6:10-11). The martyrs receive white stoles, not cushions on which to lie down and fall asleep. Those who put on white stoles have to keep watching,[27] for these "undoubtedly designate the principle of glory that the divine liberality has given the martyrs until the advent of the day of judgment." Instances of this meaning abound in Scripture.

---

23. *Haec non solum errorem istorum produnt sed etiam malignitatem contra Dei opera et virtutes, quas eum in sanctis suis operari scripturae praedicant* (p. 54).

24. *Isti non solum opus Dei ad tempus intermitunt, sed etiam exstinguunt* (p. 55).

25. *Psychopannychia*, p. 55.

26. *Pulchre vero esset cum Christo, qui desineret vivere vitam suam* (p. 55).

27. *Vigilent oportet, quae sic induuntur* (p. 56).

Moreover the Book of Revelation speaks of two deaths and two resurrections. The first resurrection takes place "before the judgment." It is no other than the liberation of the soul from the body of death. The second is "when the body rises and the soul is taken up in glory."[28] This makes the first resurrection, denied by the slumberers, "the only entrance to the blessed glory." Jesus himself affirmed this in his word from the cross when he promised the good thief entrance into paradise on that very day:

> He who is everywhere promises that he will be with the thief. And he promises paradise, for the one who has fruition of God has enough delights. And he does not delay him through a long sequence of days, but calls him that very day to the delights of his kingdom.[29]

It would be absurd to argue from 2 Peter 3:8, with the pseudo-prophets, that in God's eyes one day is like a thousand years, for the whole measurement of time is distorted if each day that is mentioned in the Bible is tantamount to a millennium![30] Nor is it a valid argument to say that when it is written, "Jesus Christ yesterday, today, and for ever" (Heb. 3:8), "today" is the time of the New Testament, and "yesterday" is that of the Old. Calvin asks, "Where," that is, in which time, "will Jesus be, he, the Eternal God who is also in his humanity the first-born of every creature (Col. 1:15) and the lamb slain from the beginning of the world?" (Apoc. 13:8). If "today" is not the day Jesus died, but is the time between the humanity of Christ and the day of judgment, then the good thief enters paradise before the souls wake up from sleep, and that which is possible only after the last judgment is given him before! The slumberers are thus pushed to the point where they deny the truth and fall into absurdities.

As he concludes this line of argumentation, Calvin turns to

---

28. *Psychopannychia*, p. 57.

29. *Ille se affuturum latroni promittit. Et paradisum promittit, quia satis deliciarum habet qui Deo fruitur. Neque illum reicit in longam dierum seriem, sed eo ipso die vocat ad delicias regni sui* (p. 57).

30. *Psychopannychia*, pp. 57-58.

those who "welcome in themselves the memory of the promises of God in the good peace of conscience."[31] He exhorts them to resist the gates of hell, for "God, who cannot deny his own truth, is their caution." God has spoken clearly. "His voice, addressed to the Church that is still on pilgrimage on earth, is not obscure at all."[32] Let no one be afraid "that all the forces of nature are believed to fail," for Psalm 92:13-14 contains the promise that they will be "vigorous in old age like trees full of sap, luxuriant, wide-spreading!"[33]

What then is the soul? "We hold," Calvin concludes,

> the faith that rests on all the prophets, on evangelical truth, on Christ himself: The spirit is the image of God, like whom it must live, understand, be eternal; as long as it is in the body it exhibits its powers, and when it escapes that prison it migrates to God, the fruition of whose presence it enjoys while resting in hope of the blessed resurrection. This rest is paradise to it. As to the spirit of the damned, as it waits for a terrible judgment on itself it is tortured by this waiting, which Paul called φοβεράν, that is, formidable. To inquire further is to plunge into the abyss of the mysteries of God, for it is enough to learn what the Spirit, the best teacher, has sufficiently taught.[34]

Again the Book of Wisdom comes handy at this point. It says: "The souls of the just are in the hands of God, and the torments of death do not touch them. They are seen to have died by the eyes of fools, but they are in peace" (Wis. 3:1-2). Further than this no human may go: "This is the end of our wisdom; being sober and subject to God, it knows that those who rise above themselves shine for ever."[35]

*   *   *

31. *Psychopannychia*, p. 59.
32. *Vox ejus est minime obscura ad ecclesiam adhuc in terris peregrinantem* (p. 59).
33. New English Bible translation.
34. *Spiritum imaginem esse Dei, instar cujus vigeat, intelligat, aeternus sit . . .* (p. 60).
35. *Hic finis est nostrae sapientiae, quae (ut sobria est et Deo sujecta) ita novit eos, qui supra se nituntur, semper corruere* (p. 61).

Several points emerge from this central part of *Psychopannychia*. The heretical denial of the survival of the soul after death as a living entity has led Calvin to make some major statements about the nature of the soul. From Greek philosophy he has retained Plato's thesis that the soul is a stranger to the body that imprisons it during the present life. He has found this notion echoed in some expressions of the Book of Wisdom.[36] From the Scriptures in the strict sense, especially from the Pauline writings, he has learned the fundamental Christian conviction that God is the life of the faithful soul. Here christology, soteriology, and spirituality converge. It is through Christ that God has revealed himself to be the life of the faithful soul. By the gift of himself to the faithful as their life God has placed in us the principle of justification and of sanctification. Thus the soul can live the divine life already on earth as it enjoys a "residence" or dwelling that is from God, and is comparable to a garment. This residence, inchoate in this life, is eternal in the heavens. When we are fully in God's heavenly mansion we will no longer walk by faith but by sight. But since this divine residence is inchoate in faith, it is built in faith during the present life, only to be perfected after death. There, in the embodied soul of our earthly living, is where the enrichment begins that will lead to the vision of God.

Calvin does not directly use the image of ascent, traditional in spiritual writings, that would find its most thorough analysis a few years later in John of the Cross's *Ascent of Mount Carmel*.[37] Yet he is close to it as he borrows the image of the way from the Psalms: The Christian soul goes *ex virtute in virtutem,* from virtue to virtue, up to the moment when "the God of gods is seen in Sion."[38] The spiritual life had previously been described as the *Ascent of Mount Sion* by the Franciscan Bernardino de Laredo (1482-1540). Sion, the mountain on which the Temple was built, was thus identified in late medieval spirituality as the mountain of the vision of God. Calvin, it is safe to presume, was not familiar with spiritual writings composed in

36. Since Calvin read the Book of Wisdom, it is superfluous to go to Plato's *Phaedo* to find the source of his "Platonism."

37. Juan de Yepes was born in 1542, the year of publication of Calvin's work as *Vivere apud Christum*. . . . The *Subida* was written in 1581-1585.

38. *Psychopannychia,* p. 52.

Spanish. He nonetheless belongs squarely in the same tradition as he further comments that the psalmist's way to Sion describes a beginning, a middle part, and the reaching of a goal. This is the traditional threefold way of beginners in the spiritual life, of the more advanced, and of those who were called, somewhat improperly, the perfect.

Deriving originally from the sixth-century writings of Pseudo-Denys, which were themselves influenced by neo-Platonism, these stages in the spiritual life had been streamlined as the "three ways" of purgation, illumination, and union. These were described as being simultaneous by Bonaventure, although most spiritual authors saw them as successive stages along the spiritual path. In the Christian literature of the Renaissance the first three books of the *Imitation of Christ* correspond to these three ways, even though the expression itself does not seem to be used by the author.

Besides the image of the way, Calvin also uses the more biological analogy of growth — *crescunt semper*,[39] — an enlargement or progression *(illo incremento)* that is followed by a passage or *transitus* through death. In this perspective there is no essential distinction between faith and glory, except, precisely, that faith undergoes an *incrementum* in the direction of the perfection that is glory. The term that Calvin uses — *incrementum* — has a quantitative connotation that is unexpected here, and that may be explained by the influence of Augustine's *De quantitate animae* on Calvin's meditation about the soul. Augustine used the word when he referred to the developments imposed on the body by the passage of time.[40] Does time, he had asked, impose similar developments on the soul? His answer was negative. He had nevertheless justified the use of temporal and corporeal images and comparisons to describe the growth of the soul's capacity to know. Thus there is, he had argued, a *longanimitas* of the soul, even using the Greek term, πακροτυμία, a dimension of grandeur that is not static and does not refer to space, but to inner power or capacity. In this context Augustine referred only to the nat-

39. *Psychopannychia*, p. 52.
40. Augustine, *De quantitate animae*, XVI, 29-30, BA, vol. V, *Dialogues philosophiques* (Paris: Desclée, 1948), p. 286.

ural potencies of the soul. It was easy enough, however, to transfer the image to the properly spiritual life and to speak of spiritual growth in a similar manner. This is precisely the point to which Calvin alludes here.

There is in the Christian life a progress toward perfection, and the last passage from progress to perfection is nothing less than death. Death should therefore be valued positively. It is an event that reveals a necessary distinction, though not a fundamental difference, between here below and hereafter, between this life on earth and the heavenly life in God. Indeed, an infinity of divine blessings can be received and experienced only when the soul has escaped its body. Nonetheless, before the faithful die, their souls have already tasted God within themselves.

Spiritual growth is a Christian experience. The gifts of divine grace, as Calvin recognizes, are progressive: "As to us, we feel and we confess mercy, since there are degrees of God's mercy: the sanctification of the elect, the glorification of the sanctified. Does not the Lord act according to his mercy when he sanctifies us more and more?"[41] At this point, three levels, inspired by Paul's letter to the Romans (8:29-30) — election, sanctification, glorification — form a continuum that unites terrestrial and celestial life, glory being given after one has died in the body to this world.

Calvin, however, is acquainted with more elaborate analyses that were developed in the tradition of Christian spirituality. It was in keeping with the principle of growth that, as they analyzed the degrees of the spiritual ascent and the stages on the way to God, monastic authors had depicted the soul as a diversified entity with seven levels or, as Teresa of Avila would write in 1577, an "interior castle" made of seven "mansions."[42] Calvin does not pursue this line of research at this time. It will recur further on.[43]

*   *   *

41. *Nos vero misericordiam sentimus et fatemur, cum sint gradus misericordiae Dei, sanctificari electos, glorificari sanctificatos. Nonne igitur misericordiam suam exercet Dominus, cum nos magis ac magis sanctificat?* (pp. 90-91).

42. The exact title of her book is *Castillo Interior, o las Moradas*.

43. See below, ch. 5, pp. 97-98, nn. 46-49.

There was an implicit question in the wish that Calvin formulated at the beginning of this section of his book: *Utinam*. . . . "If only we could, with the right faith, perceive what the kingdom of God is that is within the faithful already when they live the present life!" Does the Christian life normally include a perception of the divine kingdom in the soul? As he summed up patristic testimonies on the soul's relation to God and on its awakened survival after death, Calvin indeed affirmed that those who walk by faith toward the blessed vision of God are able to taste the kingdom, although they cannot see it. This had been the language of medieval mystics. Calvin well knew that the mystical dimension of faith was not a medieval accretion. He acknowledged one of its sources in the works of St. Augustine. According to the Christian tradition, which of course reflects the Christian experience, the life of faith is a spiritual pilgrimage toward the vision of God. In this sense, however, vision implies more than sight. As the soul advances in this life along the way to God it is given the grace to taste God. Such an experience of the kingdom of God in the soul is itself a proof that the soul never dies. This experience is the soul's life within the earthly body. And the life of the soul is God, who never dies.

V

Grace and Glory

The last and longest section of *Psychopannychia*, in both Hwang's and Schwendemann's outlines, is apparently built on two levels. The first and more obvious is the level of argumentation. Calvin refutes a number of ideas that have been put forward by adepts of the death of the soul. After the slumberers, the mortalists! The theory of the soul's sleep has been refuted. The more lethal theory of the soul's death is now carefully examined. Calvin refutes five theological arguments and a whole series of biblical arguments. Three of these are based respectively on the First Epistle to the Corinthians, the Letter to the Hebrews, and the Acts of the Apostles; seven are based on the Psalms. It is convenient to see this discussion as forming two sections, the first of which is more theological and the second more biblical.[1] In the present chapter we will look at the theological section.

Besides presenting a direct refutation of the adversaries' argumentation, this discussion provides Calvin with further occasions to emphasize several aspects of the true doctrine. As the preceding pages reflected on the spiritual experience of Christians, this part of the book evokes dogmatic perspectives that relate to creation, christology, eschatology, and spirituality. At a deeper level that may well escape readers who are not as familiar with medieval writings as he

---

1. *Psychopannychia*, First section: pp. 61-86; second section: pp. 86-105.

himself undoubtedly was, Calvin draws again on the mystical tradition to make some of his points. This constitutes a more subtle second level of attention than the straight consideration of Christian doctrine. Or, may we say, within the argumentation there flows a strong undercurrent which, without stating it in so many words, carries forward the tradition of spiritual experience that the Church of the sixteenth century had received from the Middle Ages. For the true gospel dwells in the heart of the faithful; and the heart finds powerful reasons to reject certain speculative opinions that might endanger the gospel.

*   *   *

Calvin's first discussion with the mortalists examines and rejects the thesis that, according to Genesis 1:21, animals and humans have been endowed with the same kind of soul and that, as a consequence, both humans and animals lose their soul, along with their body, when they die. In death they no longer are. With the scholastic tradition, which generally took the biology of Aristotle for granted, Calvin knows that animals have a soul by virtue of which they live, which provides their body with sensation, motion, and the instinct of doing certain things in a certain way. Their soul, however, has no intellectual capacities, and therefore animals do not live like humans.[2]

The human soul is unique in that it has been endowed with the three faculties of "reason, intellect, will, powers that are not tied to the body."[3] Because of these spiritual powers "it is no wonder that it subsists without a body and does not perish like the soul of beasts, which have nothing else than bodily senses." When St. Paul wrote that the first Adam was made "into a living soul" and the second "into a vivifying spirit" (1 Cor. 15:45), he indicated the ultimate transformation to which humans are called. Their passage from the terrestrial plane to the resurrected life is similar to the unfolding of a seed, that must be buried before it can sprout forth. The present life may be likened to a burial of the soul. The continued existence of the body in which the

2. *Aliter illae vivunt, aliter vivit homo* (*Psychopannychia*, p. 62).
3. *Psychopannychia*, p. 62.

soul is hidden depends on a multitude of external helps. It requires "food, drink, sleep, that are signs of corruption." And these necessary ingredients do not even ensure a stable material state. They do not prevent the body from being subject to "all kinds of inclinations."[4] And such a dependence of the body on the external world affects the soul that lies within and weighs it down.

Nonetheless, the human soul is also, at least through Christ, the second Adam, "vivifying spirit." That is, in Christ the human person will undergo resurrection. The body is destined to rise again, though not at the status to which it is reduced in the present life. It will be both corporeal and spiritual: "When Christ assumes us with him in glory, not only will the animal body be made alive by the soul, but so will the spiritual body, which our mind cannot conceive and our tongue describe."[5] Calvin concludes, and for this he refers to Tertullian and to Augustine: "In the resurrection we shall not be another thing, yet we shall be others."[6] In the first or earthly period of human existence the body is animated by the soul, though not to the point where its corruptibility can be eliminated, since it is "under the elements of this world" that the soul gives life to the body. These "elements" are evidently what Paul calls the "elemental powers of the cosmos," which rule over earthly life.[7]

There will be, however, a second period of human existence: "when the figure of this world passes away, participation in the glory of God will raise it [the body] above nature." The human body raised above nature is identical with the "spiritual body" of which St. Paul and the Christian tradition speak. We shall then live "in the spiritual body, when, perfectly adhering to the Lord, it [*anima:* the soul] is made a living spirit."[8] It is precisely at this incorruptible

4. *Psychopannychia,* pp. 63-64.

5. *Psychopannychia,* p. 64.

6. *Vides igitur nos non aliud futuros esse in resurrectione, sed tamen alios, detur verbo venia* (p. 64). The text gives a reference to Augustine's *Epistola 148 ad Fortunatianum* (PL 33, 622-30), though the quotation does not come from it and corresponds only to the general sense of the letter on 623.

7. *Ita et cum eramus sub elementis mundi eramus serviente* (Gal. 4:3).

8. *In corpore vero spirituali, quando adhaerens perfecte Domino vivus spiritus efficitur* (p. 64).

level that a human person is the image of God. Whatever should be admitted regarding the corruptibility of the body that is animated by the soul, "the seat of the image of God always remains secure, whether it be called soul, or spirit, or whatever else."[9] The *imago Dei* does not die.

The vision of Ezekiel provides no solid objection to this notion of immortality. The prophet used the literary device of hypotyposis when he called on the spirit of the four winds to give life to dry bones (Ezek. 37:9). The mortalists infer therefrom that the human soul is no more than the body's power of motion, that it has no substantial reality, and that this power disappears at death, though it will be revived by the Creator at the final resurrection. On the one hand, Calvin objects, this inference contradicts the prophet, who in the great inaugural vision recorded at the beginning of his book called the eternal Spirit of God a wind (Ezek. 1:4). On the other hand, it results from a crude misunderstanding of the language of prophecy. It is characteristic of prophets that "they depict (*figurant*) things that are spiritual and higher than human perception with corporeal and visible symbols." In the case of Ezekiel, the "explicit and, as it were, iconic vision"[10] that opened his ministry was intended "somehow to represent the Spirit of God and the human spirits; and because such a sight would be alien to a spiritual nature," the prophet had to borrow images from corporeal entities.

*　　*　　*

In Calvin's second discussion the reader is confronted with another aspect of the theory of the death of the soul. There are some among the mortalists who grant that the human soul was endowed with the gift of immortality when it was originally created. Yet they contend that this gift was withdrawn after the fall, as a punishment, when God pronounced the sentence on Adam and Eve: "You will die the death" (Gen. 2:17). Calvin, however, has little difficulty showing

9. . . . . *illa sedes imaginis Dei semper salva consistit, sive animam, sive spiritum, sive quidvis aliud nominent.*

10. . . . . *expressa et quasi eiconica visione* (p. 65).

that this idea runs against the evidence of Scripture. The punishment of Adam's original sin was to be the ineluctable decay of his body, not the annihilation of his soul. This point, Calvin adds, is evident by analogy with the present existence of the devil, the angel who sinned, and who, far from being dead, is ever seeking whom he may devour (1 Peter 5:8).

In addition, many biblical passages refer to another kind of death than the loss of earthly existence and life. Calvin discusses the verse, "You are dust and to this dust you shall return" (Gen. 3:19), which must have been familiar to his readers on account of its use in the traditional rite of Ash Wednesday. It is the body that returns to dust, not the soul. There is indeed a death of the soul, which is quite different from the return of the body to the original stuff of which it is made. Since it comes directly from the hands of the Creator the soul can die only from a direct action of the same Creator. This happens when God damns the soul, and such a condemnation leaves it "confused, fallen, and despairing." Damnation, however, is not annihilation. It is a spiritual catastrophe that implies the soul's continued existence. It is "a judgment, that is, by God, the weight of which the miserable soul cannot bear without total confusion, ruin, and despair."[11] Such was God's call to Adam in the garden of Eden: "Adam, where are you?" (Gen. 3:9). In the circumstances the question sounded "horrid" to Adam and Eve, for it carried condemnation. So awesome was God's voice that the ensuing horror is "easier to conceive than to express." The human mind cannot even imagine it "unless it has been experienced." Just as the divine majesty is so sublime that it cannot be described with human words, so it is not possible to tell how "terrible" is "the divine wrath for those to whom it applies." The people who have to face it would prefer to hide "in a thousand abysses," if only they could escape. There is, however, no shelter from God's voice.

This, then, as Calvin expresses it with authentic pathos, is truly the death of the soul, when it exists in God's absence: "Do you wish to know what the soul's death is? It is to miss God, to be forsaken by God, to be left to itself. For if God is the soul's life, the soul that

11. *Psychopannychia,* p. 67.

85

loses God's presence loses its own life."[12] Such a spiritual death is experienced when God's loving presence has been withdrawn. Since there is no light outside of God that is able to illumine our night, "our soul, buried in its darkness, is blind" when the divine light sets. This blindness entails other tragic defects, for by the same token the soul is dumb, "unable to make a saving confession." It is also deaf, "unable to hear the living voice." And finally it limps, being "unable to function." Calvin asks, "What more do you require for death?" All these decays of the human spirit can already be experienced by sinners in the present life. Calvin's description of the death that results from God's judgment of condemnation is strikingly close to Martin Luther's *Anfechtungen*, the abysses of anxiety that confront anyone who has truly sensed the majesty of God facing one's own littleness, and that are overcome when we are justified by faith. It may be likened to what the Mystical Doctor, St. John of the Cross, in another perspective, will soon call "the dark night of the soul."

From such a death Christ has redeemed us, as St. Paul abundantly shows. Indeed, we are like the widow of 1 Timothy 5:6, who lives amid pleasures. Left to ourselves, "living, we die," or, in Calvin's striking formulation, "we are immortal unto death."[13] As had been announced by the prophets of the Old Testament, however, Christ died for us, that we might live. Death comes from Adam, but life is from Christ. Thus the question of mortalism touches on christology directly and radically. The work of Christ and the scope of redemption are at stake in it. As Calvin says, "the hinge of the entire controversy turns around the comparison of Adam and Christ."[14] Christ did restore what had collapsed in Adam. Moreover, "as the power of grace has reached further than that of sin, so has Christ been more powerful in restoring than Adam in losing." The superiority of Christ and of his work is not only quantitative; it is above all qualitative. The Apostle even boasts: "There is no condemnation for those who are in Christ Jesus" (Rom. 8:1). Instead, the mortalists believe that death still reigns among the elect of God. If such were the

12. *Psychopannychia,* p. 68.
13. . . . *immortales sumus ad mortem* (p. 68).
14. *In comparatione Adae et Christi totius controversiae cardo vertitur* (p. 69).

case grace would have no effect, so that by implication the mortalists destroy grace. The truth is the opposite: "As death, introduced by Adam, has reigned, so now life reigns through Jesus Christ."[15] One may say: "The elect of God are now as Adam was before sin. He was created immortal, and so are now those who have been recreated through Christ into a better nature."[16]

Let us then look at the soul again. After a person dies to this world, "that will be implemented in the body which has so far begun in the soul. Or rather, what has so far begun in the soul will be implemented jointly in the body and the soul." Already in this world, in the present life, the Christian soul is being initiated to the experience of resurrection. To the elect, Calvin reflects, "a sort of passage to the highest degree of immortality is more natural" than evil or punishment, more natural even than the common necessity of bodily death. This, however, is evidently not because of the creaturely nature as such, but because of God's election.

*   *   *

Calvin's third argument turns to the image of a sleep of the soul, this time, however, in the context of its assumed death. It is absurd to maintain, Calvin affirms, that every time the Scriptures speak of sleep they really mean death, yet this is in the soul-killers' reasoning. Death, as the separation of soul and body, has indeed been called dormition *(dormitio),*[17] and in this sense the soul of Christ fell asleep when he died on the cross. While Calvin does not allude to Mary at this point, the death of the Virgin was precisely called her dormition, κοίμησις, in the early accounts of it. Such a usage he explains as a *synechdoche,*[18] the linguistic process by which a part is taken for the whole, or the whole for a part. A recurrent moment in human experience, namely bodily slumber, serves to name the disappearance of all signs of life. Already the language of dormition to

---

15. *Psychopannychia,* p. 70.
16. *Psychopannychia,* p. 71.
17. *Psychopannychia,* p. 71.
18. *Psychopannychia,* p. 72.

denote death, Calvin remarks, was frequent in the Old Testament, where it may have been borrowed from pagan authors,[19] and most of the discussion turns around dormition-language. Calvin is nonetheless aware of the deeper question that lies beneath the linguistic problem: How does the soul relate to death and dying? The soul's dormition in death is evidently quite different from what is imagined in anabaptist circles. It means that after death the soul no longer animates the body. It is itself still living, but the body is no longer there to be animated by the soul.

This discussion is all the more noteworthy in that it cannot possibly fit a Platonic view of death as liberation from the jail of the body. In spite of the Platonic backdrop to some of the earlier pages of *Psychopannychia,* Calvin does not regard bodily death as a liberation of the soul, which would be finally freed from material and temporal shackles. For the soul has a task to do on earth. At death this task ends. Seen from the earth, therefore, death is the ending of the soul's task of animating its terrestrial body. The notion of the body's animation by the soul, however, is less Platonic or neo-Platonic than Aristotelian, the body and the soul relating to each other like matter and form, the two co-principles of being that were posited by Artistotle's philosophy. As Thomas Aquinas had interpreted Aristotle, the soul brings life to the ensuing compound, the body being responsible for the concrete characteristics of this compound as it necessarily restricts the range of its life to the strictly specified limits of individuality. Although Calvin is generally not a Thomist and comes closer to John Duns Scotus on a number of scholastic questions, it does not do justice to the careful nuances of his thought to consider him simply as an adept of Platonic body-soul dualism.

*   *   *

The fourth argument begins with a discussion of Ecclesiastes 3:18-21, where the mortalists believe that humans are assimilated to ani-

---

19. Calvin mentions Catullus (c. 87–c. 54 B.C.) and Ovid (43 B.C.–A.D. 17) (p. 73), although these Latin poets could evidently not have influenced the Hebrews.

mals.[20] Solomon, however, the assumed author of the text, destroys their theory by virtue of the main lesson of the Book of Ecclesiastes: All on earth is vanity. Man's perception is vain as long as it remains merely human. The text of Ecclesiastes, as understood by Calvin, actually speaks in favor of the traditional view against the soul-murderers, for it describes the thoughts of *animalis homo,* the man who does not think spiritually. Left to itself the human mind cannot even understand any object, whether solid or liquid, by study, meditation, and reasoning *(studendo, meditando, ratiocinando),* which are the three steps of rational knowledge. True insight has to go beyond rationality. It is obtained by thinking spiritually, in the mode of faith, *fidem nostram,* which is far above the rational capacities of the mind.

Everything is vain and uncertain in this world, and it is only in Christ that the faithful receive consolation. There are of course those who look no further than their feet, and have no hope in the future or in their own resurrection.[21] If we desire certainty, therefore, "let us run to the law and the testimony (Isa. 8:20), where the truth and the ways of the Lord are." Ecclesiastes had asked, "Who knows if the spirits of the sons of Adam ascend, and the spirits of horses descend?" (Eccles. 3:21). Calvin responds: "No one who has heard the word of God doubts that the spirits of the sons of Adam ascend. To ascend I understand here simply as meaning to exist and to keep immortality."[22]

* * *

The fifth mortalist argument explicitly deals with matters of eschatology. The point it raises, and Calvin's refutation, is of substantial importance in regard to the nature of the soul. The mortalists posit that there is only one judgment, at the end of the world. In that solemn moment both the just and the unjust will receive their reward or their punishment, by virtue of which they will go to glory or to

20. *Psychopannychia,* pp. 73-76.
21. *Psychopannychia,* p. 75.
22. *Psychopannychia,* pp. 75-76.

Gehenna. Since, however, neither beatitude nor misery is mentioned before the judgment, there must simply be nothing between death and the final resurrection at the sound of the archangel's trumpet. It would of course be absurd to decree eternal beatitude for those who already enjoy it! The mortalist logic concludes from this that between death and the resurrection the soul is simply nothing. It no longer exists. The resurrection, when it comes, is not only of the body, but also of the soul. This line of thought was chiefly based on an interpretation of the eschatological passages in the Gospel of Matthew (Matt. 13:41-43; 24:34; 25:34ff.).

As Calvin challenges the mortalists' conclusion, he remarks that "not one syllable"[23] in the biblical texts about the last judgment mentions a sleep of the soul. And in any case, if the souls have been awake all along, before and after bodily death, as he himself believes with all the tradition, they can still come short of the divine glory, and in this case the last judgment keeps its proper function of sorting out good and evil. This leads Calvin to oppose the scriptural principle to his adversaries:

> Since it belongs to a senseless and even presumptuous person to define, without Scripture, what does not fall under the human sense, with what cheek do not these tipsy new dogmatists proceed to defend a sleep that they have not learned from the Lord's mouth?

The principle of sobriety is at the same time, in Calvin's eyes, a principle of security. It is neither safe nor sober to imagine a sleep of the soul "that cannot be proven with the clear word of God."[24]

Two points, Calvin pursues, should be beyond discussion. First, we must confess that "our beatitude is always in process *(in cursu)* until the day that will close and end every process." All agree that the fullness of beatitude and glory requires "perfect union with God." Yet this perfect union cannot be obtained in the present life. The day of fulfillment remains an object of hope for those who share the

---

23. *Psychopannychia*, p. 77.
24. . . . *qui aperto Dei verbo probari non possit* (p. 77).

faith: "There we all tend, there we march, there all Scriptures and promises of God send us."[25] It is there that Christian believers will share with Abraham "the possession and fruition of God, outside of which and beyond which nothing is to be desired."[26]

The second point bears on the nature of the kingdom of God that has been promised to those who believe. Precisely, "the kingdom of God, which the faithful are called to possess, is nothing other than this union with God." To be one with God is to be in God, to be filled with God, to adhere to God, to possess God. Calvin cannot have ignored that these expressions belonged to the tradition of medieval mysticism. He provides a hint of this awareness when he completes the picture of eternal beatitude with a clear allusion to the trinitarian theology of the Franciscan doctor, St. Bonaventure. To be in God, Calvin writes, is to be "in the fountain of all fullness, in which one reaches the ultimate measure of all justice, wisdom, glory, the blessings that constitute the kingdom of God." In Bonaventure's theology *fontalis plenitudo*, "fontal fullness," is attributed to God the Father, the First Person of the divine Trinity; it is the primary characteristic of Eternal Fatherhood. Calvin at this point projects Bonaventure's trinitarian insight into the eternal life of the saints: in the fountain of all fullness is "the ultimate point of the kingdom of God," when God is all in all (1 Cor. 15:28). Those whom God fills do receive thereby the plenitude of all riches.

If these two points are, as Calvin trusts, accepted by his opponents, then it is singularly absurd on their part to deny entrance to the heavenly kingdom to "the holy servants of God" who have died to the present world. Even though the kingdom will not be completely manifested before the end of the world, an incomplete kingdom is more and better than no kingdom at all. Furthermore, one should recognize that "what is to be perfected has already begun"[27] on this very earth. If this is not necessarily an allusion to the Christian mystical experience, it is at least a reference to the traditional

25. *Huc omnes tendimus, huc properamus, huc omnes scripturae mittunt et Dei promissiones* (p. 77).

26. . . . *qui cum Abraham partem habent Deum possidere et eo frui, praeter quam and ultra quam nullam aliam appetere liceat* . . . (p. 78).

27. *Psychopannychia*, p. 78.

doctrine about grace and glory. Abundant texts of Scripture attest that the kingdom of God begins, not only on the final day of God's triumph over Satan, but also whenever the powers of the enemy are subdued:

> God, to whose majesty nothing can be added, from which nothing can be subtracted, cannot reign in himself some day otherwise than as he has reigned from the start. . . . When we pray that his kingdom come, do we think that it is not now in existence? And where is it? "The kingdom of God is within you" (Luke 17:21). God already reigns in his elect, whom he leads through his Spirit. . . . He reigns already now, for the coming of whose kingdom we pray. He reigns indeed when he activates his powers in his own. . . .[28]

The text of Luke that is the background of this perspective on the presence of God's kingdom is one of the foundational texts of the mystical tradition in Christianity. Surely this is not accidental. Calvin was well within this tradition when he presented the kingdom as already at work among the elect before it reaches perfection as they enter into heaven:

> Although it is said not to have arrived yet, this kingdom may be seen to a certain degree. For those begin to be in the kingdom who in some way have the kingdom of God in themselves; and they reign with God, those against whom the gates of hell cannot prevail (Matt. 16:18). In God they are justified, those of whom it is said: In the Lord all the seed of Israel will be justified and praised (Isa. 45:25). . . .[29]

---

28. *Neque enim aliter regnare olim in se Deus potest, quam regnavit ab initio, cujus majestati nihil accedere aut decedere potest. . . . An vero dum oramus ut regnum ejus adveniat, cogitamus nunc nullum esse? Et ubi erit illud? Regnum Dei intra vos est (Luke 17:21). Regnat igitur nunc in electis suis, quos agit Spiritu suo. . . . Regnat, inquam, jam nunc, cujus ut regnum adveniat oramus. Regnat quidem, dum operatur virtutes in suis . . .* (p. 79).

29. *Hoc quidem regnum, tametsi nondum advenisse dicitur, tamen aliqua ex parte spectare licet. Nam in regno Dei incipiunt esse, qui regnum Dei quodammodo intra se habent, et cum Deo regnant, adversus quos portae infernorum praevalere nequeunt*

The interior kingdom of God, in Calvin's understanding, is therefore no other than "the upbuilding of the Church or progress of the faithful,"[30] as these grow through successive degrees toward the perfect Adam (Eph. 4:13). This allows Calvin to make two additional points. First, the gate to the kingdom being connected with justification, the upbuilding of the Church is identified with the spiritual progress of the faithful. Such a progress is interior to the soul. The kingdom of God is within, and so is the Church. In a sense, therefore, the Church is spiritual, invisible, known only to the elect who have the evidence of the gospel in their heart, of the Church in their soul. Nonetheless, the kingdom of God is also exterior, and the Church is not purely invisible, for the spiritual progress in question is that of "the faithful," of all the faithful who are visibly united in their confession of the Lordship of Christ.

Second, the difference between grace and glory, between the present moment of faith and its future fulfillment in heaven, is not a difference of essence, but only of degree. Already the faithful souls, united with God and thereby with one another, share the divine attributes that are graciously imparted to them. Whence, as Calvin insists, the Johannine doctrine of the believers' union with Christ: "Beloved, we now are children of God, but what we shall be has not yet been manifested. We know that when he will appear we shall be like him, for we shall see him as he is" (1 John 3:2). This perspective bridges the distance between this life and the next, between the beginning and the fulfillment of the believers' destiny. The children of God are already now reigning in the divine kingdom. And Calvin expresses his amazement that when his opponents hear this they do not come to their senses and realize that "the begetting that is from God, and by which we participate in divine immortality, is immortal."[31]

Such a participation, however, that is true and real in the faith of the saints, still lies hidden in their heart. The soul's present share in

---

(p. 79). Zimmerli omits the comma after *habent,* thus missing the parallelism of the sentence.

30. . . . *ecclesiae aedificatio seu profectus fidelium* . . . (p. 79).

31. *Psychopannychia,* p. 80.

the kingdom of God remains, as it were, in a state of latency, so that the eyes of the world are blind to it. The basic reason for this hiddenness is christological and eschatological: "Christ is our head, whose kingdom and glory have not yet appeared. . . ." Christ is the principle. He is the beginning, the firstborn of the new creation. The disciples shall follow him when he comes in the Father's glory and he sits at the right hand of the divine Majesty. The glory is not seen, although it is already shared and it can be sensed. Calvin can therefore affirm: "In the meantime, however, the life which is in us from God is our breath, because Christ, our life, lives."[32] This twofold perspective of the eschatological future and its anticipated presence is evidently borrowed from the Epistle to the Colossians: "Your life is hidden with Christ" (Col. 3:3).[33] It is also in line with the central stream of the medieval and Renaissance mystics.

The conclusion follows smoothly: "It would be absurd that we ourselves perish when our life lives. This life is in God and with God, and it is blessed because it is in God." Admittedly the faithful who have died in Christ are still expecting the final resurrection and the full manifestation of the children of God. For them, however, this fulfillment yet to come is already a certainty. Because "they know that God is propitious to them," one may say that, in a sense, "they see their future reward from afar."[34] We are in this world like people with bad eyes: "Where the eyes of our mind, which, being now buried in the flesh, are unperceiving, will have shed their veil, we shall see what we will have hoped for, and in that peace we shall rest." Opposite the reprobates' "formidable fear of judgment" there will be a "joyful and blessed" peace for the elect.

*   *   *

32. *Interim vivere quod ex Deo in nobis est, hoc est spiritum nostrum, quia Christus vivit vita nostra. Absurdum enim esse, ut vivente vita nostra pereamus ipsi. Vitam autem hanc apud Deum et cum Deo esse et beatam esse, quia in Deo sit* (p. 81). I take it that in this context the word *spiritus* has the sense of "breath of life."

33. *Vita vestra est abscondita cum Christo. Cum Christus apparuerit, vita vestra, tunc et vos apparebitis cum ipso in gloria.*

34. *. . . et futuram mercedem eminus vident . . .* (p. 81).

Calvin wishes to persuade, not to constrain, his opponents. To this end he explains the traditional meaning of baptism, which he finds allegorically represented by the drowning of Pharaoh in the Red Sea. Baptism is "the way of liberation through water."[35] In it

> our own Pharaoh is drowned, our old man crucified, our members mortified, our self buried with Christ, emigrating from captivity to the devil and the dominion of death, immigrating into a wilderness, a land that is dry and sterile unless the Lord send manna from heaven and make water to flow from the rock.[36]

This blessed rain is that of "his Spirit's graces." Led by Jesus, the disciples pass on to the promised land of milk and honey, where "the grace of God liberates us from the body of death through Jesus Christ our Lord. Already we are in peace and we wear white stoles." Nonetheless, "Jerusalem, the capital and seat of the Kingdom, is not yet fully built," for "Solomon, the King of peace, does not yet hold the scepter and rule over all things." His final reign will undoubtedly be celebrated in the final resurrection: "When the heavenly Jerusalem rises in its glory, and the true Solomon, Christ, king of peace, sits on high in judgment, the true Israelites will reign with their king."[37]

This passage evokes St. Bonaventure's *Itinerarium mentis in Deum,* in which the speculations of the first six chapters are so many steps leading, in the seventh, to the "throne of the true Solomon, up which one comes to peace, where the true peace-lover rests in a peace-loving mind as in an inner Jerusalem."[38] This is equivalently the propitiatory of adoration, the Pasch, or transit through the Red Sea, from Egypt to the wilderness in which those who are hungry taste of the hidden manna and those who are tired find rest with Christ in the sepulchre. At this high level of contemplation one sees

---

35. *Psychopannychia,* p. 81.

36. *Psychopannychia,* p. 82.

37. *Ubi vero surrexerit in gloriam suam coelestis Jerusalem et verus Solomon Christus, rex pacis, sublimis sederit in tribunali, regnabunt cum suo rege veri Israelitae* (p. 82).

38. *. . . . sex gradibus throni veri Salomonis, quibus pervenitur ad pacem, ubi verus pacificus in mente pacifica tanquam in interiori Hierosolyma requiescit* (*Itinerarium,* ch. 7, 1).

Christ on the cross, "through faith, hope and love, devotion, admiration, exultation, appreciation, praise, and jubilation."[39]

That Christ should be called the true Solomon is directly relevant to Calvin's argumentation, since he is refuting the contention that Solomon, in Ecclesiastes, assimilates humans to animals. Calvin is well aware of Bonaventure's use of the analogy between Solomon, the great master of wisdom in the Old Testament, and Jesus Christ, the teacher of ultimate wisdom, for he sets the symbol of the true Solomon in the very same context as was done in the seventh chapter of Bonaventure's *Itinerarium*. This context is the history of the people of God from the Exodus to the holy city. After passing the Red Sea there is a wilderness to be crossed, the heavenly manna to be eaten in the desert, the highest grace of peace and rest to be received, and this fulfillment will take place in Jerusalem, the holy city. In this holy city — Jerusalem meaning, in Hebrew, City of Peace — Christ is the king of peace. There indeed he is "the true Solomon," who not only teaches, but also saves and liberates; and he does this, as Calvin notes, "not without sweat and blood."[40]

Calvin is presumably aware that many of his readers may be unacquainted with the mystical tradition in which, at this point, he stands. For them he adds a more mundane metaphor and envisages death in light of the experience of struggle and victory. "We beat the enemy when we exit from this flesh of sin to belong entirely to God."[41] Victory over the mortalists' arguments becomes a token of the triumph and glory of Christ, "our head." This victory is obtained by those who scrutinize the Scriptures, who have learned to see God and to listen to the divine voice.

*   *   *

The eschatological perspective that has thus been opened is supported by the patristic tradition. Calvin neatly formulates the essential notion of tradition when he says: This doctrine has been "passed

---

39. *Itinerarium*, ch. 7, 2.
40. *Psychopannychia*, p. 82.
41. *Vincimus hostem, dum exuimur hac carne peccati, ut toti Dei simus* (p. 82).

on to us by hand, by those who soberly and reverently have treated of the mysteries of God."[42] He has no difficulty bringing in appropriate quotations from Tertullian, Irenaeus, John Chrysostom, Augustine, and Jerome. This patristic tradition is summed up in the Symbol of Nicaea, which, Calvin says, is a "compendium of our faith."[43] It is also notably confirmed by Augustine's analysis of the soul. For there are degrees within the soul. Calvin could have argued this point with the help of medieval authors. He preferred to go back to the Augustinian source:

> And it does not displease me that elsewhere, pedagogically, it is taught by him, if at least he has a sane and modest interpreter, that there are many degrees of the soul: first, animation; second, sense; third, art; fourth, virtue; fifth, tranquility; sixth, entrance; seventh, contemplation.[44]

This sevenfold division of the soul comes directly from the *De quantitate animae*, a philosophical dialogue with his friend Evodius which is one of Augustine's early works. The first three degrees correspond to the unfolding of natural capacities. "These are great," Augustine commented, "and entirely human, . . . common to good and evil people."[45] It is natural to the soul to animate its body, to organize its sensations, to develop a knowledge and practice of arts and sciences. At the fourth level the spiritual realm is opened, as the soul, understanding the ineluctability of death and realizing its own unworthiness before God, begins to strive for what is morally good. This marks a transition from the natural to the spiritual, from the function of the soul as psyche, related to the bodily senses, to its function as intellect, reflecting on itself and on God. The last three

---

42. *Haec etiam nobis per manus tradiderunt, qui parce et reverenter tractarunt Dei mysteria* (p. 83).

43. *In symbolo namque, quod est fidei nostrae compendium, confitemur non animae sed carnis resurrectionem* (p. 86).

44. *Psychopannychia*, p. 85.

45. *Magna haec et omnino humana. Sed est adhuc ista partim doctis atque indoctis, partim bonis ac malis animis copia communis* (*De quantitate animae*, 72, BA V, p. 378).

degrees are strictly spiritual, the soul entering into the contemplation of God, who is the ultimate Truth.[46]

Calvin could have been content with this discreet reference to the sevenfold structure of the soul. Had he gone no further, this new allusion to the mystical tradition would be an aside without great consequences for understanding his thought. He did not, however, stay there, but proceeded to add another schema, which this time did not originate with Augustine but with medieval writings in the line of monastic theology. The first degrees form a group of three, the soul relating to the body in three ways that are indicated by the Latin prepositions, *de, ad, circa:* "Or someone prefers to say: First, of the body, second, to the body, third, around the body. . . ."[47] The last four degrees are associated two by two, as the soul relates to itself and to God in terms of *ad* and *in:* ". . . fourth, to itself; fifth, in itself; sixth, to God; seventh, in God."[48] That is, the soul seeks itself and dwells in itself, and then it seeks God and dwells in God. Each forward movement (*ad,* "toward"), each seeking, is followed by an indwelling *(in),* a rest. And ultimately, the soul dwells in God, and God in the soul.

Outlines of the structure of the soul on a sevenfold pattern corresponding to seven degrees of ascent to God had been proposed by the theologians of St. Victor. Richard had spoken of three modes of contemplation, *dilatatio, sublevatio, alienatio mentis,* which are crowned by "four degrees of violent love."[49] Hugh had described three modes of vision, which he called *cogitatio, meditatio, contemplatio,* followed by three burns: by fire with flame and smoke, by fire with flame and no smoke, by fire with no flame or smoke.

Calvin's immediate reference, however, is to St. Bonaventure, who had systematized this sixfold or sevenfold division of the ascent to God: six degrees of ascent lead to a seventh which is properly

46. *De quantitate animae,* nn. 70-75, BA V, pp. 372-84.

47. *Seu quis malit: Primum de corpore, secundum ad corpus, tertium circa corpus . . .* (*Psychopannychia,* p. 85).

48. *. . . quartum ad seipsam, quintum in seipsa, sextum ad Deum, septimum apud Deum* (p. 85).

49. *Benjamin major,* book 5: Clare Kirchberger, ed., *Richard of Saint-Victor: Selected Writings* (New York: Harper, no date), pp. 181-212; *De quatuor gradibus violentae caritatis* (pp. 213-33).

ineffable. Calvin's distinction between contemplation as movement *(ad)* and contemplation as residence *(in)* once more evokes the *Journey of the Soul into God.* Where Bonaventure said *per* (through) . . . and *in* . . . , Calvin writes *ad* (toward) . . . *in* . . . Going *per* or "through," the movement of contemplation crosses over, first through the vestiges of God, second through the image of God in the natural powers of the soul, third through the divine name, Being, toward whatever lies beyond. According to the Augustinian tradition there is no being without goodness. Bonaventure's trinitarian theology carries this principle further: in God, Being is Goodness, in the sense that Being and Goodness fully express what the divine Essence is. In the journey of the knowledge of God, however, Goodness lies beyond Being. Understanding God as supreme Being leads to understanding God as supreme Goodness.

Beyond the three movements of the spiritual journey the devout come to rest and they find delight in the contemplation of God, when God is met in the divine vestiges of nature, in the gifts of supernatural grace, and ultimately in the divine name which is Goodness. By saying *ad* rather than *per,* "toward" rather than "through," Calvin emphasizes the ongoing dimension of the search for God. The first movement of this search is indeed a pilgrimage. The pilgrimage leads to a second movement, which is the arrival at a threshold, "through," and in a third movement the believer enters "in," that is, into the very object of admiration, into God.

*   *   *

No schema of the structure of the soul, however, should be taken as law, even though it has been described, and the soul's way into God has been chartered, by holy persons.[50] Nor was it Bonaventure's intention that it be so taken. The main point of the mystical tradition, which is also Calvin's, was to teach that the soul is called to make progress in this life. Against the mortalists, Calvin argued that the progress of the soul does not cease when people die to this world. All divine gifts are not given at once. The soul must remain alive in

50. . . . *ut sancti viri sensum hac in re ostenderem* . . . (p. 85).

death to receive gifts that have not been shared during this earthly life, and all the more so as the soul's ultimate goal cannot be reached before judgment day.

VI

False Dreams

It was indicated at the beginning of the previous chapter that after outlining the true doctrine on the state of the soul after death, Calvin proceeded to refute the chief arguments with which his adversaries tried to justify the theory of the sleep or the death of the soul. This was on Calvin's part a loose imitation of the scholastic method of argumentation. A *questio* normally proceeds in three steps. It first establishes the state of the question; it then posits the theologian's answer; and it finally refutes the opposite arguments. In the present case the refutation constitutes a primarily biblical section since it examines the verses from Scripture that are alleged by the soul-slumberers and the soul-mortalists to support their doctrines.

Taking account of the texts that are discussed and of the nature of the discussion one can conveniently subdivide this last part of *Psychopannychia* into a New Testament and an Old Testament subsection. The texts of the New Testament are:

1 Cor. 15:19	pp. 86-88
Heb. 11:13-16	pp. 89-90
Acts 9:36-43	pp. 90-91

The main texts of the Old Testament are taken from the Psalms, with a few citations from other writings. They are the following verses, though many others are cited in support without being examined at length:

Ps. 88:6-7	pp. 91-92
Ps. 146:4	pp. 92-93
Ps. 78:39	pp. 93-95
Ps. 88:4-6	pp. 95-96
Ps. 88:11-13	pp. 96-103
Ps. 104:33 and 146:2	pp. 103-4
Ps. 39:14 and Job	pp. 104-5

These pages could be read as early instances of the exegetical method that Calvin will later follow in his commentaries and his sermons. As my primary concern in this book turns around Calvin's doctrine on the soul and its theological presuppositions and implications, however, I will not try to compare his present exegesis with the methods of his later writings. I will only focus attention on his present treatment of the biblical texts in question.

*   *   *

The arguments from the New Testament that Calvin attributes to the mortalists are, by any standard, extremely weak. In 1 Corinthians 15:19 Paul declares believers to be the most miserable of men if the dead do not rise again. The mortalists apply this to the dead before the final resurrection. Paul, however, alludes to the situation of the living if the Sadducees happened to be right, that is, in the impossible hypothesis that there is no life after death and thus nothing to believe in beyond the present life. That there is life after death, Calvin objects, was already established by philosophers, "who strongly affirmed the immortality of the soul."[1] As to the Apostle's mind, it is made clear by the contrast that Paul establishes between the bodies of "the pious" in this life, which are exposed to "so many wounds, lashes, torments, injuries, and dire necessities," and the ridiculous spectacle of "the bodies of those who live for each day,

1. *Psychopannychia,* p. 87.

bathed in all pleasures."[2] In the midst of their sufferings the saints are already blessed by God on earth, not, however, "without the resurrection," in the hope of which they "find repose."[3] If, then, the "spirits of the saints are blessed before the resurrection, this is in view of the resurrection."

The Epistle to the Hebrews refers to the patriarchs who died after receiving God's promises, yet before it was possible to experience their fulfillment. They were people on the move, who lived as "pilgrims and guests on this earth."[4] They could have gone back to the lands they had left, but they desired better things as they looked forward to their heavenly homeland. From this summary of the stories of the patriarchs Calvin draws a striking conclusion: *Si appetunt, sunt*: "If they desire, they are." This is correct because, as he continues, "there is no desire except in a subject." Desire is a proof of existence. One century later, in 1637, the philosopher René Descartes will argue, *Cogito, ergo sum* ("I think, therefore I am"). And, attempting to find a way out of a methodical doubt about all reality, he will take this common sense observation as the basic principle of his philosophical reconstruction, going from this immediate certainty of existence to more derivative rational certainties. Both Calvin and Descartes start from an Augustinian premise, namely that personal experience is our gate of access to being. Calvin, however, places the experience of the self in desire rather than, as Descartes does, in thought.

Desire, Calvin explains, resides in "the sense of good and evil," since one has to choose between these two contraries, or at least between what seems to be good and what seems to be evil. Such a choice implies an innate capacity to distinguish between good and evil. This perspective was in fact more faithful than Descartes's rational approach to the Augustinian way of thought, which was mediated to Calvin, not only through the manuscripts that had been copied in the medieval *scriptoria* before getting into print at the end of the fifteenth century, but also through the monastic theology of

---

2. *Psychopannychia*, p. 87.
3. *Psychopannychia*, p. 88.
4. *Psychopannychia*, p. 89.

the Middle Ages. The ensuing conception of existence reflected the medieval doctrine of synderesis. Synderesis is a fundamental desire for the good that the Creator has placed at the center of the soul, and that persists even among those who, being blinded by sin, find themselves unable to identify the good and to do it.

That there is such a pure point in the soul had been inferred from a passage in St. Jerome's commentary on the prophet Ezekiel (ch. 1, n. 10). It could be found, among other loci, in Bonaventure's *Commentary on the Sentences* and in the Franciscan-Augustinian school in general. It was in keeping with the fundamental conception of God the Supreme Good, than which no higher can be desired. Thomas Aquinas, however, with his greater concern for God as Being, had identified synderesis with knowledge of the basic moral principles, thus seeing the human relation to God as a natural orientation to know rather than as a nisus to love. Calvin in this instance falls on the side of desire. His theology tends to become a theology of existence rather than, as in Thomism, a theology of being. It was only later, when he was confronted with semi-Pelagian orientations in the Nominalism of some Catholic practices of his time and with the notion of merit that remained part of the sacramental system of Catholicism, that Calvin was led to affirm such a total corruption of human nature by sin that there cannot be a pure desire to love God in the creaturely soul that has been affected by original sin.

In any case, there is "nothing more ridiculous," Calvin declares as he concludes this argument, than the adversaries' contention that the Epistle to the Hebrews (11; 13) refers to God's own desire and existence, as though something were lacking in the divine Being.

*　　　*　　　*

The story of the resurrection of Tabitha in Acts 9 comes next. The mortalists contend that if Tabitha's soul was truly alive, "living without her body in God and with God," the Apostles committed a great injustice when they brought her back "from the company of God and the blessed life into this sea of evils."[5] Since, Calvin re-

---

5. *Psychopannychia*, p. 90.

sponds, a miracle is effected only by God's power, this criticism of the Apostles implies a blasphemous criticism of the will and the mercy of God. The mortalists have not discerned that "there are degrees of God's mercy: the sanctification of the elect, the glorification of the saints,"[6] that is, election, sanctification, and glorification. Each of these three moments is an admirable instance of God's mercy. Election and sanctification, however, are events of the present life, taking place while the soul remains in her body. The divine mercy is then extended to us "when God sanctifies us more and more" and wants to be glorified on this earth "by life in our body."

This brief investigation of three passages of the New Testament is hardly sufficient to characterize an exegetical method. Nonetheless, a few principles can easily be elicited from it. First, the primary concern of a reader of Scripture should be to discover "the genuine mind of the Apostle."[7] Second, interpretation ought to agree with that of *sanos homines*,[8] "men of common sense." Third, the scope of a text may have to be evaluated in two stages, as in the case of Psalm 73:2-3, in which the psalmist refers both to the motion of his feet and to the steps he has taken. "If we look in front of his feet," we see that he declared a blessing on those to whom he spoke. We should also look further, and then we will see that "the blessed people are those whose God is Lord, to whom they go through death."[9] In other words, a text may have an immediate and concrete meaning, and a more remote and universal sense. In any case, reading Scripture is done in light of traditional Christian doctrine and of the data of Christian experience as these are interpreted by *sanos homines*, that is, those who have transmitted the tradition of reading Scripture.

*   *   *

The true Christian doctrine of immortality is developed at greater length in Calvin's discussion of the Psalms. Here attention is

---

6. *Psychopannychia*, p. 91.

7. . . . *germanam apostoli mentem* (p. 87).

8. *Psychopannychia*, p. 86.

9. *Si vero longius extendimus oculos, beatus erit populus, cujus dominus Deus est, penes quem est exitus mortis* (p. 87).

brought to seven passages to which the catabaptists have appealed in favor of their doctrine of the death of the soul. What does it mean to say, with David,

1. that the faithful are "gods and sons of the Most High" (Ps. 82:6-7)?[10]
2. that "on that day their thoughts will perish" (Ps. 146:4)?[11]
3. that "they are flesh, the spirit going and not returning" (Ps. 78:39)?[12]
4. that man in *she'ol* is "like the dead who sleep in their sepulchres" (Ps. 88:4-6)?[13]
5. that no one "in the sepulchre praises your mercy" (Ps. 88:11-13)?[14]
6. that "I will praise you, Lord, as long as I am" (Ps. 104:33)?[15]
7. that "I will be strengthened until I go and I am not" (Ps. 39:14)?[16]

Each of these texts, with a few others that are cited in addition, is taken by the adversaries to imply that the soul does not exist after bodily death. Calvin refutes this contention and brings in numerous other verses in support of his position. His first response restricts the scope of the statement, "you are gods . . . ," to the "ministers of God, the judges who have received the sword from God." These are rightly warned that they themselves will be judged and their administration scrutinized.[17] We are exhorted in Psalm 82 not to trust in men.

The next two points are more substantive. They turn around the symbolic meaning of *spiritus* in the psalmist's language. The adver-

10. *Psychopannychia,* pp. 91-92.
11. *Psychopannychia,* pp. 92-93.
12. *Psychopannychia,* pp. 93-95.
13. *Psychopannychia,* pp. 95-96.
14. *Psychopannychia,* pp. 96-103.
15. *Psychopannychia,* pp. 103-4.
16. *Psychopannychia,* pp. 104-7.
17. Calvin argues from John 10:34-35, which he reads as recording Jesus' own interpretation.

saries take it systematically in a material sense — the wind[18] — although its meaning is often symbolic and figurative, denoting the mind or soul. Psalm 146 tells us not to trust in man, for "when his spirit departs he returns to the earth; on that day his thoughts perish." If they have no thoughts, say the mortalists, it is because their soul has died. "We, however," Calvin retorts, "are not so subtle, but in our thickness we call a boat boat and a spirit spirit."[19] That their thoughts will perish means that whatever projects they concocted on earth will dissipate like the wind. One finds a similar "periphrasis," Calvin notes, "in the canticle of the Blessed Virgin."[20] The contrast lies between the subtle contortions of the catabaptists when they take literally the biblical periphrases, and the simplicity of true Christians who read the text with common sense.

As to Psalm 78, it may well be understood in the material sense. Even then, however, it contains a figure of speech: Men, like the wind, pass on and do not return. Like other biblical metaphors — for instance, men are like blossoms that do not last, passing shadows — the image points to believers' total reliance on God: "We teach that we are sustained by God's benignity and power, for he alone has immortality. And whatever is of life comes from God."[21]

*   *   *

The heart of the debate about the Old Testament turns around Psalm 88, which is examined in arguments four and five. In Calvin's reading souls are said to be dead when their memory fades and they are not remembered by God, that is, when "their names are not written in the book of life."[22] Many biblical texts, Calvin admits, refer to the silence of the dead, to the corruption that abounds in *she'ol*, to the absence of hope for those who are beyond the grave, to the fact

---

18. *Et spiritum pro vento positum ut fere ubique contendunt* (p. 93).

19. *Nos vero non ita subtiles sumus, sed pro nostra crassitie scapham vocamus scapham et spiritum spiritum* (p. 92).

20. "He has confused the proud in their inmost thoughts": *Dispersit superbos mentis cordis sui* (Luke 1:51; p. 93). The standard Vulgate text has *mente*, in the singular.

21. *Psychopannychia*, p. 95.

22. *Psychopannychia*, p. 96.

that only the living praise God. Such passages, however, do much more than simply declare that the souls that have passed away are dead. They say "in part . . . that only those who have sensed the Lord's goodness and mercy praise him, in part . . . that after death God's favors are not announced to men as they were on earth."[23] Inferno, in this case, does not designate the tomb, but rather "abyss and confusion." Indeed the Psalms do not contradict the Symbol of faith. When we confess that Christ "descended into hell" we mean that he suffered "all the pains of death for us, that he was really exposed to all its anguishes and terrors."[24] In other words, these biblical texts, like the Creed itself, refer to the Savior's redemptive work:

> Briefly: Those who hope in riches, and die in their own power, and descend to inferno, rich and poor, stupid and intelligent, will die all at once. The one who hopes in the Lord will be freed from the power of hell.[25]

Whether one reads the Psalms as the prayer of "Christ, head of the faithful, or of the Church, his body," they do speak of death as of something horrible. And yet it is by death that the saints "escape from this troubled world, from hostile temptations, from anxiety, into supreme leisure and blessed rest." Indeed, the saints never complain about their coming death. On the contrary they welcome it, because it is through death that they go to God: "The words with which they respond to the Lord who calls are quite obvious: Here I am, Lord."

The solution of the mortalists' problem lies in the mystery of redemption. Calvin briefly alludes to the patristic conception of the devil's rights over fallen humanity, and to redemption seen as a struggle between Christ and Satan. Christ indeed had to fight "the power of the devil, the torments of hell, and the pains of death," for "these had to be vanquished in our flesh, so that they would lose the

---

23. *Psychopannychia*, p. 97.

24. *Atque id est quod in Symbolo confitemur, Christum ad inferos descendisse, hoc est in omnes mortis dolores pro nobis a Patre conjectum esse, omnes ejus agustias et terrores pertulisse et verum affectum esse . . .* (p. 98).

25. *Psychopannychia*, pp. 98-99.

rights they had over us."[26] Calvin's use of these ancient images of the Redeemer is naturally indebted to the soteriology inherited from St. Anselm. Divine justice required strict compensation for sin. In the midst of his spiritual war with Satan, as he was "satisfying the rigor and severity of divine justice," Christ prayed,

> asking the Father nothing else than to free our weakness, that he bore in his body, from the power of the devil and of death. This is our faith, on which we now rely, that the pain of the sin committed in our flesh, which had to be remitted in the same flesh to satisfy divine justice, has been remitted and ransomed in the flesh of Christ, which was our own flesh.[27]

This, then, is the meaning of the Psalms. They use the word "death" to designate the "feeling of God's wrath and judgment."[28] This tallies with the psalmist's frequent recourse to "prosopography,"[29] the process by which a face is given to an abstraction or a concept in a sort of personification. The Psalms personify death under the expression "the dead." Calvin indeed admits that death is "in itself an evil, since it is the malediction and punishment of sin." It is filled with terrors and desolation. Nonetheless, "there is one remedy that moderates such a great bitterness: in the anguish of it to know that God is one's Father, that one has Christ as leader and companion."[30] The Lord will not allow the faithful to fall into the clutches of the enemy, for this would be an insult to his own name. The soul that is "sad, bent, sick," prays to God for this reason and hopes for divine assistance. And the prophet Baruch declares that "the dead who are in *she'ol* will give glory to God" (Bar. 2:18).[31] It is therefore false to affirm that the souls that have died have stopped praising God, under the pretext that praise means thinking of God's glory and proclaiming it to others. In reality, if the souls of the dead

---

26. *Quae omnia in nostra carne vincenda erant, ut jus suum, quod in nos habebant, perderent* (p. 99).

27. *Psychopannychia*, p. 100.

28. *Psychopannychia*, p. 100.

29. *Psychopannychia*, p. 102.

30. *Psychopannychia*, p. 101.

31. *Psychopannychia*, p. 102.

(as we believe) are in paradise with God, I answer: To be in paradise and to live with God is not to talk and listen to one another, but only to have the fruition of God, to experience his good will, to find rest in him.[32]

The fruition of God — *Deo frui* — is another formulation that came to Calvin from the medieval mystics. It was especially in use in the works of St. Bonaventure. It designates both the saints' eternal beatitude in heaven and the participation in beatitude that is given by the Holy Spirit in the highest experience of God that is obtainable in this life. To affirm the fruition of God is, by the same token, the highest thing that can be said of the eternal destiny of the saints. The fruition of God is the crowning of immortality. To go further and attempt to define or describe life after death is at the same time impossible and unwise. If, Calvin adds with a touch of sarcasm, "some Morpheus reveals it to them [the anabaptists] in a dream, let them hold it as certain! As to me, I will not entertain those complicated questions that are contentious and do not contribute to piety."[33] Here again one may catch an echo of Bonaventure's theological method, in which the "argument from piety" — *ex pietate* — implies the rejection of speculations that do not promote true devotion. The proper attitude before God is normative not only for Christian life, but also for Christian thought and Christian worship.

The last two arguments, about Psalms 104, 146, and Psalm 39, are treated more lightly, "as a game and a joke."[34] It is silly, Calvin points out, to say that, because the psalmist promises to praise God as long as he lives, he will no longer praise God after he dies. The poet Virgil also promised to be grateful to his host as long as he would remember him. Obviously, Virgil was not suggesting that he would forget his host! At any rate, the psalmist says elsewhere that he will praise God eternally.

As to Psalm 39:14, to which Calvin associates Job 10:20-22, it is

32. *In paradiso esse et cum Deo vivere non est alterum alteri loqui et alterum ab altero audiri, sed tantum Deo frui, sentire bonam ejus voluntatem et in eo acquiescere* (pp. 102-3).

33. . . . *nihil ad pietatem conferunt* (p. 103).

34. *Psychopannychia*, p. 103. This is said about the sixth argument. It could be applied to the seventh.

simply not to the point. Both express a sense of dread before the judgment and a prayer to God for salvation. When the psalmist speaks of "going and not being," he only indicates that the dead "are not with men and before men, though they are with God."[35] As to Job, Calvin brings in four other texts, taken, he says, at random, that contradict the mortalists' interpretation. Job wishes to see his present condition changed. He is, Calvin adds with a sense of humor, like ourselves, "if in the great heat of Summer we judge the Winter benign, and reversely, bitten by the cold of Winter, we aspire to Summer with all our wishes. . . ."[36] Rather than complain about one's present misery one should practice hope and look to the future. Death and life are related like wrath and mercy in God. "Death is in God's wrath, life in God's mercy," as is explained, "not without elegance," by Ecclesiasticus (Ecclus. 37:28). Since, however, Ecclesiasticus is a secondary biblical book, its author "is not a writer of solid authority." Nonetheless, this point is supported by many other texts of "the prophet,"[37] that is, of the psalmist. One should learn from them that there always is a way of exit out of human afflictions and despair. This is the way of prayer and calling on God's mercy.

*   *   *

The conclusion of *Psychopannychia* is short. Calvin's adversaries cite other texts that should not frighten anyone. They quote "books of uncertain faith," like 4 Esdras and 2 Maccabees 15:14, these two apocryphal books being printed in some editions of the Latin Vulgate. The first, however, Calvin considers to be entirely on his own side on the question of immortality.[38] The second is not to the

35. *Psychopannychia,* p. 104.
36. *Psychopannychia,* p. 106.
37. *Psychopannychia,* p. 107.
38. . . . *cum totus noster sit . . .* (p. 107). Four Books of Esdras were known in the Middle Ages. The official list of canonical books that was included in 1442 by the Council of Florence in the Decree for the Armenians listed Esdras without specifying which books (DS 1335). Most editions of the Latin Vulgate included Books I and II, others also keeping III and IV. IV Esdras recorded visions relating to the Last Judgment; it described the saved as a drop of water compared to the stream of the

point. The verse that is cited simply mentions that Judas Maccabee was wont to pray for the people of Israel.[39]

As he composed *Pyschopannychia* Calvin wished to neglect no argument that could make an impression on simple Christians in favor of the survival of the soul after death. Above all he wanted his readers, "if there are any,"[40] to remember the catabaptists as the authors of "this dogma" of the death of the soul. In any case, since to name them "is enough to designate all kind of scandals we should rightly suspect whatever comes from this factory, that has concocted and daily concocts so many false dreams."[41]

The strong language of this conclusion stands in a singular contrast with the rather light and humorous treatment of the last arguments against the immortality of the soul. Whoever these anabaptists were when the young Calvin's attention was drawn to their ideas about the sleep or the death of the soul, the investigation he made in 1534-35 left him with a profoundly negative impression of his adversaries. He was shocked by their doctrine to the bottom of his soul. Calvin perceived that by denying the immortality of the soul the opponents denied, or at least questioned, the work of the Creator, the Creator himself, the promises made by God in the Old Testament and confirmed in the New through Jesus Christ, and the effectiveness of the Holy Spirit. Calvin the humanist, concerned as he was, like all the humanists, about the right method of thought and the proper style of expression, was particularly incensed by their reasonings and argumentations. These had their source in a total disregard of the Augustinian and the mystical traditions, which themselves did not lie far below the literary and intellectual concerns of Erasmus, Lefèvre d'Étaples, and the French humanist movement from which Calvin came.

---

damned (IV Esdras 9:15). In 1546 the fourth session of the Council of Trent recognized I and II of Esdras as canonical, thereby excluding III and IV (DS 1502).

39. I and II Maccabees were included in the Tridentine Vulgate.

40. The qualification, "if there are any," implies that at least this conclusion was composed before the publication of *Institutio christiana,* which was an immediate publishing success.

41. *Merito enim debet nobis esse suspectum quidquid a tali officina prodierit, quae tot portenta et fabricata est et quotidie fabricatur* (p. 108).

VII

Institutio christianae religionis

The reader of Calvin's early works is faced with what has been a basic puzzle in the history of Calvinism. When did Jean Calvin clearly espouse the cause of the Reformation? When did he identify himself as a Protesting Christian? The proposals for a date vary considerably, from very early in his humanistic career to much later. If the decision was early it may have preceded Nicolas Cop's opening address at the Sorbonne on 1 November 1533, in the preparation of which several historians have thought, without any substantial evidence, that Calvin had a hand. The fact is that after this date Calvin no longer felt safe in Paris, though he made no attempt to leave the country at the time. If the decision was reached several months or a couple of years later, arguably because Calvin's writing on the doctrine of the soul does not exhibit a reforming orientation, it must have been made just before, or possibly shortly after, his flight to Basel in 1535.

In the latter case, Calvin's consent to the publication of *Psychopannychia* in 1542 without anti-papal additions may well suggest that even after his reforming ministry in Strasbourg, in the first year of his second ministry in Geneva, Calvin did not yet consider that all bridges had been drawn between the reform movement and the conservative tradition, although he certainly had no reason to be optimistic about a possible reconciliation. The question then becomes Why? or Why not? Where was the obstacle to reconciliation?

*   *   *

This amounts to asking what made Calvin decide for the Reformation, against the Roman or, more broadly, the scholastic defense of the old Church and theology, and even against the waiting stance of the many among the religious humanists who wished for a reform, who endorsed Luther's understanding of justification by faith alone, and who nevertheless did not find in these positions sufficient reasons to abandon the Roman system of government.

Calvin, it would seem, never came closer to a confidence on this point than what he wrote much later, in the preface to his *Commentary on the Psalms* (1557).

> As I was so obstinately given to the superstitions of the papacy that it was not easy to draw me out of such a deep cesspool, God, by a sudden conversion, reined in my heart and brought it to docility. . . . Having therefore received some taste and knowledge of true piety, I immediately was burning with such a great desire to profit from it that, though I did not at all give up my other studies, I treated them more loosely. Now, I was astounded that before one year had passed all those who felt some desire for pure doctrine came to me to learn, although I was only beginning myself.[1]

In this confession Calvin traces back a sudden taste and knowledge of true piety which prompted his interest in Scripture and theology, to the time of his studies in Orléans or in Bourges, that is, in the years 1533 to 1534, toward the end of which requests were made for him to explain the pure doctrine. These approaches may well be no other than the urging of some of his friends to write against the doctrine of the mortality of the soul, which led him to compose *Psychopannychia*.

In any case, as it was described by himself in 1557, Calvin's conversion implied two moments. There was a sudden taste of true

---

1. James Anderson, ed., *John Calvin's Commentary on the Book of Psalms*, vol. 1 (Grand Rapids: Eerdmans, 1963), pp. xl-xlvii.

piety, which was immediately followed by the burning of a great desire. If this is taken literally — and I see no reason to do otherwise — Calvin's experience of conversion did not open up a negative perspective regarding the old Church or even the medieval papacy. It was on the contrary a profoundly positive spiritual experience, namely a desire to deepen his interior life. In other words, Calvin underwent the kind of conversion that has often been described by Christian mystics, a sudden overwhelming sense of God's intimate presence within oneself. This taste of true piety and the burning of desire that ensued were the fruits of a mystical awareness of nearness to Christ. They implied a realization that the truth of the gospel does not hide somewhere in the distance, but dwells right here within the self, a point that is precisely exemplified in the reflections on the soul that are included in *Psychopannychia*. As is not unusual in the life of the great Christian mystics, this realization inspired a deep urge to spread the true knowledge of God, of which Calvin now had the personal evidence in himself. For reasons of circumstances and temperament, this urge became the fundamental motivation of a decisive shift to what the Puritans of England would later call "reformation without tarrying."[2]

*   *   *

The early writings that need to be considered here were composed in 1534 and 1535. They include two prefaces to Olivétan's French translation of the Bible, two letters addressed respectively to his "most beloved friend" Nicolas Duchemin and his "former friend" Gérard Roussel, and also, the most prestigious of all, the first edition of *Institutio christianae religionis*, which was printed in 1536. The two letters would be published as one volume in 1537 in Basel, before the publication of *Psychopannychia*. For reasons that will emerge as we proceed, we will begin with the *Institutio*.

After he had preached a series of ten sermons on catechetical themes in 1528 Martin Luther had issued two catechisms, called

---

2. In the early seventeenth century. This sums up the position of those who wish to do away with the Church of England's "interimistical" state.

"larger" and "shorter," which were printed in 1529. The *Larger Catechism,* a sequence of elaborate theological explanations, was suitable for mature readers and for teachers; the *Shorter,* made of brief questions and answers, was better for children or simple persons. At the opening of the *Larger Catechism* Luther cited the ten commandments, the Apostles' creed, and the Lord's prayer. These traditional texts were followed by references to the biblical basis of the sacraments of baptism and the eucharist. Luther next gave fairly long explanations on each of the ten commandments, on the three articles of the creed, on the seven petitions of the Lord's prayer, and on the two sacraments. Although they were composed several years after Luther's excommunication by Leo X, the catechisms do not, unlike his writings of 1520, echo the great reformer's struggles with himself and with the authorities of Church and State. They on the contrary reflect the inner serenity of a Christian who is at peace in the faith.

The six chapters of the first *Institutio christianae religionis,* printed in Basel in 1536, were loosely modeled on Luther's catechisms. Calvin was certainly inspired by them, and the distribution of topics in the first four chapters of *Institutio* corresponds to the sequence of the catechisms. Nonetheless, the French reformer's first major theological production differs from them to no small degree. While the scope of the *Larger Catechism* makes it more comparable to Calvin's elaborate dissertation than the questions and answers of the *Shorter Catechism,* Calvin's work is quite different in tone, method, and structure.

As treated by Calvin, the first three items — the decalogue, the Symbol of faith, the Lord's prayer — are embedded in elaborate explanations of Law (Ch. I: *De lege*), of Faith (Ch. II: *De fide*), and of Prayer (Ch. III: *De oratione*). The traditional formulations of the ten commandments, the Apostles' creed, and the Lord's prayer act as biblical or, in the case of the creed, quasi-biblical applications and illustrations of what Calvin wants to say about Law, Faith, and Prayer. Seen biblically, the commandments of the Law come first, given through the ministry of Moses. Their place was naturally welcome to a Law scholar who had lately turned to studying the Bible. Theologically, the Law sets faith and prayer in their social context. These chapters on Law, on Faith, and on Prayer offer no hint of anti-Roman bias.

Nonetheless, Calvin's commentary on the Law includes a critique of a contemporary notion that could be found in the literature of monastic communities. The distinction between commandments and counsels, Calvin reported, was based on "ignorance or malice." Critique of such a distinction was especially aimed at some unidentified persons whom Calvin simply designated as "they," who left the practice of the counsels to monks, as though monks could be "more just" than simple Christians.[3] This implied critique of monasticism, however, was by no means original. It had become commonplace among the humanists at least since Erasmus.

The same chapter on the Law ends with a rebuttal of the language of merit that had become standard in medieval theology.[4] What was at stake in this for Calvin was the gratuitousness of redemption as entirely Christ's work. Such a point, however, was anti-Roman only to the extent that it seemed, at the time, difficult to square with the sale of indulgences, against which Luther had, in 1517, directed his ninety-five theses. In fact, the entire gratuitousness of salvation and of the path to it was itself essential to what the scholastics, at least outside of the Nominalist school of the late Middle Ages, had understood merit to be. Like St. Augustine and the Second Council of Orange (529), the great scholastics had always affirmed that Christian merit grows within and as a result of the divine gift of sanctifying grace *(gratia gratum faciens)*. It is therefore itself entirely God's doing, the fruit of redemption through Christ, not the work of human effort. This was not contradicted by Calvin's statement: "This is our confidence *(fiducia)*, that Christ the Son of God is ours and has been given to us, so that in him we also are children of God. . . ."[5] The scholastics would have added that, Christ being given to us, his own merit is in us also to be shared. At this point the difference between Calvin's thought and the scholastic orientation is not substantial; it is only linguistic.

---

3. *Calvini Opera Selecta,* vol. 1, ed. Peter Barth (Munich: Chr. Kaiser Verlag, 1926), pp. 54-55.

4. *Opera Selecta,* vol. 1, pp. 63-68.

5. *Opera Selecta,* vol. 1, p. 62.

*   *   *

After presenting the Lord's prayer in the *Shorter Catechism,* Martin Luther had passed on to three other topics: "the Sacrament of Baptism," "Confession," and "the Sacrament of the Altar," which were reduced to two topics in the *Larger Catechism,* the section on confession being omitted. These sacramental themes are covered in Chapter IV *(De sacramentis)* of the *Institutio,* where Calvin follows the *Larger Catechism* and omits confession. He also replaces Luther's appellation of the eucharist, *De sacramento altaris* ("the sacrament of the Altar"), by a less liturgical but more biblical and christological designation, *De coena Domini* ("the Lord's Supper"). It was precisely in this treatment of the eucharist that Calvin inaugurated his lifelong polemic against the Mass and against traditional eucharistic teachings that had been inherited from the Middle Ages and promoted by the pope.

Following a lengthy denunciation of the Mass as an abomination, Calvin's last chapter but one, which has no parallel in Luther's catechisms, pursues an anti-Roman argumentation, even though the pope is hardly mentioned. It deals with the "false sacraments,"[6] namely the additional ceremonies of the sacramental septenary that had been systematized in the twelfth century, the theology of which had been extensively developed by the great scholastics. Although excluded from the two catechisms, the problem of the five additional sacraments had been treated at length by Luther in *De captivitate babylonica* (October 1520). This Chapter V of *Institutio christiana* is in fact much more polemical than the first four chapters, as Calvin carefully makes his way between what he identifies as the extreme positions of the anabaptists on one side, and, on the other side, several theologies and doctrinal teachings that were found in scholasticism and generally endorsed by the supporters of the pope.

6. *Institutio christianae religionis,* Ch. V: *De falsis sacramentis.* This brief title sums up a longer one: *Sacramenta non esse quinque reliqua quae pro sacramentis hactenus vulgo habita sunt declaratur, tum qualia sint ostenditur* ("It is declared that the other five, which until now have been popularly taken for sacraments, are not sacraments, and it is shown what they are").

As to Calvin's last chapter, on "Christian freedom, ecclesiastical power, and civil administration,"[7] it in part echoes Luther's concerns in *De libertate christiana* (November 1520). In spite of the three items of its title, this Chapter VI is dominated by the ideally non-polemical theme of Christian freedom. At the time of writing, however, as Calvin indicates in the very first lines, the topic has become intensely controversial: "As soon as some mention of Christian freedom is injected, evil desires are fomented or insane movements rise up, unless one turns with maturity toward these lascivious minds which otherwise corrupt the best of anything."[8] In fact, the final chapter begins with the same polemical tone that is heard in Calvin's polemic against the Mass and maintained through his examination of the other sacraments. The last two chapters of *Institutio christianae religionis* are thus marked by an adversarial mood in such sharp contrast with the serenity of the first four chapters that one may put the question: Was the *Institutio* of 1536 composed at two different moments in the evolution of Calvin's religious convictions?

*   *   *

Not counting the pages on the Lord's Supper, which have a more polemical tone, the first four chapters correspond to a time in the development of Calvin's thought when he was not yet openly critical of the Roman system, in spite of serious doubts he may already have felt about the fidelity of bishops and popes to the gospel. His explanation of the Supper, however, and his last chapters introduce a new element as they reject the sacramental theology of the scholastics, the Roman conception and practice of magisterial authority, and the obedience that is demanded of the faithful by the bishops and the pope.

Now, the only period in which Calvin had the leisure and the library resources needed for serious theological writing, whether in the polemical mood of *Psychopannychia* or in the more synthetic and

7. *Institutio*, Ch. VI: *De libertate christiana, potestate ecclesiastica, et politica administratione.*
8. *Opera Selecta*, vol. 1, p. 223.

reflective style of the first half of *Institutio christianae religionis,* was no other than the four months or so of 1534 that he was fortunate enough to spend in the peace and quiet of the du Tillet mansion in Angoulême, where the extensive library of the house was at his disposal. In other words, Calvin conceived and presumably composed the first chapters of *Institutio* while he was mulling over the topic of *Psychopannychia* and writing the bulk of what must have been the first version of this work.

Calvin's critique of specific medieval doctrines begins in Chapter IV. This critique bears on the relation of the sacraments to divine grace, on the restriction of baptismal forgiveness to those sins that have been committed before baptism, both the inherited sin of Adam and personal sins,[9] and on transubstantiation. The first point had itself been debated in the medieval schools, and there were notable differences between Thomists, Scotists, and, more recently, nominalists. Calvin, however, who was not trained in theology but in Law, must have learned from Erasmus a solid contempt for the scholastic methods of thought.[10] He also had run already into misunderstandings of the sacraments among the anabaptists and other early followers of the Reformation. In typical humanist fashion he attempted to simplify the sacramental question by bringing it back to the biblical data:

> The sacraments are actions *(exercitia)* that make our faith in the word of God more certain, and since we are carnal they are shown under carnal things, so that they teach us proportionally to our slowness and they lead us by the hand, as teachers lead children.[11]

Further than this there is no necessity to investigate how divine grace works in the sacraments, for "neither must our faith be stuck in the sacraments nor God's glory be transferred to it, but, forget-

9. *Opera Selecta,* vol. 1, p. 128.
10. Erasmus had published his *Ratio perveniendi ad veram theologiam* in 1518; it included a vehement attack on scholasticism.
11. *Opera Selecta,* vol. 1, p. 119.

ting all things, faith and confession must rise to him who is the author of the sacraments and of all things."[12] It is not the action that is important; it is the God who acts.

In regard to baptism itself, Calvin sees it as an error to restrict the sacramental grace to the forgiveness of pre-baptismal sins. Indeed, it was such a misconception that formerly occasioned the delay of baptism until late in life. Rather, it is to the grace of baptism that the faithful owe the forgiveness of *all* their sins, past, present, and future:

> This is how one should think: at whatever time we are baptized we are once for all washed and purged for our whole life. Whenever we fall the remembrance of baptism should be recalled and the soul armed with it, so that it be always assured of the forgiveness of sins, and secure.

Forgiveness, however, is not a license to sin, and there is no forgiveness for those who abuse the divine promises and who elicit from them a reason for neglecting to seek God's mercy and to walk in holiness of life. In saying this Calvin is manifestly reacting against the medieval practice of sacramental confession, in which he sees a downgrading of the baptismal grace. Since the Roman system of indulgences, which had prompted Luther to make the original protest of the Reformation, was itself based on the view that Calvin rejects, his doctrine in this section of *Institutio* is definitely anti-Roman. But it is not yet, I would say, anti-Catholic. On the one hand, Calvin's entire purpose is to give an explanation of the faith of the Catholic Church. On the other, his understanding of baptism is quite defensible in the context of Catholic theology.

It is not so, however, with the eucharistic doctrine that is expounded in the second half of Chapter IV. Calvin is not wrong when, following his reading of St. Augustine, he highlights the spiritual aspects of the Lord's Supper, which place the faithful face to face with Christ giving his life for them. It would be superfluous at this point to examine all the nuances of Calvin's presentation of the

12. *Opera Selecta,* vol. 1, p. 122.

Supper of our Lord, which is, even in the short treatment of it in the first *Institutio,* extremely sophisticated. Calvin is negative regarding what he regards as excessively carnal views and practices of the sacrament. Along this line he condemns the adoration of the consecrated bread and the doctrine of transubstantiation. In itself, however, this was not necessarily at the time an anti-Roman position. Calvin was presumably acquainted with the use of the passive verb, *transubstantieri,* in the decree for the Jacobites that had been adopted by the Council of Florence (4 February 1442), and he certainly knew the main theories of scholastic theologians regarding the exact nature of transubstantiation. This must have been quite enough, in the context of his humanistic training, to bring the doctrine of transubstantiation into disrepute,[13] for the scholastics were not in agreement, and the humanists strongly reacted to what they regarded as undue intrusions of rational speculation in what could not but remain a mystery. In any case, what Calvin describes as transubstantiation is hardly what was taught by Thomas Aquinas or Bonaventure. As he saw it in his *Petit traité de la Sainte Cène,* composed in 1539, Calvin judged it essential to the integrity of the sacrament that bread remain fully bread. But the point of the great scholastics was precisely that the consecrated bread is physically bread, for physical characteristics do not reach to the level of substance.[14]

However this may be, Calvin goes on to condemn the Mass as an abomination, polluted "by every kind of impiety, blasphemy, idolatry, sacrilege."[15] He rejects the sacrificial nature of the eucharist as it was intended by Christ, the popular reduction of the whole faith and piety to the Mass, the medieval and contemporary rule of not

13. Calvin of course wrote these pages before the Council of Trent, which would declare at its thirteenth session (11 October 1551): "By the consecration of the bread and wine a conversion is made of the entire substance of the bread into the substance of the body of our Lord Christ, and of the entire substance of the wine into the substance of his blood." By the same token, the conciliar decree had not yet endorsed the term "transubstantiation" as being "conveniently and properly" used to designate such a conversion of substance.

14. *Petit traité de la Sainte Cène* (Paris: Les Bergers et les Mages, 1959), pp. 48-49; Thomas Aquinas, S.T. III, q. 75, a. 3.

15. *Opera Selecta,* vol. 1, p. 157.

sharing the cup with the laity. He concludes that the Mass has not only replaced, but also completely abolished the participation in the Last Supper that the eucharist was intended to be by the Lord. At this point Calvin takes his stand by the contentions of the *Placards* regarding the unbiblical, erroneous, and idolatrous nature of the Mass. Implicit in this is of course a condemnation of the priests, bishops, and popes who promote and, Calvin would say, exploit the Mass for their own worldly purposes.

The contrast between the tone of the first three and a half chapters of *Institutio christianae religionis* with the treatment of the eucharist in the last part of Chapter IV and with the dismissal of the "false sacraments" in Chapter V supports the notion that the first three and a half chapters were written before, and the rest of the book after, the episode of the *Placards* in November 1534.

*   *   *

Let us at this point recall the positive teaching of the *Institutio* about the heart of the Christian life:

> Having received the gospel, the faithful have this peace [previously described as "tranquility and security of conscience"] when they see that God, whom they previously thought of as a judge, is a father to them, that they are children of grace instead of children of wrath, that the bowels of God's mercy are poured out *(effusa)* in them, so that they expect nothing else from God than goodness and kindness.[16]

Calvin had also written that when faced by the anguish of dying the faithful "know that God is to them a father."[17] This, then, is for him the heart of the Christian faith and life: to believe that God is my very own Father, and to learn so to call him.

Precisely, the entire purpose of the Law, in the context of the *Institutio,* is to teach love: "It is easy to perceive where all the com-

16. *Opera Selecta,* vol. 1, p. 42.
17. *Opera Selecta,* vol. 1, p. 101.

mandments tend, namely to teach love."[18] And this love, *caritas,* is twofold. Directed toward God it means that "we fear, love, worship, trust God, invoke and pray to God, expect everything from God, rest in God," which is the topic and purpose of the first table of the Law, while the second table teaches us to love our neighbor. Calvin remarks that "not one syllable in the entire Law can be read" to the effect that we should seek our own welfare:

> It is most clear from this that observation of the commandments is not the love of self, but of God and the neighbor, that he lives in the best and holiest way who lives and strives for self as little as is possible; and that on the contrary he lives in the worst and most evil way who lives and strives for self, who thinks and seeks what is his own.[19]

Along with other passages that are germane to it this text unveils a key that opens up Calvin's teaching and his understanding of the necessary reform of the Church. The Christian life consists in truly becoming a child of God, so that the proper appellation of God ought to be "my Father," on the model of Christ's own prayer. The discovery of this filial relation to God was at the heart of Calvin's conversion. Without undergoing the painful *Anfechtungen,* the anxieties, that had marked Martin Luther's rejection of the system of salvation implied in the sale of indulgences, Calvin was hit by the sudden evidence that the episcopal system of government, at least as it had become in the hands of venal bishops, could not promote the holiness necessary for the faithful to call God "my Father." Calvin could no longer read the essential Christian message in the behavior of bishops who made themselves, by their vestments, their gestures, their sermons, the center of the eucharistic liturgy instead of being simply its facilitators for the faithful people of God, especially when many of them, in addition, drew the income of several bishoprics

---

18. *Facile autem est percipere quo tendant omnia, nempe at docendam caritatem (Opera Selecta,* vol. 1, p. 53).

19. *Opera Selecta,* vol. 1, pp. 53-54.

that they never visited, the administration of which they entrusted to their delegates.

*   *   *

The Apostles' creed is "as it were an epitome of the faith in which the Catholic Church is one."[20] There are two kinds of faith, Calvin explains. A merely historical faith believes the history and the truths of Christ as facts that need not be considered relevant to one's personal life. This is the faith of demons. With the true faith, on the contrary, "we do not only believe that there is a God and there is a Christ, but we do believe in God and Christ, truly acknowledging God as our God and Christ as our Savior."[21] This faith is inseparable from hope, for it not only believes what is written or said of God and of Christ, but "it places all hope and trust in one God and Christ." This is the salvific faith, that is based on the word of God. By it we are convinced that all we need for our soul and body will be given us by God, and that "through the forgiveness of sins and the sanctification that come from the Savior we shall be led to the Kingdom of God that is to be revealed in the last day." Commenting on the definition of faith as "the substance of the things hoped for," in Hebrews 11:1, Calvin uncovers two aspects in this salvific faith. Already now it is a "sure and secure possession of all that God has promised us." And also, as turned to the future,

> until the supreme day on which the books will be opened, it is higher than what our sense can perceive or our eyes can see or our hand can seize, which in the meantime cannot be possessed unless we exceed the entire scope of our intellect and we aim our gaze above all that is in the world, and finally transcend our own selves.

The mystical tone of this description of the Christian faith and life is unmistakable. What Calvin points to here is the *excessus mentis*

---

20. . . . . *breviter compendium collectum est, et quasi epitome quaedam fidei in qua consentit ecclesia catholica* (*Opera Selecta*, vol. 1, p. 68).

21. *Opera Selecta*, vol. 1, p. 69.

of the medieval mystics, when the mind is raised above itself and above the whole creation into union with God. Seen in this light, the Christian life is a pilgrimage along the way to the eschatological opening of the books. These are evidently the book of life, concealed in heaven, in which the names of the elect are already listed, and also, on this earth, the books of nature, of the soul, and of Scripture, in which medieval theology, especially that of St. Bonaventure, had found a threefold revelation of God.[22] Whatever nature tells us of the Creator, it cannot by itself discern the mysteries of God. These have to be seen in Scripture read as *verbum Dei,* the word of God, and "their truth must be so ingrained in us that whatever is said [in the word] is held as done and implemented."[23] Creation is indeed the necessary background of faith; Scripture reveals the full scope of creation; and the soul realizes the profound truths of both creation and Scripture over and above the truths of reason. The gaze in question *(acies),* by which the first two books are now read, is the operation of the pupil of the eye acting as physical symbol of the highest level of the soul, of the acme or "fine point" of the human spirit. Thus Calvin's perspective on salvific faith does include the mystical ascent. It joins analogy and anagogy, faith and hope, the here and now together with the anticipation of the hereafter. As in medieval mystical writings and in the later writings of the Catholic mystics, all of this is the work of God's grace alone, *sola Dei gratia.*[24]

This faith Calvin found stated in the Apostles' creed. The first three articles of the creed are focused on the divine Persons, the Father, the Son, and the Holy Spirit. They give Calvin the occasion to discuss the fundamental objection that trinitarian theology is only a matter of arbitrary terms that are used for God without biblical warrant; to discuss also the Arian and Sabellian heresies, the communication of idioms, the status of Christ as King and Priest, and the meaning of the descent into inferno, which he considers to be a metaphor for the sufferings of the Messiah.

The fourth article is focused on believing "the Holy Catholic

22. See above, chapter 2, p. 33.
23. *Opera Selecta,* vol. 1, p. 70.
24. *Opera Selecta,* vol. 1, p. 70.

Church, that is, the universal number of the elect, both angels and humans, whether dead or still living on earth. . . ." All these form "one Church and society and one people of God, of whom Christ our Lord is the leader and prince and, as it were, the head of one body, in that by God's goodness the elect have been established in him before the foundation of the world in order to be gathered as one into the Kingdom of God."[25] The Church is holy, "because as many as have been elected by God's eternal providence to be co-opted as the Church's members are all sanctified by the Lord."

In this Church the faith is not idle. It bears fruit, thanks to its two companions, hope and love. As Calvin has already explained, faith and hope are inseparable. "Faith believes that God is to us a Father, hope expects him always to behave like one."[26] Hope contributes directly to the strength of faith. "As it waits for the Lord in silence and patience, hope constrains faith, lest it be excessively festive, and confirms it, lest it weaken and hesitate about the promises of God." There is nonetheless a major difference between hope and love. Love, the keystone of the divine charisms, is directed outside, given for the edification of the Church. It is not by love that we are justified, but by faith, that is, "by the mercy of God, which is said to justify when faith receives it."[27] Love, however, bears fruit in that it is active in the service of the neighbor and the Church. All three, the traditional theological virtues, are gifts of the Holy Spirit, and we should beg God to bring them to perfection in us:

> We need that they constantly increase as long as we are in this life, which is nothing else, as long as things go best for us, than a way and a progress until we fully reach God, in whom all our perfection is located.[28]

Thus the parameters of Calvin's understanding of faith are set between the Catholic consensus that is manifest in the creed, and

25. *Opera Selecta*, vol. 1, p. 86.
26. *Opera Selecta*, vol. 1, p. 94. *Haec ergo spes nostra est quod filii Dei sumus* (p. 78).
27. *Opera Selecta*, vol. 1, p. 95.
28. *Opera Selecta*, vol. 1, pp. 95-96.

the fullness of our own perfection in God. The Christian pilgrimage goes from faith to perfection; it is lived in hope; and, as befits the children of God, it bears fruits in acts of love.

*   *   *

The mystical dimension of *Psychopannychia,* which has been echoed in the second chapter of *Institutio christianae religionis,* "On Faith," also pervades the third chapter, "On Prayer." As in Luther's catechisms, this chapter includes a commentary on the Lord's prayer. Unlike the catechisms, however, Calvin's commentary is enshrined between the invocation of our Father in heaven and the final doxology. The starting point is therefore personal and christological. Because Christ has been given to us as "a brother," he wishes us to call God "our Father," as he himself does.[29] The "great sweetness of this name" derives from God's immense love for us. God will not abandon us, since he is, as the Scriptures declare, "the father of mercies and the God of all consolation."[30] And there is more: "Not only is God a father to us, if we are Christians, he also wants to be called by name our own Father." In this case everything should be common in fraternal affection among those who so recognize their Creator. Hence the necessarily communal dimension of prayer: "All prayers must be such as to concern the community that our Lord establishes in his Kingdom and his home."

The beginning of the chapter, however, sets the tone of prayer, which again is reminiscent of medieval mysticism and of *devotio moderna.* "If someone," Calvin declares, "seeks the means to assist his poverty, it is necessary to exit the self and to buy what is needed from another."[31] The image of going out of oneself is standard in mystical literature. The one from whom one buys is of course God, except that nothing can be paid for, since all has already been given to us in Jesus Christ. In this way the context of Christian prayer is twofold. It is, on the one hand, human misery and, on the other, the

29. *Opera Selecta,* vol. 1, p. 105.
30. *Opera Selecta,* vol. 1, p. 106.
31. *Opera Selecta,* vol. 1, p. 96.

infinite generosity of the Father which is manifested in the Savior. In him indeed

> God offers us all felicity instead of our misery, riches instead of our poverty, in whom he opens the heavenly treasures to us, that our whole faith may look at this beloved Son, our whole expectation hang on him, our whole hope cling to him and rest in him. This is a secret and hidden philosophy that cannot be deduced with syllogisms; but those master it whose eyes God has opened so that they may see the light in his light.

All prayer should be prayed in the horizon set by the prophets. Calvin quotes Daniel and Baruch along with the Gospel of Luke to the effect that we should seek God in all things. Our very shortcomings, our sins, the confession of our unworthiness should be incentives to the kind of prayer that is entirely focused on the glory of God. Drawing on Melanchthon's argumentation against the invocation of saints in Article XXI of the *Apology for the Augsburg Confession* (1531), Calvin adds several pages on the same topic. Christ is "the only way."[32] Indeed, the saints in heaven pray for us when they say, as we also do, "Thy Kingdom come." Yet they themselves are not the way. In the line of Calvin's starting point, this is less a polemic against the Catholic understanding of prayer and the saints than a drawing out of the implications of the centrality of faith and hope, which are, in prayer, entirely turned to God in Christ. Faith excludes all ways to God that would not go through the divine Word made flesh, Jesus Christ.

Calvin's sequence of thought in this context is not unlike that which will be followed by St. John of the Cross in the *Ascent of Mount Carmel* (composed in 1581-85). For the Mystical Doctor faith is "the only proper and proportional means of union with God." It follows that those who seek God must be unattached to all that is not God, including "supernatural goods," holy pictures, statues of the saints,

---

32. *Quantum ad sanctos attinet, qui mortui in Christo vivunt, ne somniemus iis ipsis aliam esse rogandi Dei viam quam Christum, qui solus via est, aut alio nomine Deo esse acceptos* (*Opera Selecta*, vol. 1, p. 99).

129

chapels and oratories.[33] The Doctor of Carmel admits the invocation of saints, for he understands that such a prayer is really addressed to God through Christ who is present in his saints. Like Melanchthon, however, Calvin would not accept this, because, he says, there is now "no communication by speech or hearing"[34] with the saints in heaven, in spite of a persistent unity in faith and in love. The different conclusions that were reached by the reformer and by the Mystical Doctor on this relatively secondary point do not detract from the importance of their common principle.

On the basis of this principle "we should ask for nothing unless it promotes the glory of God." It is in light of this that Calvin understands the petitions of the Lord's prayer. In the first three petitions we should have in mind "only God's glory, omitting our reason and not looking at our own welfare,"[35] and so we testify that we are "God's servants and children." The sanctification of God's name, which is focused on the divine majesty, includes thanksgiving for all that is God's and all that comes from God. Anticipation of the coming of God's kingdom expresses the desire that God reign and act everywhere through his Holy Spirit, the perception that the Word of God, raised "like a royal scepter," is triumphing "under the cross," the vision of the kingdom that is not of this world flourishing nonetheless *in* this world, and the expectation of its eschatological fulfillment. Praying that the divine will be done implies not only that we "give up all our own wishes," but also that we ask God to annihilate everything that in us opposes his will, and to create new minds and new souls for us.

The last three petitions turn to our own needs, both bodily and spiritual. Asking "our bread from our Father"[36] implies total trust in God's providence. Our spiritual needs include the forgiveness of sins and protection from temptation, both those that come from

33. *Ascent of Mount Carmel*, part III, ch. 30-45, Kieran Kavanaugh and Otilio Rodriguez, eds., *The Collected Works of St. John of the Cross* (Washington: ICS Publications, 1991), pp. 323-49. This section of the book is unfinished.

34. . . . *nullum tamen remanet nec linguae nec auditus commercium* (*Opera Selecta*, vol. 1, p. 100).

35. *Opera Selecta*, vol. 1, p. 110.

36. *Opera Selecta*, vol. 1, p. 111.

the right (the temptations of wealth, power, honor) and those that come from the left (poverty, indecency, contempt, afflictions that lead to despair).

As to the concluding doxology, *quia tuum est regnum et potentia et gloria . . . ,* it expresses "the solid and tranquil repose of our faith,"[37] for no one can steal "the kingdom, the power, and the glory from our Father." Likewise, in the perspective of St. Bonaventure, the ultimate point that can be reached in the spiritual ascent is peace. And it was in the same line of thought that the author of the *Imitation of Christ,* who addressed God as "Beloved Father,"[38] also exclaimed, "Above all, O my soul, always find your repose in God, for he is the eternal repose of the saints."[39]

*   *   *

Repose is a good label for the atmosphere that is conveyed by these first chapters of *Institutio christianae religionis.* The faithful who have truly known God are at peace. But if it is permissible to read the story of Martha and Mary analogically, there are some among the true believers who are in repose in their knowledge of God, who live, as it were, like Mary, focusing their attention on the only thing necessary, listening to Christ who addresses them, and thus knowing God as their own Father in whose embrace they rest. And there are those who are also pushed by the Spirit to tell others of what they have heard, seen, and touched of the Word of God — who live, as it were, like Martha, keeping close to their internal vision, yet at the same time busy with all the things of God in this world. Jean Calvin definitely belongs among the latter. He may get involved in theological polemics, in problems of administration, in debates with the magistrates of Geneva, yet he never loses his interior vision. And the purpose of his theology in the first version of *Institutio christianae religionis* is no other than to lead others to the threshold of their own

---

37. *Opera Selecta,* vol. 1, p. 115.

38. *De Imitatione Christi,* III, xv, 22, Tiburzio Lupo, ed. (Vatican City: Libreria Editrice Vaticana, 1982), p. 268.

39. *De Imitatione Christi* III, xxi, 1 (p. 188).

intimacy with God, to what, drawing on St. Augustine's expression, *intimior intimo meo,*[40] one could call their "intimiority," where they will know God as their very own Father.

---

40. *Tu autem eras intimior intimo meo et superior summo meo* (*Confessions,* III, vi, 11, BA XIII, p. 382). See VII, x, 16: *intravi in intima mea* (BA XIII, p. 614).

VIII

The Case Against the Bishops

It was precisely while Calvin was writing the first chapters of *Institutio christianae religionis* that he found himself having to struggle with the fundamental question: Are the Church's bishops leading the people of God toward the fullness of Christian life? Rather than to help them listen to the Spirit of God in their heart, are they not concerned primarily with keeping and even increasing their privileged status in society? Where can the faithful find the proper spiritual guidance?

A minority of the faithful, those who were literate and comfortable with spiritual reading, could find suitable writings, though chiefly in Latin, the language of the intellectual and clerical elite. Although I am not aware that Calvin ever quotes it, the *Imitatio Christi* was a well-known product of the *devotio moderna* that was familiar to many in humanistic circles. The examples and writings of chancellor Gerson (1362-1428) were not outmoded. Nearer in time, Erasmus (1467-1536) had promoted a gentle approach to the spiritual life that was remote from monastic and ascetic practices and attuned to the needs of the laity. His *Enchiridion militis christiani* (1503) was popular among the religious humanists. The piety of Marguerite de Navarre, the king's sister, and that of Renée de France, the king's cousin, shared this orientation. For those who had the taste for more esoteric compositions, a great number of mystical writings were available. One of these, the *Theologia deutsch,* an anonymous work in German, Martin Luther had found so congenial that he had two versions of it, short and long, printed after he discovered their manuscripts in a library in Frankfurt. Calvin, however, did not care for this work when he read it in a Latin translation. He was too concerned about clarity in thought and expression to relish this sort of literature.

Whether or not the mystical writings of the times offered suitable reading for simple Christians, Calvin's *Psychopannychia* shows him to be deeply concerned about the welfare of ordinary believers, those precisely who were targeted by "anabaptist" propaganda and insinuations, and unable by themselves to determine if the soul dies, sleeps, or is fully alive in God after bodily death. The simple faithful had to rely on oral instructions from priests and bishops. But was the average priest or bishop in the sixteenth century equipped, able, and eager to provide the required guidance through the recesses of the Christian soul struggling with its tainted nature? By and large, the bishops, as Calvin observed, seemed more eager to keep the people in obedience than to lead them along the spiritual way. It was this point, it would appear, that brought Calvin face to face with a choice that he could not elude.

* * *

In June 1535 the French version of the Bible that had been put together by Pierre Robert (c. 1506–c. 1538), a relative of Calvin, who was known by the Greek-sounding name of Olivétan, was published in Neuchâtel.[1] This translation belonged squarely in the camp of the Reformation, composed as it was in response to a request for a French Bible that had been made by the Waldensian Synod of Chanforans (12 September 1532). Olivétan's "translator's apology" was addressed to the Basel reformers Farel, Viret, and Saunier, designated by names that were also constructed from ancient classical languages, here Hebrew and Greek: Chusemeth, Chlorotes, and Almeutes. Calvin himself, when he arrived in Basel,

---

1. S. L. Greenslade, ed., *The Cambridge History of the Bible: The West from the Reformation to the Present Day* (Cambridge: Cambridge University Press, 1963), pp. 116-20.

wished to be known as Lucanus, though this may have been less a humanist's conceit than a means to protect his privacy. This frequent Renaissance practice of forging ancient-looking names emphasizes the elitism of the humanists, which stands in sharp contrast with their wish to make the Bible available to all. At any rate, Calvin contributed two prefaces to Olivétan's translation. The first, in Latin, took the form of a letter to "the Emperors, Kings, Princes, and all Nations that are subject to the Dominion of Christ."[2] In it Calvin referred to Chusemeth and Chlorotes as "holy men and witnesses of the unvanquished word."[3] The second, much longer, preface, written in French, was intended for all "those who love Jesus Christ."[4]

It is evident that these two pieces in such a setting identified Calvin, like Olivétan, with the Reformation. Their tone and their content, however, hardly do. Admittedly, the Latin epistle regrets that there are today no disciples resembling "the prophets whom the Lord called from a sheepfold or the apostles from a fishing boat." It mentions as one of the manifold heresies of the time the idea that "the people's obedience is better than doctrine."[5] But this sort of rhetoric was by no means unusual among the Catholic Evangelicals, who professed justification by faith without forsaking the traditional structure of the medieval Church.[6]

Written in part in an ironical tone, the Latin letter qualifies the gospel, *evangelium*, as

> smell of death unto death for those who perish, scandal to Jews, stupidity to Greeks: therefore let it be neither read nor heard! Yet it is the power of God for salvation to every believer, Jew as well as Greek. Christ is a stone of offense on which many stum-

---

2. CR IX, p. 787.
3. CR IX, p. 790.
4. This is its title: *Addresse aux amateurs de Jésus-Christ.*
5. CR IX, 789.
6. The expression "Catholic Evangelicals," though not widely used, conveniently designates those who, like Lefèvre d'Étaples or Bishop Briçonnet, sympathized with the reformers, but thought that a true reform could still be effected without upsetting the structures of the Church.

ble and many are crushed: therefore let there be no Christ! But he is the eternal life, the only way to the Father, and the truth.[7]

Such a text establishes a quasi-identity between the gospel, the word of God written, and the Savior. It implies a christological understanding of the scriptural principle, even though the formula, *Scriptura sola,* is not used. In the perspective of the "address to those who love Jesus Christ," the biblical revelation does not contradict the testimony of creation. On the contrary the text explicitly argues: No one can "claim ignorance of so magnificent a Lord," who "in all the sections of the world, in the sky, and on earth has written and as it were imprinted the glory of his power, goodness, wisdom, and eternity."[8] Indeed, "all creatures, from the firmament to the center of the earth, could be witnesses and messengers of his glory to all men."[9] This is precisely the central theme of the address: Jesus Christ is in the Bible today as he was in Hebraic and Jewish history. In a remarkable synthesis Calvin reverses the biblical typology, traditional in medieval exegesis, that saw the heroes of the Old Testament as types of the promised Messiah. Rather than look forward, from the Old Covenant to the Messiah, he looks from the living eternal Christ to the text. Christ is the eternal reality, the universal Person, behind the images and figures of the former revelation:

It must be most certain and manifest to you that the treasuries of paradise are open to you in it, and the riches of God displayed, and eternal life revealed. For this is eternal life, to know the only true God and the one he has sent, Jesus Christ, to whom he has entrusted the beginning, the middle, and the end of our salvation. He is Isaac, the beloved Son of the Father, who was offered in sacrifice and yet did not succumb to the power of death. He is the watchful shepherd Jacob, who has such a great care of the

7. *Evangelium est odor mortis in mortem iis qui pereunt, Judaeis scandalum, Graecis stultitia: ergo ne legatur, ne audiatur. At est virtus Dei in salutem omni credenti: Judaeo simul et Graeco. Christus est petra offensionis, in quam multi impingunt et qua multi eliduntur: ergo ne sit Christus. Sed est vita aeterna, unica ad Patrem via et veritas* (CR IX, p. 789).

8. CR IX, p. 793.

9. CR IX, p. 795.

ewes in his charge. He is the good and merciful brother Joseph, who in his glory is not ashamed to recognize his brothers, however humble and abject they were. He is the great sacrificator and bishop Melchisedech who offered the eternal sacrifice once and for all. He is the sovereign lawgiver Moses writing his Law on the tables of our hearts through his Spirit. He is the faithful captain and guide Jossuah who leads us to the promised land. He is the noble and victorious King David subjecting all rebellious power under his hand. He is the magnificent and triumphant King Solomon governing his kingdom in peace and prosperity. He is the strong and virtuous Samson who by his death crushed his foes.[10]

One question is left open. Would Calvin, at the time he wrote these lines, have been able to make a similar analogy between Christ and the Church of his own day? Did Paul III, Bishop of Rome in 1535, convincingly embody some aspect of Christ's Person and mission? Bent on Church reform, he appointed the special commission of cardinals and bishops which presented him, in March of 1537, with its recommendations, the *Consilium delectorum cardinalium et aliorum prelatorum de emendanda ecclesia*,[11] which, however, proved to be too radical for implementation. This program for reform *in capite et in membris* included drastic measures like forbidding some religious Orders, considered to be irreformable, to admit novices. Nonetheless, the *consilium* would inspire the convocation of the Council of Trent, which was effectively launched on its course by Paul III. This pope also showed great concern for the plight of the American Indians under the harsh rule of the Spanish conquistadors. None of this, however, would have convinced Calvin that the current Bishop of Rome was truly the legate of the Savior who was described at the beginning of Olivétan's Bible.

The French preface, which was meant to be read by all, did not openly criticize the hierarchy. The Latin preface, however, which

10. CR IX, p. 913.
11. English translation in John C. Olin, *The Catholic Reformation: Savonarola to Ignatius Loyola, 1495-1540* (New York: Harper and Row, 1969), pp. 186-97.

could be read only by the well-educated, is more revealing of Calvin's mounting criticism of ecclesiastical structures. Indeed it praises the deacon Philip and his four daughters, who were prophetesses of Christ; Jerome, who was not loath to count women as his co-students; Chrysostom, who declared that Bible-reading was more useful to lay people than to monks; Augustine, who exhorted the people to read the Scriptures; Pamphilus, who kept a number of Bibles that men and women were free to borrow from him; and Eusebius, who praised Pamphilus for so doing. At the same time Calvin bemoans the attitude of unnamed "Rabbis (who are such by their pomp or their ferocity), who would be ashamed of learning together with the people and the vulgar."[12] It is not that he wishes to "take away the order of teaching and learning from the Church, for one must acknowledge God's splendid kindness when it [the order of teaching] is shaped by prophets, doctors, interpreters sent by him." The gospel has to be taught, and there should be qualified teachers in the Church. Authentic teaching, however, must have its source in God.

It is easy to read something else between these lines, for it cannot be by mere oversight that Calvin did not include bishops in his list of teachers. Designated by the biblical image of the "shepherds," which had been used of bishops in the early Church,[13] bishops appear in a critical light in the next point of the letter. True Christian liberty, Calvin reports, lasted many years, until the people, corrupted and eager for pleasure, abandoned the study of the Bible. Only recently has a new hunger for the word of God been felt. And how, he asks rhetorically, has it been received?

> Now, however, where the people have begun to request them [these biblical studies], this tyranny has emerged that keeps the people from the good that belongs to all. . . . Who would have thought that the cruelty of shepherds (for they want to be con-

12. CR IX, p. 788.
13. Thus the *Shepherd of Hermas*, c. 140, referred simply to the "presbyters who are in charge of the Church" in Rome (vision 2, n. 4): *Apostolic Fathers*, vol. 2, Loeb Classical Library (Cambridge, Mass.: Harvard University Press, 1965), pp. 24-25.

sidered and called shepherds) was so great that they are not horrified at snatching the food of life from the sheep's mouths?[14]

Calvin's interest in presenting his cousin's French version of the Bible was inspired precisely by his concern that all believers have access to the word of God: "This only I ask, that the faithful people be allowed to hear their God speaking and to learn from his teaching."[15]

*   *   *

On 23 August 1535 Calvin had finished the address to King François I that would preface the *Institutio christianae religionis* of 1536. This book was going to be at the same time the basic theological statement and the first public document by which he took his distance from the Roman religious system. The letters to Duchemin and Roussel were written a few months later, between February and April of 1536, either when Calvin was on the way to Ferrara to visit the duchess Renée de France, the reform-minded daughter of King Louis XII, or during his brief sojourn at the duke's court in Ferrara. Calvin left for Ferrara shortly after signing the First Helvetic Confession (3 February 1536), which was the decisive formal gesture by which he identified himself with the Reformation. He was accompanied by Louis du Tillet, who was trying to hide his identity under the name of M. de Haultmont. At the time, the *Institutio* was in the last stages of printing, since it went on the market in Frankfurt in March of the same year.

The itinerary of Calvin's conversion can thus be reconstructed to a great extent. As a university student Calvin had plunged into the erudite humanism that is manifest in his study of Seneca's *De clementia*. From there he was led to the religious humanism that found expression in a moderate form in Nicolas Cop's Sorbonne discourse of November 1533, and that Calvin saw at work at the court of Marguerite de Navarre. In October 1534, however, the *affaire des placards* had centered the basic conflict of the French Refor-

14. CR IX, pp. 788-89.
15. CR IX, p. 789.

mation on the theology of the eucharist and the liturgy of the Lord's Supper. According to the *placards,* the Mass was, by its false doctrines, and notably by the implication of idolatry that Antoine Marcourt read in transubstantiation, the abomination of desolation; it brought antichrist, that is, the Roman priesthood, into the Temple. To many, the scurrilous tone of the *placards* may have seemed more incendiary than persuasive. In 1534, however, Marcourt also explained his position more theologically in a *Petit traité de la sainte eucharistie.* The problem that was thus raised in France about the chief of the sacraments was evidently indebted to one of the basic reformatory writings of Martin Luther, *The Babylonian Captivity of the Church* (1520), which offered a perceptive critique — more balanced than Marcourt's — of the sacramental system and theology inherited from the Middle Ages.

Precisely, the letters to Duchemin and Roussel illustrate Calvin's conviction that pontifical pomps and circumstances, visible wherever a bishop, rather than the Lord, becomes the center of attention in worship, had entirely distorted the meaning of the Last Supper and the reality of the eucharist, theological and political justifications for the centrality of the bishop in the local Church notwithstanding. Duchemin and Roussel, however, were not the only friends of Calvin's who disappointed him by settling down, if not also gaining advancement, in the Roman system.

This was also the case with Louis du Tillet, the rector of Claix, his close friend, in whose ancestral home Calvin had been a welcome guest in 1534, the large library of which he had used extensively. Calvin was, it seems, staying at Claix when the *placards* affair exploded. In Louis du Tillet's company he had traveled to Basel in late 1534. With him he had visited Renée de France in Ferrara. Louis du Tillet had even accompanied Calvin to Geneva. Prompted by his older brothers, however, Louis had returned to France in January 1537 and renounced the Reformation.[16] He nonetheless kept a

---

16. Alexandre Crottet, *Correspondance française de Calvin avec Louis du Tillet* (Lausanne, 1850). Louis had two older brothers called Jean, who both died in 1570. The elder became a distinguished lawyer and an officer (*greffier*) in the Parliament of Paris. The other, a historian and linguist, was made Bishop of St. Brieuc in 1553

friendly correspondence with Calvin until December 1538, when his last letter remained unanswered, and this for an obvious reason: Du Tillet gave it as his firm opinion that Calvin had not been called by God to the ministry! He was to be made chaplain to Queen Catherine de Médicis in 1552.

In the chronological sequence of publication the letters should be examined after the *Institutio* of 1536, which was on the verge of hitting the market when Calvin wrote to Nicolas Duchemin in answer to a now lost communication from his friend. Although the letters are focused on specific items relating to each of his two correspondents, they properly fit in the wider doctrinal horizon of Calvin's *Institutio*. In fact, their polemical mood, though subdued, is germane to that which emerges in Chapter IV of the *Institutio*, where Calvin explains the doctrine of the eucharist, and which prevails in Chapter V, on "the false sacraments." Taken in its totality, *Institutio christianae religionis* responds to two different concerns and reflects two moods. Explanation dominates up to the first half of Chapter IV. Criticism starts in the second half of IV and largely dominates Chapter V. This clearly suggests that the book is likely to have been composed at two different times, the first before, and the second after Calvin's full endorsement of the Reformation.

*   *   *

Nicolas Duchemin, some ten years younger than Calvin, had been a student in Orléans when Calvin studied there. Both had taken magisterial courses in Law from Pierre de l'Estoile (c. 1480-1537) in 1528. They had moved together to Bourges in 1529 to follow the lectures of the Italian humanist Andrea Alciati (1492-1550) and of the Greek scholar from Germany, Melchior Wolmar (1486-1561). Alciati having criticized and made fun of de l'Estoile in an *Apologia*, Duchemin who, like Calvin, admired de l'Estoile, had penned a response in 1531, *Antapologia*, the publication of which Calvin super-

---

and of Meaux in 1564; he attended the later sessions of the Council of Trent. Both were distinguished scholars and deeply involved in the struggle against the Reformation. Another brother, Séraphin, was also a lawyer.

vised when he spent time in Paris after leaving the Angoulême region in 1534. Calvin had also composed a preface for Duchemin's piece, in the form of a letter to a certain Franciscus Connanus, who was also a scholar in Law.

The tone and the topic are typical of humanist style and concerns. Stella (Pierre de l'Estoile), however, while undoubtedly a distinguished humanist and a marvelous teacher of Law, was also a somewhat conservative churchman. It therefore comes as no surprise that his defender against the critique of an Italian scholar who despised French scholarship was offered the prominent function of *officialis* in a diocese. Nicolas Duchemin thus became the chief canonical adviser of the Bishop of Le Mans. This was René du Bellay (c. 1496-1546), Bishop of Grasse in 1532 and of Le Mans in 1535 after the resignation of his predecessor, Louis de Bourbon-Vendôme (1493-1557). Both Bourbon-Vendôme and du Bellay were aristocrats and typical Renaissance bishops, who were not above collecting huge revenues from numerous benefices and even from several episcopal sees that they hardly ever visited. This may explain why Duchemin felt a twinge of scruples as he accepted this promotion, and that he shared his problem with his friend Calvin. Calvin's unambiguous response to his lost letter emphasizes the responsibility of bishops and their collaborators in the promotion of what he now regards as idolatry. No true Christian can take part in the papal rituals without betraying the teachings of Christ. Calvin, who addresses Duchemin as "my brother, . . . sweetest brother, . . . excellent man," is eager to draw his correspondent away from such a spiritually dangerous position.

In a long introduction Calvin expresses his sympathy with his friend in the dilemma on the horns of which he is caught. He appeals to Scripture and to the example of St. Cyprian for suitable models of the courage that is necessary to true faith. He then sets out to describe the "true piety of heart," which is entirely devoted to listening to the "all but boisterous exhortation to desire the knowledge of God"[17] that resounds in the Scriptures. True knowledge of

---

17. *His verbis (ut videmus) inest paene clamosa ad appetendam Dei cognitionem cohortatio* (*Calvini Opera Selecta*, vol. 1, ed. Peter Barth [Munich: Chr. Kaiser Verlag,

God is incompatible with idolatry, which is absolutely condemned in the Old Testament. And it is not possible to indulge in external idolatrous practices while interiorly keeping the true faith, since the New Testament clearly demands the external profession of true faith.

This is precisely the peg where Calvin hangs his relatively new anti-papalism. He is now convinced that papal commandments and ceremonies are not authentic confessions of true faith, but new forms of idolatry that are destructive of the Christian faith. Abundant examples are given. The prohibition of meat at certain times destroys Christian liberty. The rites of unction with oil, the cult of pictures and statues, the sale of indulgences, the exorcisms, the blessings with water that has been exorcized,[18] imply the identification of spiritual grace with material elements. The use of holy chrism and the practice of exorcism are given extensive critical treatment. Above all, however, the celebration of the Mass, which is at the heart of the Roman system, is analogous to the episode of the Golden Calf, for it is grounded, as Calvin formulates it, in the contention that God becomes bread, and, Calvin asks, What is the difference between becoming a statue and becoming a piece of bread? In the Mass, priest and people adore bread that has been renamed God, under the false pretense that "God himself passes into bread that has been bewitched by an obscure and as it were magic murmur."[19]

The personal implications of the harmony of external behavior with interior faith are inescapable, as the end of the letter makes clear:

> From me, or rather from the Lord through my hand, you have the advice you requested. For your body it is dangerous indeed and hardly attractive, but for your soul true and salubrious, and,

---

1926], p. 295). The letters were published in 1537, in Basel, as *Epistolae duae . . . ;* they take up pp. 284-328 of *Opera Selecta,* vol. 1.

18. *Opera Selecta,* vol. 1, p. 305.

19. *Ac si non illa potius nefaria sui nominis usurpatione bis irriteretur Dominus: quod et eo nihilo secius relicto, ad idolum curritur, et transire ipse in panem fingitur, obscuro ac velut magico murmure incantatum* (*Opera Selecta,* vol. 1, p. 314).

I will add, most necessary to you, unless you decide to throw off the Lord's yoke from your shoulders and to abjure his religion.[20]

In the circumstances of the kingdom of France in 1535, the recommended gesture of publicly renouncing Roman idolatry could lead to martyrdom. Deliberately to choose a way that might occasion one's violent death is of course a humanly desperate decision. It is nonetheless unimpeachable, if indeed involvement in papal rituals and ceremonies, be it only as a witness, amounts to the idolatry that is solemnly condemned in the Scriptures. This is precisely, at this time, Calvin's conviction. True faith can lead to death. But what is death? "Taught by the word of God, we affirm that it is nothing else than, through a momentary sense of pain, the peaceful entrance into the immortal and blessed life. . . ."[21] The unwelcome perspective of martyrdom ought to be balanced with the expectation of the blessed immortality that God keeps in store for the faithful soul. That the soul is immortal by creation was of course the central topic of *Psychopannychia*. The conviction that this immortality will be, for Christians, blessed, derives from the gospel.

*   *   *

Gérard Roussel (1480-1550) had been, in 1524, an admiring correspondent of Guillaume Farel. In 1526 he had become chaplain to Marguerite de Navarre at Nérac, where he felt free to preach about justification by faith. In 1533, as we have seen, he had preached at the court of François I. Calvin got to know him when he visited Marguerite's court during the Lent of 1534. In February 1536 Roussel had been made Bishop of Oléron. As a bishop he remained a prominent humanist.

Calvin, however, was profoundly shocked when Roussel accepted his election to the bishopric of Oléron. He wrote to Roussel, not in congratulation, as he himself noted in the first lines, but in reproval. Roussel had been his friend. Twice, at the beginning of his letter

20. *Opera Selecta,* vol. 1, p. 327.
21. *Opera Selecta,* vol. 1, p. 228.

and in the last pages, Calvin calls him, *vir mihi amicissime*,[22] "man most dear to me." He evokes "our old friendship, our all but brotherly union."[23] Once he says, possibly with some irony, *o vir eximie*[24] ("O eminent person"). As he starts to write, however, he uses an ambiguous formula that betrays his hesitancy about the present state of their friendship: "John Calvin, to an old friend, now a lord, greetings." The letter, which was later given a somewhat grandiloquent title, *De Christiani hominis officio in sacerdotiis papalis ecclesiae vel administrandis vel abjiciendis* ("On the duty of a Christian in administering or rejecting the priestly honors of the Papal Church"), is at the same time a serious analysis of episcopacy, and a virulently antipapal pamphlet.

A long introduction outlines Calvin's personal dilemma. In the eyes of most people Roussel deserves congratulations, for he has received the highest honors in the Church. Calvin, however, asks himself: Has his friend been, like many others, poisoned by "drinking from this chalice of the Roman table?"[25] Has he lost his mind? For surely he knows that "all this complex of Roman wealth, from the Highest See itself to the smallest chaplaincy (as they call it), has been gathered from impostures, robberies, plunder, sacrileges, and the most evil maneuvers *(artibus)*." Against "the Roman Pluto," however, one should trust the word of God: "Great is the strength of the word of God, more powerful than anyone dare to esteem it unless he has experienced it. . . ."[26] This power, however, can have contradictory outcomes: it leads either to death or to life. The purpose of Calvin's letter is to help his friend find life in the word of God.

Calvin describes the task of a true bishop and its inherent difficulties,[27] the dilemma of a bishop in the Roman system in which he is forced to cooperate with evil and idolatry,[28] whose wealth im-

22. *Opera Selecta*, vol. 1, pp. 331, 355.

23. *Opera Selecta*, vol. 1, p. 330.

24. *Opera Selecta*, vol. 1, p. 353.

25. *Opera Selecta*, vol. 1, p. 330.

26. *Magna sane vis est verbi Domini, potentiorque quam reputare quisquam temere queat, nisi expertus . . .* (*Opera Selecta*, vol. 1, p. 331).

27. *Opera Selecta*, vol. 1, pp. 333-37.

28. *Opera Selecta*, vol. 1, pp. 337-41.

pedes the fulfillment of his duties,[29] who promotes all the Roman superstitions.[30] Calvin urges Roussel to realize that episcopal wealth comes from four evil sources: distortions of the biblical tithing, yearly donations made for "the sacrilege of the Mass" and the "utopian jail of purgatory," voluntary and extraordinary offerings, and enforced exactions imposed by the papal canons.[31] The common excuse for participating in this venal system — the money that is not spent for legitimate living expenses belongs to the poor — is not valid since the clergy actually live in luxury and spend much more than they need.[32] This diatribe leads to a bad pun, in which the four letters of the city of Rome *(ROMA)* become initials of *Radicem Omnium Malorum Avaritiam* ("Root of All Evils Avarice").

Roussel's choice is clear. Either he will do what is expected of a Roman bishop, or he will give up his episcopal see. In the first case, "lingering in the camp of Antichrist,"[33] he will become "a murderer"[34] and a disciple of "the Roman Archpirate."[35] He will be "neither a good man nor a Christian."[36] In the second case he will lead "in poverty a holy life worthy of his calling."[37] Then he will be among those of whom Calvin declares:

> Those, I say, we embrace with brotherliness with their faults and their lapses, those we count in the number of our brothers, those we cherish in our bosom, who are shown by their Christianly organized life to aspire with their whole soul to the kingdom of God.[38]

29. *Opera Selecta*, vol. 1, pp. 341-47.
30. *Opera Selecta*, vol. 1, pp. 347-53.
31. *Opera Selecta*, vol. 1, pp. 353-58.
32. *Opera Selecta*, vol. 1, pp. 358-59. Calvin was evidently more familiar with city clergy than with the impoverished priests of the rural countryside.
33. *Opera Selecta*, vol. 1, p. 361.
34. *Opera Selecta*, vol. 1, p. 341.
35. *Opera Selecta*, vol. 1, p. 356.
36. *Opera Selecta*, vol. 1, p. 362.
37. *Opera Selecta*, vol. 1, p. 361.
38. *Eos, inquam, cum suis delictis et lapsibus fraterna benignitate complectimur, eos fratrum in numero retinemus, eos in sinu nostro fovemus, quos vita christiane instituta toto animo adspirare ad Dei regnum apparet* (*Opera Selecta*, vol. 1, pp. 361-62).

*   *   *

There have been, Calvin admits, many good bishops in the Church. There are still "not a few who are not bishops by name only, but deserve the praise and admiration of all,"[39] although he does not know anyone now who can be compared to St. Paul. Since episcopacy was instituted by God, it consists in what God planned for it, not in what men have made of it. Therefore episcopacy resides neither "in the miter . . . the crozier . . . the pallium . . . the ring . . . ," nor in "domestic splendor . . . a numerous retinue . . . an elegant table . . . and every kind of pleasure and magnificence. . . ."[40] Rather, a true bishop is a "guardian of the people of God," entrusted with its care, watching over its salvation. His administration is geared to the dispensation of the divine mysteries and the building of the house of God. Since "preaching is itself called 'power of God for salvation to every believer' (Rom. 1:16) and 'kingdom of God' (Matt. 4:17)," the chief duty of bishops is to proclaim the word of God. They must give the people "the taste of the word of God," not any kind of taste, but the one that the Lord wants. They have also to become the providence of the people, their voice, and "the eyes of the Church." As "shepherds" they must be more than "father, president, leader, or guardian." Or rather, "the shepherd not only has the task of leading, ruling, and serving, but somehow also of being father."[41] This may be summed up in three functions:

> to feed the Church with the food of the word, to protect it from Satan's incursions with the resources of the word, and then through holiness of life to show the way that should be followed by those who aspire and strive after the kingdom of God.[42]

---

39. *Quin potius et permultos fuisse olim, et hodie esse non paucos dico, non episcoporum nomine solum, sed laude etiam admirationeque omnium dignissimos . . . (Opera Selecta,* vol. 1, p. 340).

40. *Opera Selecta,* vol. 1, p. 332.

41. *Opera Selecta,* vol. 1, p. 334.

42. *Opera Selecta,* vol. 1, p. 335.

This positive description of a bishop's calling places the accent exclusively on the function of teaching and leading. In several perceptive pages Calvin draws a picture of a bishop and his role according to the gospel. He does not include in this role, however, the traditional function of presiding over the liturgy. This, I suspect, is deliberate, and it offers a key to Calvin's understanding of the Church when he was writing the two letters to his friends or former friends.

Christianity implies a desire for the kingdom of God. But neither in the official shepherds of the believers nor in what the Roman liturgy and the sacraments had become did Calvin observe the simplicity of Christ, the way of the Spirit, the worship of the Father, the purity of faith, the true shepherding of the faithful. The presidency of the eucharist was a spectacle that exhibited the ostentation of riches, the hybris of ecclesiastics. No parity was visible between God's call and the celebrant's performance. Hence a negative view of bishops in their most public function came to darken Calvin's overall perspective on the Catholic Church. In the rulings of bishops, the popes' decrees and decretals, and the synods' canons, Calvin detected the pride of power and the tentacles of an all-invading tyranny. In the choirs of chapters and monasteries he heard the false claims of self-made holiness.

How then did Calvin, in these early years of his theological career, understand the eucharistic doctrines of the scholastics? The Platonism that he shared with many a humanist did not help him at this point. He denied transubstantiation, the doctrine that the substance of bread and wine is, in the proper context of liturgical worship, by the power of the Holy Spirit, transformed into the substance of the body and blood of Christ. He did not, however, understand it in the Aristotelian horizon of the scholastics, but on the background of a Platonic dualism, familiar to the Renaissance, between the invisible and the visible, between divinity and the material world. It was this unbridgeable chasm between the Creator and the creature that allowed him to speak of the liturgical consecration as bread and wine falsely becoming God, and of the consecrated host as an idol. In his eyes the eucharist had been made an idol, idolatry being disguised as adoration. In a word, the liturgical face of the Church was hidden in his eyes by what would be called triumphalism at Vatican Council II.

148

If this was the Roman doctrine, then Calvin was certainly justified in calling the Mass idolatry and the most horrible sacrilege. The bishops, then, were not protecting the faithful from Satan's attacks, and their accouterments with miter and crozier could be seen as Satan's own disguise. As Calvin wrote to the Bishop of Oléron,

> And nonetheless from you and from the men of your order I hear these voices immediately claiming: the priesthoods that you bear under the name of bishops are nothing less than the episcopate. They are rather positions of power, or civil appointments, or honorary pensions, or anything you like, as long as they are not thought to be episcopacy.[43]

* * *

The tone of these writings of 1535 and 1536 marks a sharp contrast with that of *Psychopannychia*. It must have been between his pamphlet on the immortality of the soul on the one hand and, on the other, the prefaces to Olivétan's Bible and the letters to Duchemin and Roussel that Calvin adopted his anti-Roman stance. At the most, *Psychopannychia* betrayed Calvin's hostile reaction to a reform movement that, as he saw it, was going astray. Admittedly, there would have been little incentive to be concerned about small circles of anabaptists, unless Calvin was already eager to see the reform movement on the right path. Nonetheless, *Psychopannychia* was not a reforming document. The position it defended was identical with Catholic teaching, and it did not contain one word that was critical of the medieval Church or of the papacy.

In contrast, the prefaces to Olivétan's French Bible and the two letters to Duchemin and Roussel clearly identified the gate of true reform: This is the opening of the word of God to all believers, and not only to scholars. Paradoxically, *Psychopannychia* is relevant to such a reforming path. When Calvin underlined the interiority of the gospel written in the heart, the indwelling of the Word in the soul, the inner experience of the Spirit, Christianity as desire for

---

43. *Opera Selecta*, vol. 1, p. 337.

God and expectation of the divine kingdom, he hinted at the reason why he could not follow the examples of du Tillet, Duchemin, Roussel, and of the many reform-minded humanists who remained in the Roman fold. Calvin did not trust the official shepherds of the Christian people, the bishops, to place the service of the gospel above their own advantage, comfort, wealth, honors, and pomps. What he saw in their public appearances and their government was ill-gotten wealth and unlawful tyranny. He was interested in doctrine, for doctrine shapes the interior of a Christian. The bishops, however, were more concerned about effective obedience than about true doctrine.

*   *   *

The same recognizable tone of voice with which Calvin addressed his friends or former friends Duchemin and Roussel reappears in Chapter V of *Institutio christianae religionis*. After speaking of the two main sacraments, baptism and the eucharist, Calvin takes up a medieval question that dealt with the historical and theological status of the "five other sacraments." He gives it a radical answer. These are "false sacraments," instituted by men and therefore without efficacy. Since "a sacrament is a seal by which God's testament or promise is sealed,"[44] it can exist only by the power of God, and it must be attested by the word of God.

Calvin looks at confirmation first. In *The Babylonian Captivity of the Church,* Luther had treated the problem of confirmation with restraint. He could not figure out why "the Romanists" had made a sacrament out of the imposition of hands that followed baptism in the early Church. He could not find a divine institution of it. But he did not thereby condemn and wish to abolish confirmation. It is a "rite or ceremony of the Church," a usage, however, that does not bring salvation.[45]

---

44. *Sacramentum sigillum est quo Dei testamentum seu promissio obsignatur* (*Opera Selecta*, vol. 1, p. 163).

45. John Dillenberger, ed., *Martin Luther: Selections from His Writings* (New York: Doubleday, 1961), pp. 324-25.

Calvin's reflection is much more critical than Luther's. Confirmation originated in "human temerity."[46] It includes a "beautiful and old" prayer, which, however, is not supported by any promise of God to send the Holy Spirit. It also uses chrism, but this is only "oil, a greasy thick liquid," and there is no scriptural command for such an unction. As to the imposition of hands, there are many different ones in the Scriptures, and no reason to see them as sacraments. The urge to behave like the Apostles and to impose hands is no more than κακοξηλία,[47] an "unholy envy" on the bishops' part. The Lord's true sacraments require two elements, "the substance of a material thing that is proposed to us, and a form that is imposed upon it by a word of God, in which the whole power resides."[48] In the absence of a word of God the unction breeds monsters, namely the belief that it brings strength for the struggle of Christian life, that it perfects baptism, that it is such a noble sacrament that "simple priests" cannot confer it, but only bishops. The argument from long usage has no value if it neglects the fundamental principle that a sacrament must be attested in Scripture by a promise made by God in relation to it. Calvin actually advocates a kind of "Christian catechesis by which children or those who verge on adolescence would explain the reason of their faith before the Church."[49] They would be interrogated and would respond. They would be then taught what they do not yet know. This, however, would be "like a method of Christian doctrine," and not a sacrament. In fact, Calvin's arguments and ideas were hardly new in his time. Bonaventure had answered them substantially when he taught that sacraments were given to the primitive Church by Christ or by the Holy Spirit.

46. *Opera Selecta,* vol. 1, p. 163.

47. The word is presumably coined by Calvin.

48. *Opera Selecta,* vol. 1, p. 165. Calvin continues: "Insofar as bread, wine, water, that are offered to our viewing in the sacraments retain their substance, the word of Paul always applies: food for the belly, and the belly for food; God destroys both. They pass away and vanish with the figure of this world. But insofar as they are sanctified by the word of God in order to be sacraments, they do not consign us to the flesh but truly teach us spiritually." Calvin failed to notice that this could be an argument for transubstantiation!

49. *Opera Selecta,* vol. 1, p. 169.

What is new in Calvin's view of confirmation is the hostile tone, which is also in sharp contrast with the style previously used in *Institutio christianae religionis*. The holy chrism, says Calvin, is "oil polluted by the devil's lie";[50] confirmation is a "malicious and grievous fraud of Satan,"[51] a sacrilege, an "aborted larva of sacrament,"[52] a "false promise of the devil";[53] the responses given by the Holy See are "the oracles of the apostolic tripod"[54] spoken by "the mouth of sacrileges"; the bishops are "charlatans"[55] and "monkeys,"[56] who act out of "libido" and suffer from "dizziness in the head."[57]

We have no need at this point to go through Calvin's consideration of the other "false sacraments." His concerns and his tone are the same as for confirmation. One should nonetheless note an expression that sums up the dilemma of all would-be reformers: "This is a Gordian knot, which is easier to cut than to labor with great difficulty to undo."[58] Calvin had become impatient.

*   *   *

As a humanist, Calvin would stop at nothing in his search for truth. As a Christian he could not recognize the bishops, such as he saw them, as exemplifying the interior experience of God that he had come to desire and, at least in part, to understand. They could well be the Apostles' successors. But the external order of the hierarchy could not be placed above the evidence and the desire of the kingdom of God in the soul. When the moment came to choose between the external order and the internal reality, that is, when he no

50. *Opera Selecta*, vol. 1, p. 166.

51. *Videte malitiosam et sonticam Satanae fraudem, qui ex Deo estis* (*Opera Selecta*, vol. 1, p. 166).

52. *Opera Selecta*, vol. 1, p. 169.

53. *Opera Selecta*, vol. 1, p. 166.

54. *Opera Selecta*, vol. 1, p. 167; the Sybil at Delphi sat on a tripod when she gave her oracles.

55. *Histriones* (*Opera Selecta*, vol. 1, p. 164).

56. *Simiae* (*Opera Selecta*, vol. 1, p. 165).

57. *Opera Selecta*, vol. 1, p. 168.

58. *Nodus gordianus est, quem abrumpere satius sit quam in dissolvendo tantopere laborare* (*Opera Selecta*, vol. 1, p. 168).

longer felt safe in France under François I, Calvin could only opt for the interior kingdom, a choice that found ready support in the Platonic idea, common among the humanists, that the invisible has priority over the visible. When the bishops generally supported the king's persecution of true religion they were clearly unfaithful to their apostolic task and mission. This was the chief reason why Calvin heard the call to become an active reformer.

If this may not have been, as his former friend Louis du Tillet contended, a call to the ministry, it was at least a prophetic call to announce the interior kingdom of God, to assist the faithful in their desire for God, to shield the interior and invisible Church from the corruption that was rampant in the exterior and visible Church, and to attempt, in the context of Geneva, to reshape the exterior Church on the model of the interior Church.

IX

Christian Liberty

The last chapter of the *Institutio christianae religionis* of 1536 is of another nature than the preceding chapters. It does seem at first sight to amount to a sequence of remaining unrelated questions. At least the title conveys such an impression: "On Christian Liberty, Ecclesiastical Power, and Political Administration." The pattern of ideas is nonetheless quite clear as one reads through. The central Christian doctrines having been explained in the previous sections of the book, it now remains to look at their practical consequences for the self-understanding of the faithful as they lead a Christian life in the human city. In turn, reflection on Christian liberty leads to an investigation of authority in its relation to liberty. Does it function as a support or as an obstacle? Since authority is exercised in both Church and State, the ensuing considerations cover ecclesiastical power and civil authority.

This approach would appear to be slanted toward a critical view of authority as this is seen from the perspective of the spiritual freedom just described — the liberty of the soul that is highlighted by Christian doctrine and experience — on the horizon of redemption, justification, and sanctification by God through Jesus Christ.

Calvin's point of view is essentially theological and biblical, not social and political, in spite of his early interest in the art of government that was the chief topic of Seneca's *De clementia*. It is in fact entirely possible, but outside the scope of the present research, that

Calvin's familiarity with Seneca's Stoic principles helped him to discern radical differences between the demands of the Christian conscience and the best of political government. It is not, in Calvin's eyes, the achievements of human reason but the requirements of Christian liberty that must set proper boundaries to the legitimate use of power, both in the organization of the Church and in that of civil society.

*   *   *

Martin Luther had treated germane topics in his reform writings of 1520. Unlike Calvin, he had done it separately, extolling Christian liberty in the spiritual perspective of *The Freedom of a Christian,* and calling on civic authority to assist the necessary reform of the Church in his *Appeal to the Christian Nobility of the German Nation.* His more mature considerations on political power, however, stemmed from his horrified reaction to the turmoil of the Peasants' Revolt in 1525. Luther was then led to stress the distinction between spiritual freedom and political subversion, when, unable to control a movement that found support in a misreading of the gospel, he called on the nobility to put down the uprising by force. This lay behind his distinction of the "two kingdoms" in which Christian believers have to live, that is, the realm of spiritual authority and that of political responsibility, the latter having the obligation to support the former without being directly subject to it, the former being itself bound to inspire and support the lawful exercise of political power.

Because it was written for the enlightenment of Emperor Charles V on the doctrine of the Protestant princes and estates of the Holy Empire, the *Confession of Augsburg* had simply, against the anabaptists, affirmed the right of Christians to hold political office as "magistrate, prince, and judge," and to "pronounce sentence and render justice according to imperial law and other applicable laws . . ." (Art. XVI). It had not attempted to discuss the nature of law or justice and the limits of the corresponding power. There remained a gap at this point in the reformed teaching. Calvin tried to fill this gap in the last chapter of *Institutio christianae religionis.*

*　　*　　*

In spite of the turmoil in Calvin's life which led him to search for a stable and safe city to live in, his approach to the question of freedom and authority reflected a calmer context than that of the Peasants' Revolt which had served as a backdrop to Luther's reflections on the police powers of princes. If there was an emergency in 1535-1536, it was that of persuading François I to tolerate the reformed conventicles along with their doctrine and their style of worship. In his early experience as a student of Law who got interested in the religious questions posed by the reformers, it was the King of France who had recurred to force, and not, as in Luther's experience, a rebellious mob. Even after the posting of the inflammatory *placards,* the king's authority in the political order was not challenged by the reforming party. Addressing the king, directly in the introductory epistle of the *Institutio,* and indirectly in the rest of the book, required a more serene tone than that of Luther's embattled writings.

The question needed to be posed: Was the king's use of force to subdue the open advocacy of the reforming ideas that lay behind the *placards* compatible with the Christian gospel? The context of the question shaped the framework of Calvin's answer: Deriving from the spiritual empowerment of faith, Christian liberty should determine, if not exactly the nature, at least the limits, of both ecclesial *potestas* in the community of believers and civil responsibility for good order in society. What, however, is Christian liberty, if not an essential quality of the soul that has committed itself to the Savior?

It is not necessary in the context of the present book to examine Calvin's last chapter in all its details. It will satisfy our purpose, first, to understand the nature of Christian liberty as Calvin describes it; second, after a brief survey of his conception of ecclesial and governmental authority, to indicate the relation of liberty to the point of departure of his theological reflection in *Psychopannychia;* and third, to assess the connection of Calvin's view of Christian freedom with the anti-papal stance that was illustrated in the letters to Duchemin and Roussel. This should enable us to look for lingering traces of *Psychopannychia,* should there be any, in the main articulations of Calvin's final theological system.

*   *   *

Calvin sees three aspects of Christian liberty: liberation from law, obedience to God out of love, and freedom from unnecessary man-made regulations. The first aspect characterizes "the conscience of the faithful, when they are to seek the assurance of their justification before God, when they ascend and rise above the law, and when they forget the whole justice of the law."[1] Each of these three points has its relevance. The faithful relate to the Savior when they seek for the assurance of being justified in God's eyes. As a result of this assurance they are lifted up to a realm above the Law, and they are not concerned any longer about legal requirements. The soul's spiritual freedom is thus the direct outcome of justification as God's sovereign action and gift. Only when they have given up every self-reliance and every thought of being capable of a good action can the faithful adhere totally to God's mercy. Then, looking away from themselves, they can see Christ only.[2] The Law indeed keeps a positive function in the Christian life, for it never ceases to invite believers to holiness and to the desire of what is good. "The entire life of Christians must be a sort of meditation on piety, for they are called to sanctification."[3] The Law calls the faithful to be holy, even though it is radically unable to lead them to holiness because they lack the power to respond as they ought. For this they must rely wholly and only on God's action, which is extended to them in Jesus Christ.

The second aspect of Christian liberty follows. Since they are called to holiness, true Christian believers should fulfill God's will in all things out of love. Only when "every other concern and thought has been voided can we love our God with all our heart, all our soul, all our forces."[4] In Article VI of the *Confession of Augsburg* the eagerness to do good works as the will of God with no reference to rewards had been called *nova obedientia,* "the new obedience." At

1. *Institutio christianae religionis,* 1536, Ch. VI; *Opera Selecta,* vol. 1, p. 224.

2. . . . *unum Christum intueri* (p. 224).

3. *Tota Christianorum vita quaedam pietatis meditatio esse debet, quoniam in sanctificationem vocati sunt* (p. 224).

4. *Opera Selecta,* vol. 1, p. 225.

this point of *Institutio christianae religionis* Calvin makes this new obedience the mark of Christian behavior. His primary polemic, however, is not, as was the case in Luther's writings, with the notion of merit and of expected reward, but with the frequent occurrence of thoughtless routine and with the fear of punishment. The true Christian acts only for love of God and neighbor.

Again, the third aspect of Christian liberty follows. Those who have been freed from the Law must not be subjected to new external regulations that would replace the old ones. As a humanist, Calvin was familiar with the Stoic concept of *adiaphoron*, of what is morally indifferent, which was to play an important role in later intra-Lutheran discussions of the obligations of the Law.[5] The term would then be used primarily of ritual ceremonies that were considered permissible but not necessary. From this primary meaning the notion was easily applied to problems of food and drink, fast and abstinence, the observation of certain times and periods.[6]

Calvin's perspective also goes beyond the question of ceremonies. The heart of the matter, for him, is simple: Points that are in themselves indifferent, that is, as one might say today, valueless, must not be allowed to become a burden on the Christian conscience. The creatures that God placed at our disposal in the process of creation are there to be used, but only in peace and thanksgiving, without either attachment to them or selfishness in regard to other users. In sum, as he writes,

> one should observe that Christian liberty is spiritual in all its parts; its power resides in the pacification of terrified con-

5. See Bernard Verkamp, "The Limits upon Adiaphoristic Freedom: Luther and Melanchthon," *Theological Studies* 36 (1975): 52-76. Without the Greek term the concept played a role in the *Confession of Augsburg*, Article XV, where Melanchthon argued that many points, that are "neither commanded nor forbidden" in Scripture, should not be imposed on the faithful. Canon 19 of the Tridentine decree *De justificatione impii* touched on this, but in a polemical way that misrepresented the doctrine of the *Confession of Augsburg*.

6. The term would be featured in the *Formula of Concord* (1581), *Solida declaratio*, 10:5-9.

sciences before God, whether these are disturbed and worried in regard to the forgiveness of sins, or anxious that their imperfect works, tainted by the vices of our flesh, may not please God, or hesitant about the use of matters that are indifferent.[7]

Liberty is not license, and a free person will not indulge in demonstrations of freedom by deliberately departing from the accepted laws of society. One should be concerned about what God sees, not about what men see or believe they see. One may eat indeed meat on Friday with a good conscience. Eating meat on Friday, however, is not an act of freedom if it is done in order to shock our neighbor; and those also "are free who abstain with a free conscience."[8] The scandal of the weak is not identical with the scandal of the Pharisees, "and thus we will moderate the use of our liberty, so that it may cede to our weak brothers' ignorance. . . ."[9] The proper use of Christian liberty is therefore a norm and a mark of the Christian soul. It provides a rule of thumb to distinguish between true Christians and those hypocrites who claim to be followers of Christ while they do not live by his gospel. Calvin concludes:

> Let us see in summary where this liberty tends, namely, that we use God's gifts with no scruples of conscience and no perturbance of soul for the purpose for which they have been given us, in which assurance our souls will have peace with God and will acknowledge his generosity toward us.[10]

*   *   *

It is in light of his reflection on Christian liberty that Calvin approaches the twofold question of authority in Church and in society. If indeed liberty is a "prerogative" given by God to the faithful conscience, then in principle "we have been exempted from the

7. *Opera Selecta,* vol. 1, p. 228.
8. *Opera Selecta,* vol. 1, p. 229.
9. *Opera Selecta,* vol. 1, p. 230.
10. *Opera Selecta,* vol. 1, p. 227.

domination of all men."[11] What then are we to think of the necessary organization *(regimen)* of human society, in which specific officers wield spiritual power, and others political power? That the two powers were distinct had been embedded in the medieval mind. Conflicts between bishops and temporal lords had indeed marked the history of Europe on both the large and the small scale. On the large scale emperors and popes had quarreled over the domination of the one over the other. There are two swords, the popes had commonly affirmed since Boniface VIII (bull *Unam sanctam,* 18 November 1302), and the temporal sword must be subordinate to the spiritual. At the highest human level the spiritual sword was in the hands of the pope and the bishops, the temporal sword in those of the emperor, of kings, and of lesser lords at their recognized feudal rank. On the small scale, bishops had also quarreled with lay lords since Carolingian times, over the extent of episcopal jurisdiction, over the right to appoint to ecclesiastical offices, over the ownership and income of churches, chapels, and land. Such quarrels had also spread to relations within the Church's hierarchy itself, in and outside of synods, over the proper authority of archbishops, over the autonomy of abbots and abbesses, over an imbroglio of competing and overlapping territorial and parochial jurisdictions.

The power of the emperor had come to be considerably restricted, as kings more and more wielded the totality of the temporal sword in their kingdom without reference to the emperor. In addition, the kings of France tended to claim a share in the spiritual sword, on the ground that they were traditionally anointed with the quasi-sacramental chrism of the *Sainte Ampoule.* Since Philip the Fair's opposition to Boniface VIII and the doctrine of the bull *Unam sanctam* (1302), the kings of France admitted little more than a largely nominal subordination to the pope, a situation that had been made official in the Pragmatic Sanction promulgated by Charles VII in 1437. Subordinating the application of papal decrees to the king's authorization, the Pragmatic Sanction had brought a practical solution to the problem of relations between the spiritual and the temporal power. The king being, in principle, a faithful

11. *Opera Selecta,* vol. 1, p. 232.

Christian in good standing, the Pragmatic Sanction did not question the authority of the Bishop of Rome; it only subordinated the application of the pope's decrees to the king's prudential political judgment.

This restriction on papal power had been formally condemned by the Fifth Council of the Lateran and Pope Julius II at the fourth session of the council, on 21 February 1512, largely because the King of France, Louis XII, was then promoting a rival conciliarist council in Pisa. Their successors, however, Pope Leo X and King François I, were able to reach an agreement in a concordat that was approved at the eleventh session of the council, on 19 December 1515. Although it abolished the Pragmatic Sanction, the concordat accepted several of its major features, and subsequent kings still took the Pragmatic Sanction as the model of their relations with the Holy See.

That such problems had been inherited from the medieval period could not have been without influence on Calvin's thought when he confronted "the double regimen . . . spiritual . . . and political . . ."[12] that still ruled the society of his time. As he pointed out in the *Institutio*, the two powers were generally known as "spiritual and temporal jurisdiction." The first had its seat "in the interior soul, while the other regulated external mores." In an apparent allusion to Luther's vocabulary and his doctrine of the two kingdoms, Calvin noted that the two powers may also be called "the spiritual kingdom and the political kingdom."[13] Each, however, has commonly despised the other, a fact which, given the human condition, he himself did not find astonishing, for the division of the two powers reflected, he believed, the interior partition of the human person in "two worlds, in which various kings and various laws can dominate." In other words, recurring conflicts between the two realms flow directly from the split condition of the human person, the soul being spiritual while the body is necessarily temporal.

It was in keeping with this correspondence between the macrocosm of society and the microcosm of the human nature that Calvin

12. *Opera Selecta*, vol. 1, p. 232.
13. *Opera Selecta*, vol. 1, pp. 232-33.

should take the question of the twofold areas of government most seriously. His discussion of spiritual authority fills as many as twenty-six pages (232-58), that of political authority the following twenty-one pages (258-80). In contrast, the previous analysis of Christian liberty occupies only nine pages (223-32). Whether ecclesial or secular, spiritual or temporal, however, the principle of authority derives directly from the doctrine of these first pages. Spiritual or ecclesial authority exists in order to promote the gospel and to protect the liberty of Christian consciences. Political or governmental authority exists to organize and protect the proper order of society, not only so that the people may live in peace, but also that the gospel be preached, the sacraments administered, and the faithful free to follow their conscience in keeping with the liberty of the children of God. It is within the conscience, in the soul itself, that one should find the norms that are to regulate the exercise of authority in both Church and State. Thus, without stating it, Calvin is still thinking, when he composes these pages of the *Institutio* of 1536, along the lines of the central concern of *Psychopannychia*. Even when it has been liberated from itself and its sin by Christ and the grace of God, the Christian soul is still the immortal *anima* which is the essence of the human person. Both the temporal order and the ecclesial order must protect and promote the life of the soul even as they erect the proper setting for the life of the body.

In this way the first *Institutio* carries the doctrine of *Psychopannychia* into the specific situation of the Christian soul in human society. What Calvin has affirmed of the immortality of the soul is confirmed by the basic Christian revelation about the three divine Persons, the incarnation of the Word, and the process of justification and salvation. It would be absurd and derogatory of Christ and of God's redeeming action that a soul which is alive in Christ would either itself die or fall asleep at the death of its body. The soul's undelayed immortality is alone fully congenial with what Calvin declares to be the revealed doctrines. This eternal dignity stands in judgment over unjust restrictions that civil authorities are able to impose on the people they rule.

*　　　*　　　*

Given the perspective in which Calvin has posited the question of authority, it is logical that much of his discussion of spiritual authority amounts to a vehement critique of the exercise of power by bishops and popes. This was precisely his case against the bishops in the letters to his former friends Duchemin and Roussel. What was at the time of St. Paul a call to preach the gospel had in the sixteenth century become a confusing and bitter dilemma: How can the two of them in conscience agree to share an authority which, in the Roman system, has been and is being systematically abused? This question was due to remain at the heart of Calvin's case against the Nicodemites when he thought of all those, like the king's sister Marguerite de Navarre, who externally remained loyal within the Roman fold while they interiorly favored the reforms of the Church that were being advocated and implemented in Geneva and elsewhere.

The critique of Rome and the bishops is made explicit in the last chapter of the *Institutio* by way of contrast. The positive, original aspect of ecclesial authority is not neglected. Spiritual authority operates in the realm of conscience, "so that conscience be educated in piety and the worship of God." Calvin's terms, *quo conscientia in pietatem et cultum Dei instituitur,*[14] are particularly significant at this point. Education of the Christian conscience for piety and the worship of God is the proper task of bishops. But these generally neglect it, as Calvin would soon affirm in his response to the Bishop of Carpentras, Cardinal Jacopo Sadoleto. Such an education is precisely what Calvin wishes to do through his *Institutio christianae religionis*. In Calvin's Renaissance Latin, *Institutio* connotes an act of creation or formation, that is, an institution in the original sense of the verb, *instituere:* "to establish, to install, to institute." It has a double dimension as it designates both the very origin of the Christian religion in God's design that was implemented in Jesus Christ, and the continuing formation of the Christian conviction and conscience by education. Concern for spiritual formation as being the episcopal task par excellence will in fact become the basis for Calvin's own ecclesial authority, even though, when he wrote his first version of the book, he was far from anticipating his future career as

14. *Opera Selecta,* vol. 1, p. 232.

the spiritual director and guide of the city of Geneva and of the entire reformed Church in the kingdom of France.

The Christian *magisterium* — the word is used explicitly by Calvin[15] — belongs to Christ. That Christ is the teacher evidently limits whatever spiritual authority has been passed on to "the apostles and to their successors."[16] These were to use only the "spiritual weapons" that were contained in the "word of God," in the light of which our faith, according to St. Paul, was to be "liberated from all the traditions and figments of men, since faith, as he said, is by hearing, and hearing through the word of God."

In contrast with the task they had received from the Lord, however, popes and bishops have done the opposite of what was expected of them. They have behaved as though power was their own, as though it could properly be used for themselves. As Calvin says, they have wanted "our faith to stand and fall according to their will."[17] These words are presumably an echo of Luther's frequent insistence that justification by faith constitutes the heart of the gospel,[18] which led later Lutherans to call justification the *articulus stantis et cadentis ecclesiae,* the one article on which the Church stands and falls. In other words, it is the one article that is absolutely essential to the very existence of the Church. In Calvin's eyes the bishops have betrayed the gospel by restricting the liberty of Christian consciences, and have betrayed Christ himself by substituting their authority for his. In these pages of the *Institutio* Calvin confirms what he has written about the bishops and the pope in his letters to Roussel and Duchemin, though his language is more moderate than when addressing his falling-away friends. It is, however, no less telling for being more subdued.

*   *   *

As to temporal authority, Calvin's basic conception was already explicit in the letter to François I with which he opened *Institutio*

15. *Opera Selecta,* vol. 1, p. 236.
16. *Opera Selecta,* vol. 1, p. 236.
17. . . . *suo arbitrio stare et cadere* . . . (p. 237).
18. Tavard, *Justification: An Ecumenical Study* (New York: Paulist Press, 1983), pp. 56-67.

christianae religionis. In this letter Calvin fully acknowledged the royal authority in its realm, and he assured the king: "Moreover, being now driven away from our homes, we do not cease to pray God for your prosperity and that of your reign."[19]

Since the last chapter of *Institutio christianae religionis* was not written in the kingdom of France, however, but in Basel, a free city of Switzerland that was run by several layers of magistracy, Calvin did not focus his reflection on imperial or royal power, but on the legal authority of magistrates and on the laws that were to regulate the city. Yet this could not change his dominant point of view, already expressed in *Psychopannychia,* in regard to the primacy of the spiritual in relation to all levels of political power — local, regional, regal, imperial, and even, insofar as Calvin, safe in a Swiss canton, was also concerned about spiritual liberty over the border in the kingdom of France, international. Whether imperial, royal, or magisterial, temporal power, understood in a Christian perspective, has only one purpose. It has the twofold task of assuring the peaceful coexistence of the inhabitants and of protecting true religion. And since Calvin could not find true religion in the papal regimen of the Church, he held that the magistracy of a free city, like the king in his domains, has the duty to reform the Church according to the gospel — as already suggested in Martin Luther's *Appeal to the Nobility of the German Nation* in 1518.

It was in this spirit that after speaking about Christian liberty in Chapter VI Calvin presented what he identified as the three components of the temporal order: the magistracy, the laws, and the people.[20] While he systematically avoided subordinating the temporal sword of the magistracy to a spiritual sword held by the local ministers of the gospel, he more than anyone else in his time taught that magistrates must not attempt to interpret the gospel, but should strive to apply it as it is expounded by the Church's ministry. It was admittedly an ideal situation that Calvin envisioned. He knew as

19. "Epître au Roi," *L'Institution de la religion chrétienne,* vol. 1 (Geneva: Labor et Fides, 1955), p. xxxvii. The two introductory epistles of the first *Institutio* were kept in all subsequent versions.

20. Respectively, *Opera Selecta,* vol. 1, pp. 258-67, 367-70, 270-80.

well as anyone that magistrates, legislators, and the people themselves are subject to human failures, sin, and ignorance, and are constantly tempted to substitute the idolatry of their own conceptions to the injunctions of the gospel. He was nonetheless convinced that there can and should be a *christiana politia*,[21] drawn from the Scriptures, that would ensure good order, peace, and justice, and also promote the faith, while respecting the liberty of the Christian soul. In the ensuing state of Christian society the attitude of the people to their leaders should be one of *reverentiae atque adeo pietatis affectus*, "a position of reverence and even piety,"[22] *pietas* being, in the Latin that was Calvin's theological language, the attitude of mutual love and respect that unites parents and children. The ideal of the Christian city is no other than that of a family that is closely united in the true faith.

It would therefore be a grave misreading of Calvin's doctrine to identify his conception of Christian liberty with the philosophy of the freedom of consciences that was shaped later, through the Enlightenment, the French Revolution, and the liberal thought of the nineteenth century. The liberty that sets the parameters of administrative responsibility, ecclesiastical authority, and political power is not that of eighteenth-century deist philosophers, who assumed, as it was written in 1776 in the American Declaration of Independence, that "all men are created equal." Nor is it the *liberté de l'homme et du citoyen* proclaimed in 1793 by the Constituant Assembly of the French Revolution. It is rather the liberty of a Christian soul, understood in the Augustinian perspective, in which *liberum arbitrium* is not *libertas*. Liberty is not the right to choose among alternatives. It

21. *Opera Selecta*, vol. 1, p. 267.
22. *Opera Selecta*, vol. 1, p. 277. It is intriguing to note that at the fourth session of the Council of Trent (1545) *pietatis affectus* will describe the Catholic attitude to Scripture and the apostolic traditions, which should be venerated *pari pietatis affectu*, "with an equal position of piety." Since the word *pietas* expresses the basic relationship that should unite parents and children, Calvin's use of the term at this point implies that magistrates and people ought to be together like parents and children. The context of the council gave the term a more metaphorical meaning: The faithful read the Scriptures and apostolic traditions like the writings of their parents in the faith.

is the gift of God, which has been earned by Christ for all the elect, and is given to them in the Holy Spirit when they are justified by faith. *Libertas christiana* is a spiritual gift. Because it is spiritual and it directly affects the soul, all social institutions gain their authentic standing from their relation to it — the institution of the Church, as the visible "mother of the faithful," by teaching them the gospel and nurturing their faith, and the institutions of the City and the Nation by ensuring that the Christian faithful enjoy the proper conditions of justice and peace.

Our survey of Chapter VI of the *Institutio* of 1536 can end at this point. It has shown that Calvin's view of authority in both Church and Nation is indebted to his conception of the predominance of the spiritual element in the human person, a conception that he already had formulated forcefully in *Psychopannychia*. Because the human *anima* is spiritual it is also immortal. Because it is spiritual and immortal it is in principle not subject to anything that is material and mortal, even though the human condition requires that the soul accommodate itself to the material conditioning of its bodily existence and in so doing respect the limitations that human coexistence in society imposes on the autonomy of each person. There is in this a clear continuity between *Psychopannychia* and the last chapter of *Institutio christianae religionis*.

The original sin of humanity subjected the soul in the present life to the power of Satan. The liberation of the soul from sin and Satan, and its restoration to the full scope of immortality, came through the birth, life, death, and rising of Jesus Christ — the Word made flesh. Only in Christ and by God's grace has the spiritual state of the soul been fully restored. No human power or authority, therefore, whether it be in the Church or in society, may lawfully restrict the *libertas* that God has entrusted through Christ to all those who believe the gospel, whatever the conditions of political freedom or unfreedom may happen to be in a given time and place.

X

The Main Theses of Calvin's Theology

I n August 1539, when Calvin was acting as pastor to French-speaking Protestants in Strasbourg, the magistrates of the city of Bern invited him to respond to a letter that their colleagues in Geneva had received the previous March, from Cardinal Jacopo Sadoleto (1477-1547), Bishop of Carpentras.

Sadoleto was a distinguished humanist. He had written on education in 1530 and commented on Paul's Epistle to the Romans in 1535. A member of the commission that was responsible for the *Consilium de emendenda ecclesia* in 1537, he both understood the doctrine of justification by faith and was eager to promote the reform of the Church. He was, however, opposed to breaking with the traditional institutions and the see of Rome. Carpentras was not too distant from Geneva, and after Calvin had been expelled from it by the magistracy Sadoleto wrote to the city, urging it to return to the Roman fold, and assuring its citizens that one could obtain the "blessing of complete and perpetual salvation by faith alone in God and in Jesus Christ,"[1] and at the same time remain in the one and unchanging Catholic Church,

---

1. I quote from the English translation by Henry Beveridge (*Tracts and Treatises*, vol. 1, 1844; Grand Rapids: Eerdmans, 1958) as reprinted in John C. Olin, ed., *A Reformation Debate* (New York: Harper, 1966), p. 35; the following quote is from p. 41.

which in all parts, as well as at the present time in every region of the world, united and consenting in Christ, has been always and everywhere directed by the one Spirit of Christ; in which Church no dissension can exist; for all its parts are connected with each other, and breathe together.

As presented by the cardinal, the choice was between the "general consent" of the Catholic Church, united "for more than fifteen hundred years," or, if one insists on strict documentation, "for more than thirteen hundred years," and "innovations introduced within these twenty-five years by crafty or, as they think themselves, acute men; but men certainly who are not themselves the Catholic Church."[2] Sadoleto correctly perceived that the reformers felt "a just indignation" when beholding "the manners of ecclesiastics almost everywhere corrupt."[3] But he did not consider this a sufficient reason to break the unanimity of faith and charity that is of the essence of the Church.

At two points in his argumentation the Bishop of Carpentras introduced consideration of the human soul. First, as he pointed out, the very soul of all believers is involved in the choice that is now placed before them. It was for the sake of the human soul that the Word of God became incarnate: "This possession, therefore, so large, so dear, so precious to everyman as is his soul, we must use every effort to retain. . . . This one good of a preserved soul is not only ours, but we ourselves are that very good."[4] Second, Sadoleto was aware of those who insinuate that "the soul perishes along with the body."[5] If, however, the soul is indeed immortal, the death of the body is not able to break the communion that ties together the dead and the living, the souls in heaven and the souls they have known and loved on earth.

Whether one should read this as a direct allusion to *Psychopannychia* is of course a moot question. The cardinal's letter was not addressed to Calvin, but to the magistrates and citizens of Geneva,

2. Olin, *Reformation Debate,* pp. 40-41.
3. Olin, *Reformation Debate,* p. 44.
4. Olin, *Reformation Debate,* pp. 34-35.
5. Olin, *Reformation Debate,* p. 41.

where Calvin was no longer, and not yet again, *persona grata*. But Sadoleto may well have been acquainted with Calvin's contribution to the debate on the immortality of the soul.

After presenting a justification of his own ministry as a doctor and pastor who has been called by God, Calvin focuses his response on two major questions: What is the "purer teaching of the Gospel?" What is the "better form of the Church?"[6] We need not examine the details of his remarkable answer to Sadoleto. One point, however, ought to be lifted up. Calvin explains that the Church and people of Geneva are assailed by "two sects," which outwardly have nothing in common, "the Pope and the Anabaptists," who, however, use the same weapon, for in claiming to follow the Spirit they both neglect the Word of God.[7] In regard to the intercession of the saints, Calvin agrees that the saints do pray for the Church, though this is no reason to pray to them. As to the immortality of the soul, however, he not only objects to being accused of believing "that the soul perishes with the body," but he also retorts:

> That philosophy we leave to your Popes and College of Cardinals, by whom it was for so many years most faithfully cultivated, and ceases not to be cultivated to the present day.[8]

This is a much more forceful allusion to Pope John XXII than was featured in *Psychopannychia*. Calvin now feels a hostility to the papacy and to the entire Roman system of teaching and government that he did not yet share when he refuted the aberrant doctrine of a few anabaptists, though I fail to see what makes him add that this erroneous teaching on the soul is still cultivated by popes and cardinals.

* * *

Investigation of *Psychopannychia* and of its influence raises a further question about possible traces of it in the later theological writings

6. Olin, *Reformation Debate*, p. 57.
7. Olin, *Reformation Debate*, p. 61.
8. Olin, *Reformation Debate*, p. 72.

of the French reformer. In the limits of the present work, however, such an inquiry cannot be exhaustive. It would be hardly feasible to survey the successive versions of *Institutio christianae religionis,* Calvin's extensive biblical commentaries, along with his numerous sermons, minor writings, and letters. Our research will be restricted to the main theses of Calvin's systematic theology, as these are illustrated through the final edition of *Institutio.* Since, however, the consideration of the soul is carried out in light of Calvin's methodological approach to the knowledge of God as outlined in the opening pages of *Institutio christianae religionis,* we will begin with the basic principle of Calvin's method, from where we will go on to look at his treatment of the soul.

Our first chapter already indicated that the beginning of the *Institutio* of 1536 is indebted to the insight that Augustine had put in the form of a wish and a prayer in the *Soliloquies: Noverim me, noverim te.*[9] Should I know myself, Augustine had written shortly after his conversion, I would know you. Self-knowledge implies an awareness of God who creates me and is present in me. A certain self-knowledge is obtained by close attention to one's interior life. Calvin's reflection on immortality in *Psychopannychia* already made this clear. His reading of Augustine gave him the further insight that self-knowledge and God-knowledge are inseparable, even if, as Calvin remarked in the final *Institutio,* it is not easy "to discern which comes first." Each one in fact leads to the other, so that one may speak of a truly dialectical relationship between self-knowledge and God-knowledge. No one, as Calvin states,

> can contemplate the self without immediately turning attention to God from whom one lives and has strength, for it is not unclear that the gifts where all our dignity resides are by no means from us: even our forces and firmness are nothing else than a subsisting in and a leaning upon God.[10]

9. See above, chapter 1, pp. 4-7.
10. *Inst.* of 1559/61, I, ch. 1, n. 1. I translate the French text. The Latin is more strongly reminiscent of the vocabulary of mysticism: . . . *se nemo aspicere potest quin ad Deum, in quo vivit et movetur, intuitum sensus suos protinus convertat.* . . .

In a first movement of self-knowledge our little drops of good accumulate, forming rivulets from which we can reach back to their source in God. The littleness of our own gifts — mere drops — suggests its opposite, the immensity and the perfection of God, thus convincing us, in a second movement, of ignorance, vanity, and perversity.

The self-knowledge that is not based on God-knowledge can only be an illusion. "It is manifest that man never reaches to pure self-knowledge until he has contemplated the face of God and has from this vision descended to look at self."[11] What Calvin has in mind here is neither a mere rational conviction of the existence of God nor an intellectual construct regarding God's nature and attributes. Potentially given in faith, it comes to life and increases through further gifts of the Spirit, when *Veritas intus loquitur sine strepitu verborum*[12] ("the Truth speaks interiorly without the noise of words"). This saying of *De Imitatione Christi* expressed a commonplace of late medieval mysticism.

As Luther had identified justification by faith as the criterion of everything that is truly Christian, so Calvin, drawing from a deeper level in the tradition of the medieval mystics, found the standard of Christian authenticity in the contemplation of the face of God, *aspiciendo faciem Dei,* in the inner life of the soul that is being overwhelmed by God's gifts. As he did so, Calvin took his stand squarely in the Bonaventurian version of the Augustinian tradition, for which spiritual experience is essential to theological reflection. He did so, however, while steering clear of the excesses of the catabaptists, the *fanatici* of his later works. It was his originality among the great Reformers to make the experience of the Spirit the rule and model of the interpretation of Scripture, of Christian thought, practice, and Church order.

In practice the dialectic between self-knowledge — *noverim me* — and God-knowledge — *noverim te* — is evidently an unequal dialectic, as appears in the conclusion of the first chapter of the final *Institutio:* "Nonetheless, although there is a mutual link between the knowl-

11. "Vision" renders the French *regard* and the Latin *intuitum.*
12. *Imit.,* III, ch. 2, title.

172

edge of God and of ourselves, and each is related to the other, the order of good teaching demands that in the first place we treat the knowledge of God so as to reach the second point."[13] All subsequent chapters of the first part are precisely devoted to explaining the knowledge of God.

The "order of good teaching" that Calvin intends to follow cannot be reduced to a mere matter of pedagogy. A pedagogical point of view could indeed favor starting where the people are, in their awareness of themselves, their existence, their dreams, their shortcomings. Precisely, the first degree of self-knowledge leads to seeking God as the source of the good we have. It does not imply self-congratulation, for it unveils the evil in one's heart: "As one finds in man a world of all miseries since we have been stripped of the ornaments of heaven, our nakedness uncovers with great shame such a heap of filth that we are entirely confounded."[14] This discovery should act as an incentive to find God: "It is necessary that our conscience impress us with our evil in order at least to come near to some knowledge of God." The point is founded, as Calvin's anthropology will show, on the doctrine of sin and the depravity of human nature after the fall.

*   *   *

Given Calvin's methodology and his ensuing point of departure, the section of *Institutio* that best evokes the topic of *Psychopannychia* is in Chapter 15 of Book I, where the doctrine of creation includes a reflection on the human soul. It is certainly not accidental that the very opening of this chapter recalls the principle of Augustine's *Soliloquies*: "We cannot know God clearly and in a precise sense unless the knowledge of ourselves is joined to it, and as it were reciprocal."[15] Self-knowledge is twofold, in keeping with the two early states of humankind: "in our first origin," and after the fall. The original state of humanity points by contrast to the post-lapsarian depravity of the offspring of Adam. In this state human beings received "two parts, that

13. *Inst.* of 1559/61, I, ch. 1, n. 3.
14. *Inst.* of 1559/61, I, ch. 1, n. 1.
15. *Inst.* of 1559/61, I, ch. 15, n. 1.

is, the body and the soul. . . . By this word, soul, I understand the immortal spirit, though created, which is the nobler part."[16] Scripture, Calvin explains, makes a distinction between spirit and soul when it compares the two terms, but when the word appears by itself it simply designates the soul. Unlike the opponents of Calvin in *Psychopannychia*, the chief adversaries he now has in mind are the philosophers who maintain that the soul is only the body's breath or strength and "has no essence." This opinion is promptly refuted:

> Conscience, which by discerning between good and evil responds to God's judgment, is an infallible indication that the spirit is immortal. For how could an essenceless motion enter God's judgment and inspire in us fear of the condemnation we have deserved? For the body will not fear a spiritual punishment, and such a suffering pertains only to the soul; hence it follows that it is not without an essence.[17]

Further, the knowledge of God shows that the souls, "since they go beyond the world, are immortal, for a vanishing inspiration would not reach the fountain of life." The virtues themselves that adorn the soul point to "some I-know-not-what that is divine, and is imprinted in them." Even the sleep of the body shows up the spirituality and immortality of the soul, since we have dreams "of what has never happened" and others that announce the future, feats that would be impossible if the soul was bound to the limitations of the material world.

There are two main differences between this treatment of the soul and what was said so much earlier in *Psychopannychia*. In the first place, Calvin does not now refer to the catabaptists and the theory of the soul's sleep or death after the present life. Calvin's adversaries in this chapter are proponents of extravagant theories on the image of God, namely, some followers of John Duns Scotus's view of the incarnation if Adam had not sinned, though Scotus himself is not named. For them it is Jesus in his soul and body who is the image of

16. *Inst.* of 1559/61, I, ch. 15, n. 2.
17. *Inst.* of 1559/61, I, ch. 15, n. 2.

God.[18] Another adversary is the reformer Osiander, for whom it is not the human soul, but the whole of Adam, that is the image of God. Others still are Michael Servetus and the Manichaeans with their view that the soul itself shares the divine essence,[19] and Aristotle for his idea that the will has priority over the intellect among the faculties of the soul.[20] Calvin's main adversaries now go astray on the origin rather than on the destiny of the soul. In the second place, the argument in favor of the immortality of the soul is philosophical rather than, as was the case in *Psychopannychia,* biblical. While it leads to the biblical teaching that the soul is made in the image and likeness of God, it is based on the soul's capacity to think and to desire beyond the confines of the material world. It has similarities to the argument of Thomas Aquinas on the infinite desire to know.[21]

Thus the considerations on the soul in *Psychopannychia* and in *Institutio christianae religionis* are inspired by distinct concerns that were related to the theological situation in reforming circles at the time of writing. The differing horizons of the two works, however, should not suggest that Calvin no longer cared for his early defense of the immortality of the soul when he put forward the final form of his systematic theology. In the first place, immortality is still presented as being integral to the nature of the soul: "By this word, soul, I understand the immortal spirit, though created. . . ." In the second place, the publication of the Latin *Institutio* in 1559 followed shortly the appearance on the market of the French translation of Calvin's first work, *Psychopannychie,* in 1558. While this translation was not made by Calvin, it certainly would not have been published, in Geneva itself, without his explicit approval.

* * *

It was one of the dramas of Calvin's early years in Geneva that some adherents of the Reformation threw doubt on the orthodoxy of his

18. *Inst.* of 1559/61, I, ch. 15, n. 3.
19. *Inst.* of 1559/61, I, ch. 15, n. 5.
20. *Inst.* of 1559/61, I, ch. 15, n. 7.
21. Tavard, "Reflections on the 'Unrestricted Desire to Know,'" *The Josephinum Journal of Theology* 4, no. 1 (1985): 3-18.

trinitarian doctrine. Shortly after the text of *Vivere apud Christum* . . . was turned over to its publishers, Calvin was denounced at the disputation of Lausanne, in October 1536, as being more Arian than trinitarian. While reformed ministers from Bern and Neuchâtel, and three representatives of Geneva — Farel, Calvin, and the less prominent Couraud — were disputing with defenders of the old Church, the Genevans were taken to task for their doctrines by Pierre Caroli (c. 1480–c. 1550). The debate with the defenders of the Catholic system took place in the cathedral. The followers of the Reformation, however, also caucused in the Franciscan church. As they did so Caroli openly accused the three Genevan ministers of Arianism. As told in an account[22] published in 1545, presumably under Calvin's inspiration, Caroli attacked the Genevans "on the question of the nature of God and the distinction of Persons in God." His mannerisms made him proclaim the creeds of Nicaea and of Athanasius in an extravagant way at which everyone laughed. Calvin reacted with passion, questioning Caroli's belief in God, accusing him of having no more faith than a dog or a pig.

Caroli's accusation rested in part on his ignorance of the still unpublished dissertation on the immortality of the soul, in which, as our chapter 3 pointed out, the doctrine of the Trinity was clearly affirmed.[23] The ensuing polemic lasted several months, and somehow, in spite of Calvin's frequent and perfectly orthodox trinitarian formulas, Caroli's accusation lingered for a long time. Several of Calvin's interpreters have been at pain to show that his doctrine of God was indeed trinitarian even before his explicit treatment of the Trinity in the last version of *Institutio religionis christianae*. In subsequent history Calvinist theology has been strongly trinitarian. A striking confirmation of this is the fact that the hostility of William

22. Jean-François Gounelle, *Défense de Guillaume Farel et de ses collègues contre les calomnies du théologastre Pierre Caroli par Nicolas Des Gallars* (Paris: Presses Universitaires de France, 1994). The text has been attributed to Calvin, but his authorship is unlikely.

23. See above, ch. 3, p. 64, and footnotes 66-68. The non-polemical language of the trinitarian passage of *Psychopannychia* (Zimmerli, pp. 46-47) evidently shows that the reference to the Trinity was not added in order to counter Caroli's critique; it was there before the polemic started.

Channing (1780-1842) to Calvinism lay at the origin of American Unitarianism.

The doctrine of the Trinity was in fact closely related to the opening lines of *Institutio*. For as Calvin, in his first chapter, outlines the movement by which contemplation of the face of God brings about a higher degree of self-knowledge, his point of departure is strictly theological. It has its source in the conviction that God is three Persons, for the "contemplation of the face of God" without which no one obtains a pure knowledge of self is no other than the trinitarian experience that pertains to the life of faith. The "face of God" is the face of the Father, which is known to the faithful through Christ, the Word made flesh, while the Third Person, the Holy Spirit, enables them to recognize and contemplate it.

Other traces of *Psychopannychia* persisted in Calvin's mature trinitarian theology. The originality of his presentation of trinitarian doctrine emerges from his understanding of the notion of "person" in God. This had been a point of debate in medieval speculation. The stream of thought that originated in the writings of Boethius and was chiefly represented by Thomas Aquinas understood personhood as "a distinct subsistence in a rational nature." A person is that entity which is endowed with reason and subsists in itself. On the whole, reflection on the dogma of the Trinity has mostly followed this line of approach.

Another stream of thought, however, that goes back to Richard of St. Victor in the twelfth century, and was chiefly emphasized by John Duns Scotus at the end of the thirteenth, understood personhood as, seen negatively, the incommunicability, or, positively, the uniqueness, of a spiritual or rational being. A person is that spirit which is itself and no other. Personhood belongs to the order of existence rather than of subsistence. In the God of the Christian revelation it designates a dimension of divinity that is so unique that it cannot be communicated and shared. That there are in God three such dimensions is at the core of the revelation of Christ. *Abba*, the Father of the *Logos* incarnate, is neither the Son nor the Spirit, and vice versa twice repeated. The Father is known to believers in a glass, darkly, through the further revelation of the filiation of the Second Person and the procession of the Third.

The *Institutio* of 1559 would seem to join the two approaches. Starting with the Greek term *hypostasis* used in Hebrews 1:3, Calvin explains, in the Latin version: "There is no doubt that he [the Apostle] designates some subsistence in which he [the Father] differs from the Son."[24] This is further clarified with the remark: "Person I call a subsistence in the essence of God, which, related to the others, is distinguished by an incommunicable property."[25] The French version of 1561, however, introduces a remarkably new element that points in a complementary direction as it explains the philosophical term "subsistence" by reference to the Christian experience of the presence of God in the soul: "This word [hypostasis] implies a subsistence residing in one God." And again, more explicitly: "I call Person a residence in the essence of God, which, being related to the others, is distinct from them by virtue of an incommunicable property."

In other words, Calvin is not satisfied with the French word, *subsistance,* as obviously equivalent to the Latin, *subsistentia.* Indeed, the term is philosophical, and its use in the Latin theology of the Trinity is backed up by a long tradition that is likely to be familiar to the readers of Calvin's Latin works. Many readers of the French *Institution,* however, may not be so well acquainted with medieval scholasticism. For their sake Calvin explains subsistence by the totally different term, *residence,* that is evidently borrowed from the well-documented spiritual experience of sensing God "indwelling" in the Christian soul. This indwelling is the fulfillment of the promise of Jesus that is made in the Gospel of John: "If someone loves me, he will keep my word, and the Father will love him, and we will come to him and make a dwelling in him" (John 14:23).

In the commentary of the Johannine Gospel that he published in January of 1553, Calvin translated the verse as: . . . *Et nous viendrons à lui, et ferons demeure en lui.*[26] *Faire demeure,* "to live in, to inhabit," refers to the profound reality that is the source of the experience, and that is believed before it can be sensed: The three Persons dwell in

24. *Inst.* of 1559/61, I, ch. 13, n. 2.

25. *Personam voco subsistentiam in Dei essentia quae, ad alias relata, proprietate incommunicabili distinguitur* (I, ch. 13, n. 6).

26. Jean Calvin, *Commentaires sur le nouveau testament. Evangile selon saint Jean* (Geneva: Labor et Fides, 1968), p. 406.

the faithful soul. The commentary, as it saw the Christian believers in the perspective of obedience to God and Christ, explained that the passage refers to their filiation as children of God by adoption. It also specified that as a result of this indwelling "the faithful must be persuaded with certainty that the obedience they practice toward the Gospel is pleasing to God," and that they should "expect from him new increases of his gifts."

Because he was above all eager to guide the people in the witness of a Christian life, Calvin gave his biblical commentaries a moral orientation that has been more effectively echoed in later Calvinistic theology than the mystical background of his trinitarian perspective. Nonetheless, the indwelling of the three Persons in the soul was the model he followed when he explained the Father, the Son, and the Spirit as three mutual indwellings in the divine *ousia*. Each Person is a specific indwelling, a residence, in this essence of God. "But as it [*la Parole*, the Word] can have been in God only as residing in the Father, this shows the subsistence of which we speak, which, though it is joined with the essence by an inseparable link, nonetheless has a special mark by which to be different from it."[27] The divine Word subsists and dwells in God the Father.

Undoubtedly, Calvin could well have arrived at this understanding of the divine Persons without his early interest in the immortality of the soul. It remains that the writing of *Psychopannychia* had turned his theological perspective in the direction of the soul's interiority, exactly in that inner dimension of humanity — Augustine's "intimiority"[28] — in which Christian faith and experience have located the indwelling of Three Persons.

*   *   *

Closely related to Calvin's trinitarian theology is the christological point of view that came to be called the *extra Calvinisticum*. This expression was forged by Lutherans during discussions, in the second half of the sixteenth century, of the traditional question of the

---

27. *Inst.* of 1559/61, I, ch. 13, n. 6.
28. See above, chapter VII, note 40.

"communication of idioms," the sharing of divine and human qualities between the two natures of the *Logos* incarnate. In the course of these discussions the Lutheran Martin Chemnitz (1522-1586) carefully distinguished between three sub-questions, which correspond to three ways of speaking of Christ.[29] In the *genus idiomatisticum* one presents the qualities of the two natures as belonging to the divine Person of the Word. In *genus apotelesmaticum* the qualities and works of the Person are attributed to either of the two natures. In the *genus majestaticum,* some of the attributes of divinity are predicated of the human nature. The first two modes raised no special difficulty; the third proved to be more contentious: Is it only a form of speech, or also a description of the reality and experience of the divine Savior?

While Lutherans were divided in their opinions Calvinists looked for an answer in the works of Calvin, where they found the operative principle that while the humanity of Jesus is entirely dependent on the divinity, the divinity is not dependent on the humanity.[30] The divine *Logos* retains his total integrity as the Second Person of God even as he takes flesh of the Virgin Mary, lives, dies, and rises again in Palestine, and in his risen humanity now sits at the right hand of the Father. Incarnate, he is necessarily also *extra carnem.*[31] His humanity is inseparably associated to his divinity as

29. *De duabus naturis in Christo,* 1571. This was written against the "cryptocalvinists" of Saxony, who rejected all *communicatio idiomatum.*

30. The elucidation of the *extra calvinisticum* has been a minefield in Calvin studies. The most thorough treatment is by E. David Willis: *Calvin's Catholic Christology: The Function of the So-called Extra Calvinisticum in Calvin's Theology* (Leiden: E. J. Brill, 1966). The question seems to have originated in the Colloquy of Maulbronn (1564); it was discussed extensively at the Colloquy of Montbéliard (1586). See Willis, pp. 8-25; Jill Raitt, *The Colloquy of Montbéliard: Religion and Politics in the Sixteenth Century* (New York: Oxford University Press, 1993), pp. 110-26.

31. In the context of the Sacramentarian controversies the alternative to the *extra* was the paradoxical doctrine of the ubiquity of the body of Christ, to which Luther had been led in his struggle with Zwingli's purely symbolic understanding of *Hoc est corpus meum.* Although this became a common thesis in Lutheran orthodoxy, it is far from certain that Luther intended it to be taken literally. Ubiquity can be understood locally (the body of Christ is in every place) or sacramentally (the body of Christ is wherever the sacrament is offered to the faithful). This second reading is germane to Thomas Aquinas's presentation of the sacramental presence.

180

the Word, who has an eternal essence and existence regardless of his temporal experience as Jesus of Nazareth. As he shares the divine immensity with the Father and the Spirit, the Word is outside — *extra* — his flesh no less than in it.

This christological and trinitarian statement evokes a principle of the theology of creation: *Finitum non capax infiniti*. That is, nothing and no one that is created is able to contain the Infinite, infinity being one of the essential attributes of the divine Being. In Calvin's christology this principle applies also to the hypostatic union, for reasons, however, that are more soteriological than philosophical. The Redeemer is first of all, as God, the Creator. Knowledge of the Redeemer implies knowledge of the Creator. Through the humanity of Christ the believers are saved by the powers of his divinity, which are infinitely beyond the merely human, however holy the humanity of the Word made flesh. The Redeemer is the divine Word in his divinity and not only in his humanity. It follows that, in spite of the Word incarnate being the only Savior and Mediator, the prayer, adoration, and contemplation of the elect place them face to face with the totality of the divine Essence, which is equally present in the three Persons. As the scholastics put it, God indeed dwells in the believing soul in totality. This interior presence, however, neither limits nor exhausts the divine immensity: God is in the creature *totus sed not totaliter*.

That this approach to the incarnation relates to *Psychopannychia* and its discussion of the immortality of the soul is not immediately evident. Nonetheless, the *extra Calvinisticum* identifies the presence of Christ in the believing soul as the indwelling of his divinity as eternal Word along with his humanity, and this is not due to the "concomittance" of the two natures, as in the scholastic understanding of the eucharist. It is because the soul is spiritual and immortal by creation, that by grace it can be united to the divinity of Christ no less than to his humanity. Given by the Father through the Word, enlivened by the Spirit, faith has indeed been earned for all believers by Christ in his human nature, and it has been given to them for his sake alone. As it is alive in their soul, however, faith relates them, through the mediation of the human nature of Jesus, to the divine nature *extra carnem*, which has also made its dwelling in

181

them. The divine presence opens a perspective on the soul's *unio mystica* with the divinity as such. This point, which is clearly related to the mystical leanings of *devotio moderna,* had already been made possible by the argumentation of *Psychopannychia* against the catabaptists.

*   *   *

The doctrine of the Church that is formulated in *Institutio christianae religionis* is based on the tradition of *Ecclesia mater,* which goes back to patristic theology. "It is not licit to separate these two things that God had joined together, that the Church be the mother of all those whose Father he is."[32] In the translation of the creed, Calvin opts for the formula, "I believe the Church," rather than "in the Church."[33] The Church's foundation is the eternal and secret election of its members by God, so that the Church is really known to God alone. There is only one Church, which is "the body of Christ," whose members "live by one and the same faith, hope, and charity by the Spirit of God." This is the "Catholic or universal Church." This invisible Church, however, is also the "communion of the saints," and as such it is visible, for "the saints are so gathered in the society of Christ that they must mutually exchange all the gifts that are given them by God." There is indeed a diversity of spiritual gifts, yet only "one heart and soul in the multitude of believers" (Acts 4:32), "one body and one spirit" (Eph. 4:4). God is "their common Father," and Christ "the only head of all of them." This visible Church, the gathering of the saints on earth, is the true mother of the faithful,

> inasmuch as there is no entry to the permanent life unless we are conceived in this mother's belly, and she begets us, she feeds us from her breasts, and finally she keeps us in her guidance and governance until, freed from this mortal flesh, we are similar to the Angels.[34]

32. *Inst.* of 1559/61, IV, ch. 1, n. 1.
33. *Inst.* of 1559/61, IV, ch. 1, n. 2.
34. *Inst.* of 1559/61, IV, ch. 1, n. 4.

Scripture, Calvin remarks, speaks of the Church in these two ways. The Church "as it is in reality" includes only those who "by the grace of adoption are children of God, and by the sanctification of his Spirit are true members of Jesus Christ." Such are "not only the saints who inhabit the earth, but all the elect since the beginning of the world."[35] Scripture also speaks of the Church as the multitude of people in diverse regions of the world "which professes to honor God and Jesus Christ, which practices baptism to witness to its faith, which, in participating in the Supper affirms unity in doctrine and in charity, is faithful to the word of God. . . ." This visible Church is a mixed body, for it includes "hypocrites mixed with the good." Nonetheless, "just as it is necessary for us to believe the Church that is invisible and known to God alone, it is also commanded to us to hold this visible Church in honor and to remain in its communion."

Admittedly, the mature Calvin's description of this Church as it is visible on earth and his emphasis on its role as mother of the faithful have no direct connection with his early interest in the immortality of the soul. There is, however, a clear parallelism between the primacy of the spiritual and immortal soul over the body which is its abode on earth, and that of the invisible Church over the visible. Calvin's early view of the ties between the soul and the body provided him with a pattern that remained in his mind, ready to be applied in other areas of theology. Calvin undoubtedly drew upon it in his theology of the Church, invisible and visible.

*   *   *

Closely related to his ecclesiology is Calvin's controversial view of election and predestination. God knows his own because he has chosen them from all eternity. Indeed, the theory of double predestination that had been put forward by Augustine in the collective perspective of humankind becoming a *massa perditionis* through original sin had been generally abandoned in medieval theology. The form in which it had been revived in the ninth century by the

---

35. *Inst.* of 1559/61, IV, ch. 1, n. 7.

Saxon monk Gottschalk had been vehemently opposed by Raban Maurus (776-856), Archbishop of Mainz, and Hincmar (d. 882), Archbishop of Reims. It had been condemned in 853 by the Synod of Quierzy, which was soon contradicted by the Synod of Valence (855). Although the most learned theologian of the period, John Scot Eriugena, who wrote in the light of Greek theology, had taken his distances from both sides, the ensuing controversy between the northern bishops and the southern bishops of Gaul ended in a compromise at the Synod of Tusey, in October 860. The bishops agreed, first, that there exists a predestination of the elect, and, second, that one cannot speak of a predestination of the damned!

Broadly speaking, this compromise had held through the scholastic reflection on the problem of predestination. Thus, when Thomas Aquinas discussed the nature of prophecy he treated predestination as a variant form of foreknowledge, which could itself be understood as a subdivision of prophecy. God's foreknowledge, *praescientia*, knows in advance the destiny of both the good and the evil, while predestination refers only to the good because it is the knowledge of what God himself does, and the evil of the damned is done by themselves, not by God.[36]

Calvin, however, did not accept this compromise, and his considerations on divine Providence brought back the theology of double predestination.[37] In fact, he formulated this doctrine early in his career. It appeared implicitly in the treatment of "election" or "eternal Providence" in the first *Institutio*, where, drawing on Romans 8:30, Calvin presented justification and glorification as the fulfillment of the "eternal election" of the saints "before they were born."[38] More explicitly though briefly, predestination was prominent in the *Brève instruction chrétienne* (1536) that was to serve as the model of Calvin's catechisms. The Word of God "calls all men" but is not equally received by all. Many, who are "blinded and hardened by incredulity, disdain it," while the faithful receive it with joy: "Being given to

---

36. *Summa theologiae*, II, 2, q.174, a.1.

37. *Inst.* of 1559/61, I, ch. 18, and III, chs. 21-24; *Tractatus de aeterna praedestinatione Dei*, 1552 (CR VIII, pp. 249-366).

38. *Opera Selecta*, vol. 2, ch. 2, n. 21.

them they do not reject it; being called by it they follow it."[39] Why the difference? Calvin's answer is unambiguous:

> It is necessary to consider the great secret of the counsel of God. For the seed of the Word of God takes root and bears fruit only in those whom the Lord, through his eternal election, has predestined to be his children and the heirs of the heavenly Kingdom. To all others, whom God, before the constitution of the world, has rejected by the same counsel of God, the clear and evident preaching of the Truth cannot be other than a deadly smell that leads to death.

The reason for merciful election and just reprobation must be "left to be known by God alone. . . . For neither could the uncouthness of our spirit bear such great light nor could our smallness understand such great wisdom."[40]

These aspects of the question are fully elaborated in the last *Institutio*. Since election by God is not due to human merit, the predestination of the elect and also of the damned is a logical necessity. In spite of appearances it is also, and this seems to be Calvin's most personal contribution to the debate, a doctrine of consolation:

> This matter seems perplexing to many because they find no reason why God predestines the ones to salvation, the others to death. Now it appears by their reasoning that they themselves are confused by their lack of common sense and discretion. Moreover, in the darkness that frightens them we shall see how, not only useful this doctrine is, but also sweet and savory by the fruit it produces.[41]

What, then, is the sweet-tasting fruit of such a harsh doctrine? It is in the first place the conviction that God's gifts do not amount to a

---

39. Pierre Courthial, ed., *Brève instruction chrétienne* (Paris: Les Bergers et les Mages, 1957), part 1, ch. 1, p. 31.
40. *Brève instruction*, p. 32.
41. *Inst.* of 1559/61, III, ch. 21, n. 1.

185

salary for services rendered, but are pure graciousness on God's part. As a consequence it makes for a greater adoration of God and a more thorough self-abandonment to divine Providence, without any forethought or afterthought of merits and rewards. Calvin of course is aware of the objections. He formulates and refutes many of them.[42] Yet no objection can nullify the fact that predestination is clearly taught in Scripture, both in the Old Testament and in the New.[43]

Calvin formulates the doctrine without any compromise:

> We call predestination the eternal decision of God by which he has determined what he wants to do with each man. For he does not create them all in the same condition, but directs the ones to eternal life, the others to eternal damnation. Thus, according to the end for which a man is created, we say that he is predestined to death or to life.[44]

The silver edge of the dark cloud of predestination is that it has to be entirely compatible with God's justice. One must therefore maintain, however paradoxical it may seem, that those who have been predestined to damnation will be justly condemned and will therefore not find in themselves a reason to protest God's decision. God's sentence is "equitable" even when it also is "incomprehensible" to us.[45]

Predestination is a doctrine of holiness, for it urges the believer to surrender totally to God's will and glory even in the midst of an ignorance that is truly a learned ignorance: "Let us confess that the reprobate does not suffer anything that does not conform to God's just judgment. That the reason escapes us we must take with patience, and we must not refuse to be ignorant of something where God's wisdom shows its loftiness."[46] The conviction that "predestination, if it is properly reflected upon, should not trouble or shake

42. *Inst.* of 1559/61, III, ch. 21, nn. 2-4; ch. 22, nn. 8-10; ch. 23, nn. 1-13; ch. 24, nn. 15-16.

43. Old Testament: III, ch. 21, nn. 5-7; New Testament: ch. 22, nn. 1-7.

44. *Inst.* of 1559/61, III, ch. 21, n. 3.

45. *Inst.* of 1559/61, III, ch. 24, n. 14.

46. *Inst.* of 1559/61, III, ch. 24, n. 14.

the faith, but rather confirm it well"[47] implies a distinction between the "universal call" and the "special call" of God. The universal call comes from the outside. It "resides in the external preaching of the Gospel, by which the Savior called all humans to himself indifferently, even those to whom he presents it as smell of death and matter for grievous condemnation."[48] The special call, meanwhile, is addressed only to the faithful, "when, through the interior light of his Spirit, he ensures that the doctrine is rooted in their hearts." This special call, which alone is efficacious, resounds in the depths of the soul.

The pattern that appeared in *Psychopannychia* at the beginning of Calvin's theological career has been at work once more. The primacy of the soul over the body, which is manifest in its spirituality and immortality while the body decays and dies, is now put in terms of interiority and exteriority. The elect experience the Spirit's interior witness, to which they respond with joy through the testimony of their life; the reprobate hear no more than external calls from the prophets, the apostles, or the visible Church, and they do not respond in their heart.

Whatever hesitancies and outcries the doctrine of predestination occasioned in subsequent polemics, it was seen by the reformer as a source of consolation in the struggles of the present life. The ensuing conviction was to be the principle of a deep spirituality through the unselfish trust it should inspire in God's eternal wisdom. As early as 1536 Calvin had written: "One cannot find the eternal and immortal life anywhere but in God. Therefore the principal care and concern of our life must be to seek God and to hanker after God with all the affection of our heart, and to find rest nowhere but in God alone."[49] Standing in adoration before God alone is what should remain after debating the pros and cons of the doctrine of predestination. This was still the ultimate import of the doctrine in the final edition of *Institutio christianae religionis:* "Once one has brought in many arguments and debated back and forth, we must

47. *Inst.* of 1559/61, III, ch. 24, n. 9.
48. *Inst.* of 1559/61, III, ch. 24, n. 8.
49. *Brève instruction,* p. 32.

come to this conclusion, that we are ravished in astonishment with St. Paul. . . ."[50]

Predestination was not directly implied in the vindication of the immortality of the soul and in the polemic of *Psychopannychia* against the peculiar thesis of a few anabaptists. It nevertheless provides a paradoxical evidence of the lasting impact on Calvin's theological method and conclusions of the principle that had been highlighted in *Psychopannychia:* Since the soul is spiritual and immortal, its reality escapes the concerns and rules of earthly desires and reasonings. To the end of his life was Calvin faithful to the outlook of his first theological writing.

*   *   *

As he found himself at the same time having to give the tone and set the parameters of biblical exegesis, and building up the most impressive systematic theology of the sixteenth century, the mature Calvin got also more and more deeply involved in the politics of the canton of Geneva and in the encouragement and support of reformed communities in France. This would have given him little time for self-introspection and inspired no eagerness to review the historical basis and the genesis of his theological development, had he felt any taste for this. While he was forced by his poor health to pay a reluctant attention to the needs of his body, he was never inclined to study his soul for its own sake, to assess his ecclesial and theological achievements at the service of the gospel, or to trace the curve of his theological thought since the writing of *Psychopannychia*. Whatever the circumstances, and however assertive the tone of his theologizing, his personal experience of God and of Christ was not a matter to be shared with others, still less with adversaries.

The sobriety that Calvin advocated in all things may have been grounded in the native shyness of a retiring scholar. It was also in line with the medieval notion of *pietas,* a concept that was related to

---

50. *Inst.* of 1559/61, III, ch. 24, n. 16. Latin: *Porro ubi multa ultro citroque adducta fuerint, sit haec nobis clausula, ad tantam profunditatem cum Paulo expavescere* . . . (n. 17; nn. 15 and 16 of the Latin text become n. 15 in the French).

the proper relationships between child and parent, pupil and teacher, creature and Creator. The immortality of the soul had to be defended precisely as a matter of *pietas*. Since the immortal God has decided to be a Father to his creatures he has established a permanent and unceasing tie between his eternal being and their temporal, successive existence. This unbreakable link requires the creation to continue in immortality. Witnessing to the creaturely link in the eternal adoration of God is precisely the vocation of the immortal human soul. Calvin's whole theological system confirms his conclusions in *Psychopannychia*. And it is to a large extent indebted to this early foray into theology.

Conclusion

The investigation that nurtured the present book was started partly out of curiosity, because I was puzzled that Calvin's first theological writing should have dealt with such a peripheral, though important, question as the immortality of the soul; and partly out of disappointment, because the bilateral conversations between the Catholic Church and the Reformed churches did not seem to herald any form of breakthrough.

Regarding the first point, I have come to realize that Calvin's exploration of the question of immortality was largely the fruit of his participation in the humanist movement of the Renaissance, in which the nature of the soul had been a favored topic for a long time. When some reform-minded friends drew his attention to the strange teachings of a small group of anabaptists, it was not uncongenial for him to look into the matter. Comparing the central principle of *Psychopannychia* with the mature synthesis of *Institutio christianae religionis* shows that the contribution of Calvin's early reflection to his final system was far from negligible. Given the fact that the human *anima* is spiritual by creation, it follows that it is immortal; consequently all human questions will find their ultimate answer at the level of immortality, in the eternal kingdom of God to which the Christian faithful have access by faith through Jesus Christ, when the Spirit within them testifies to the truth.

This basic insight grew and bore fruit in Calvin's final writings, the major theses of which are easily related to the basic idea of *Psychopannychia*. As Calvin had learned from the late medieval tradition and *devotio moderna,* the *anima* is the locus of true Christianity, and the central importance of the Church — mother of the faithful — derives from its task of nurturing souls in the life of the Spirit. Everything in personal life and in the Church needs to be evaluated in light of the Spirit of Christ who is continuously active in the believing heart.

In the sixteenth century the contrast between the spiritual requirements of the soul and the institutional realities of the Church militant was too blatant to be ignored. Immediate total reform, or the planting of a seed of reform that would grow slowly over years and decades — this was the choice that Calvin faced, the same choice that would be faced in a twentieth-century context by the participants of Vatican Council II. If Sadoleto and others adjusted their hopes to the possibilities of a gradual evolution, Calvin opted for revolution. It was urgent to cut drastically into the corrupted limbs of the body. That this choice was rooted in the mystical trends of late medieval theology went mostly unnoticed; and it became irrelevant in the wars of religion and in the polemics that followed, in the course of which Calvin's Catholic adversaries were blinded to the fundamental catholicity of his thought.

Regarding the second point, those who today are eager to pursue an ecumenical dialogue between the Calvinist tradition and Catholic theology can learn something from the great reformer's first theological writing. Each side, adopting the style of the Groupe des Dombes, should ask what sort of a conversion it is called on to undergo in order to reach beyond the stage of controversy. As is illustrated in the recent dialogue on "Mary in the design of God and the communion of saints,"[1] some type of conversion would seem to be appropriate at the three levels of attitude, doctrine, and cult.

In terms of attitudes, Catholic theology will understand Calvin and his movement better if not only his biblical concerns but also the medieval roots of his thinking are made clear. Given the primacy

---

1. Groupe des Dombes, *Marie dans le dessein de Dieu et la communion des saints,* vol. 2, *Controverse et conversion* (Paris: Bayard Editions, 1998).

of the soul in the human compound and therefore in the Christian community, the public life and the external forms of the Church are not absolutes. They must bow to the spiritual demands of the gospel, even to those that appear to be new because they have recently been elicited in light of the signs of the times. If, however unthinkable it may seem, there appears to be a conflict between the soul and the body, should the organizational structures prevail, or should the Spirit be allowed to shape new structures? This question was faced in the sixteenth century, and the answers that were given at the time still divide the churches of today. The eventual outcome of the ecumenical movement and of the bilateral dialogues inspired by Vatican Council II may well hinge upon the attitudes adopted in the twenty-first century as the churches face the question again.

In terms of doctrine, it is not sufficient to obtain a better understanding of the teaching of the reformers and of the churches that have inherited their insights. There is an urgency to go beyond mutual understanding, beyond polite apologetics, in order to discover equivalencies or analogies between the traditions where this is at all possible. And where it is not possible, the churches and their theologians have to seek a common vantage point that will do justice to the past while building towards a joint position for the future.

In regard to cult, if this term is taken in the broad sense of the sacrifice of praise offered to God by the testimony of a devoted life, openness to new forms of Christian service would seem to be unavoidable. As was already suggested in 1968 by the Malta Report of the Anglican–Roman Catholic Joint Preparatory Commission,[2] the churches should no longer act unilaterally as they formulate their affirmations and their denials and as they determine their policies.

---

2. "In every region where each Communion has a hierarchy, we propose an annual joint meeting of either the whole or some considerable representation of the two hierarchies. . . . We further recommend constant consultation between committees . . . agreements for joint use of churches . . . agreements to share facilities for theological education. . . . We should cooperate and not take unilateral action, in any significant changes . . ." (*Anglican/Roman Catholic Dialogue: The Work of the Preparatory Commission,* ed. Alan C. Clark and Colin Davey [London: Oxford University Press, 1974], nn. 8, 9, 13, p. 110; also in *Called to Full Unity: Documents on Anglican–Roman Catholic Relations, 1966-1983* [Washington, D.C.: USCC, 1986], pp. 9-10).

They should rather establish regular structures of consultation between their hierarchies with the purpose of arriving at common positions. The very different structures of the churches make such regular consultations somewhat difficult to establish, though this is by no means an insuperable obstacle. However reluctant one may be to open new paths, it will be increasingly necessary to do so if the old or new gaps that separate the churches are to be narrowed or bridged over.

These remarks do not flow directly from the study of *Psychopannychia* or of Calvin's mature theological system. They reflect the conviction that it will be imperative for all churches, in the first few decades of the third millennium, to abandon their defensiveness, to give up the determination to preserve at all cost their traditional forms and formulations, and to claim as their own many of the traditions that they have until recently too systematically opposed.

APPENDIX

The Structure of Psychopannychia

ZIMMERLI'S OUTLINE			HWANG'S PLAN
First thesis: *Incipiemus* ...	p. 26		
Second thesis: *id quod secundo loco* ...	p. 33		
Dives et Lazarus	38		
1. *Primum* ...	41	in	I.2.2.2
Cum autem ...	44	in	2.2.2
Christus resurrexit ...	45		2.2.3
2. *Aliud argumentum* ...	48	in	2.2.3
3. *Praeterea* ...	49		2.2.4
a. *Objiciunt primum* ...	61		II.1.1.1
b. *Objiciunt secundo* ...	65		2.1.1
c. *Tertio loco afferunt* ...	71		2.2
d. *Quarto* ...	73		2.1.4
e. *Quintum argumentum* ...	76		2.3.1
i. *Primum* ...	77		2.3.2
Respondemus ...	91	in	4.2.4.1
ii. *Audiamus alterum* ...	92		4.2.4.2
iii. *Tertium* ...	93		4.2.2.3
iv. *Quartum* ...	95		4.2.4.4
v. *Quintum* ...	96		4.2.4.5
vi. *Sextum* ...	103		4.2.4.6
vii. *Septimum* ...	104		4.2.4.7

SCHWENDEMANN'S PLAN:

MY OUTLINE:

Index